This is a study of Greek mythology in relation to its original contexts. Part One deals with the contexts in which myths were narrated: the home, public festivals, the *leschē*. Part Two, the heart of the book, examines the relation between the realities of Greek life and the fantasies of mythology: the landscape, the family and religion are taken as case-studies. Part Three focuses on the function of myth-telling, both as seen by the Greeks themselves and as perceived by later observers. The author sees his role as that of a cultural historian trying to recover the contexts and horizons of expectation which simultaneously make possible and limit meaning. He seeks to demonstrate how the seemingly endless variations of Greek mythology are a product of *this* community, situated in *this* landscape, and with *these* institutions.

The book aims to engage with the latest work in this field (e.g. the structuralist and myth-and-ritual approaches developed by European scholars) in a style as free as possible from unnecessarily obscure terminology. All Greek is translated.

IMAGINARY GREECE

[Frontispiece] Paris, on a rock, greeted by Hermes.

IMAGINARY GREECE

The contexts of mythology

RICHARD BUXTON

Reader in Ancient Greek, University of Bristol

CAMBRIDGE
UNIVERSITY PRESS

Published by the Press Syndicate of the University of Cambridge
The Pitt Building, Trumpington Street, Cambridge CB2 1RP
40 West 20th Street, New York NY 10011–4211, USA
10 Stamford Road, Oakleigh, Melbourne 3166, Australia

First published 1994

Printed in Great Britain at the University Press, Cambridge

A catalogue record for this book is available from the British Library

Library of Congress cataloguing in publication data

Buxton, R. G. A.
Imaginary Greece: the contexts of mythology/by Richard Buxton.
   p.   cm.
Includes bibliographical references and index.
ISBN 0 521 32978 7 (hc)
1. Mythology, Greek. 2. Greece – Civilization – To 146 B.C.
1. Title.
BL782.B87   1994
292.1′3–dc20   93-27412
                                        CIP

ISBN 0 521 32978 7 hardback
ISBN 0 521 33865 4 paperback

SE

For George

May you always find time for stories

CONTENTS

PLATES

PREFACE

This book has been several years in the writing. During that time the author has accumulated personal and intellectual debts too numerous to mention. But a few exceptions must be made, and I am happy to make them.

Successive groups of final-year and post-graduate students in the University of Bristol have listened to and modified my ideas with good humour and appropriate scepticism. Participants in the research seminars which I gave in the University of Strasbourg during 1991–2 opened up new perspectives for me and offered much valuable criticism of detail; in addition, my Strasbourg colleague Gérard Siebert gave me help well beyond the call of duty. It is a real pleasure to thank Jan Bremmer, Frank Shaw and Thomas Wiedemann for many years of friendship, during which they have given unstintingly of their knowledge of matters mythological; indeed Professor Bremmer read and commented on a draft of the present book. Conversations with Fritz Graf, and more recently with Claude Calame and Philippe Borgeaud, have confirmed the impression which I had formed from my reading, that Switzerland has become the focus of much of the best work in this field. Throughout, Pauline Hire of Cambridge University Press has been a wise and tactful guide. I hope she feels that her patience has in some measure been rewarded.

RGAB
June 1993

ACKNOWLEDGEMENTS

Part of Chapter 6 is adapted from my article entitled 'Imaginary Greek mountains', published in *JHS* for 1992. I am grateful to the Council of the Society for the Promotion of Hellenic Studies for granting me permission to reuse this material.

Passages from Homer are usually cited in the translations by Richmond Lattimore (*The Iliad*: University of Chicago Press, © 1951 by The University of Chicago; *The Odyssey*: Harper & Row, © 1965, 1967 by Richmond Lattimore). For Pindar, I have drawn on the versions by (p. 118) C. M. Bowra (Penguin Books, © C. M. Bowra 1969), and, again (pp. 149 and 176), Richmond Lattimore (University of Chicago Press, © 1947 by the University of Chicago Press). For other authors, in cases where I have taken over or adapted existing translations, I have tried always to acknowledge the fact. Otherwise, the version given is my own.

For acknowledgements relating to illustrations, see under list of plates above.

ABBREVIATIONS

AAntHung	*Acta Antiqua Academiae Scientiarum Hungaricae*
ABSA	*Annual of the British School at Athens*
AC	*L'Antiquité Classique*
AJA	*American Journal of Archaeology*
AJPh	*American Journal of Philology*
ARV²	J. D. Beazley, *Attic Red-figure Vase-painters²*, Oxford, 1963
ASNP	*Annali della Scuola Normale Superiore di Pisa, Cl. di Lettere e Filosofia*
BCH	*Bulletin de Correspondance Hellénique*
BICS	*Bulletin of the Institute of Classical Studies of the University of London*
CPh	*Classical Philology*
CQ	*Classical Quarterly*
CR	*Classical Review*
DK	*Die Fragmente der Vorsokratiker⁶*, edd. H. Diels and W. Kranz, Berlin, 1951–2
FGrH	*Die Fragmente der griechischen Historiker*, ed. F. Jacoby, Berlin, 1923–
FHG	*Fragmenta Historicorum Graecorum*, ed. C. Müller, Paris, 1841–70
HSCP	*Harvard Studies in Classical Philology*
HThR	*Harvard Theological Review*
JAPA	*Journal of the American Psychoanalytical Association*
JDAI	*Jahrbuch des Deutschen Archäologischen Instituts*

xv

JHS	*Journal of Hellenic Studies*
LIMC	*Lexicon Iconographicum Mythologiae Classicae*, Zurich, 1981–
MAL	*Memorie della Classe di Scienze morali e storiche dell' Accademia dei Lincei*
MDAI(A)	*Mitteilungen des Deutschen Archäologischen Instituts (Ath. Abt.)*
MDAI(R)	*Mitteilungen des Deutschen Archäologischen Instituts (Röm. Abt.)*
MH	*Museum Helveticum*
OCT	Oxford Classical Text
OJA	*Oxford Journal of Archaeology*
PCG	*Poetae Comici Graeci*, edd. R. Kassel and C. Austin, Berlin, 1983–
PMG	*Poetae Melici Graeci*, ed. D. L. Page, Oxford, 1962
QUCC	· *Quaderni Urbinati di Cultura classica*
RA	*Revue Archéologique*
RE	Pauly/Wissowa, *Real-Encyclopädie der classischen Altertumswissenschaft*, Stuttgart, 1894–
REG	*Revue des Etudes Grecques*
RhM	*Rheinisches Museum*
RPh	*Revue de Philologie*
SAWW	*Sitzungsberichte der Österreichischen Akademie der Wissenschaft in Wien, Philos.-Hist. Klasse*
SIFC	*Studi Italiani di Filologia classica*
SO	*Symbolae Osloenses*
SSR	*Studi Storico-Religiosi*
TAPA	*Transactions and Proceedings of the American Philological Association*
TrGF	*Tragicorum Graecorum Fragmenta*, Göttingen, 1971–
WSt	*Wiener Studien*
WüJbb	*Würzburger Jahrbücher für die Altertumswissenschaft*
ZPE	*Zeitschrift für Papyrologie und Epigraphik*

Although in the main text I have in general preferred transliterations which give a 'Greek' rather than a 'Romanised' impression (thus 'Herakles', not 'Hercules'), for *abbreviations* of names of authors and titles of works I have followed the widely accepted system adopted in the standard *Greek-English Lexicon* of Liddell, Scott and Jones.

Introduction

Greek myths look familiar enough: we seem always to have known about Oidipous, Elektra, Medea. But a moment's consideration of the question, 'How do we go about interpreting a Greek myth?' is enough to make us pause. For twenty-five centuries, thinkers of rare insight and imagination have adopted a bewildering range of strategies towards the stories, and good reasons for preferring one approach to another can seem hard to come by. Yet the last thirty years have seen an explosion of interest in mythology.

Structuralism led the way. The French took less time than others more positivistically minded to realise the value of the analogy between myth and language, and to dedicate themselves to analysing the structure, the systematic organisation, which gave myths meaning. It was this structure which J.-P. Vernant, P. Vidal-Naquet and M. Detienne claimed, with one or both eyes on Lévi-Strauss, to be bringing to light.[1] Vernant's account of Hermes and Hestia is the classic illustration: the two divinities can only be fully understood if seen as complementary in relation to the Greeks' perception of space – to the goddess of the fixed, central hearth corresponds the boundary-crosser, the god who moves to and fro.[2] Despite nagging doubts about the indifference to history which sometimes crept into this work, and about the tendency to treat each variant as equally significant (even if mythology is like a language, it may still contain spelling mistakes), Paris was the only place to be.[3]

---

[1] Some key works: Detienne 1977, Vernant 1980 and 1983, Vernant and Vidal-Naquet 1981, Vidal-Naquet 1986.   [2] Vernant 1983, pp. 127–75.

[3] On attitudes towards history, it is important to distinguish between the members of the trio: cf. the Introduction to Gordon 1981.

Those doubts were expressed, in language of formidable compression, by Walter Burkert, who sought to reintroduce history – but history of an exceptionally *longue durée*. For Burkert, Greek myths had to be understood in relation to mankind's biological nature.[4] 'Programs of action' grounded in human biology found a dramatised continuity in ritual, which was in turn reflected and paralleled in mythology. With *Homo Necans*, ritual returned to occupy the central position which it had left with Sir James Frazer and Jane Harrison. In the work of Jan Bremmer and Fritz Graf, the emphasis on rites has continued. While their work may lack the vast chronological perspective built into Burkert's vision, their use of, in particular, initiation ceremonies as a means of decoding Greek myths has deservedly claimed attention. In thirty years' time the vogue for initiation will certainly be seen to have been overdone, but there is a good deal of staying power in analyses such as Bremmer's of the scapegoat and maenadism, where a prising apart of the elements pertaining to myth and ritual permits a clearer view of the interrelationship between these two modes.[5]

Several other strategies have affected current thinking about Greek myths. One approach, concentrating on the distinctions and overlaps between oral and written communication, has highlighted the contrast between myths in performance and myths as texts, and towards the difficulties embedded in that contrast.[6] With a different but not unrelated emphasis – though the preferred explanation for change is located this time in politics rather than in media of communication – a series of works by G. E. R. Lloyd has probed the interrelations between the areas conventionally segregated as 'myth' and 'science', raising fundamental questions about the types of explanation characteristic of each.[7] Next, in direct lineal descent from structuralism's stress on significant contrast, we have a series of studies

---

[4] Cf. Burkert 1979, pp. 14–18.
[5] Bremmer 1983a and 1984a. Graf's approach is illustrated by Graf 1985b.
[6] See Goody and Watt 1963, Finnegan 1977, Goody 1977, Havelock 1982, Detienne 1988. Havelock's views about the essential orality of Greek culture until the arrival of Plato have been questioned by, for example, Pöhlmann 1988 and Kullmann in Kullmann and Reichel 1990, pp. 319–20.   [7] Lloyd 1966, 1979, 1983, 1987, 1990. See below, pp. 207–11.

preoccupied with the notion of 'otherness' and 'difference'.[8] Then there has been deconstruction, with its playful syntax, its contrived obscurity, and its tendency to elide the difficulty of assigning some meaning into the impossibility of assigning any. But there is a baby as well as bath water: the certainty with which structuralists and others have spoken of Nature and Culture, of The Greeks and Greek Thought, has been deflated in favour of a healthy awareness of differences. In the spirit if not the style of deconstruction, M. Detienne and then C. Calame have shown just how problematic is the category of myth(ology): 'Very probably invented and at all events articulated by the Greeks, *muthos* was for them neither a type of narrative, nor an ethnocentric concept, nor a mode of thought. It was emphatically *not* an indigenous category.'[9]

Three more interpretative developments may be mentioned. The first originates with critics working under what may crudely be called a 'feminist' umbrella. Thanks to them, a beginning has been made in the attempt to coax a voice from that half of the population which had remained almost mute; the fact that it is phenomenally difficult to answer questions about women's perceptions of and through the myths of antiquity does not make the questions any less worth pressing.[10] Then, there has been an advance in the sophistication with which visual representations are interpreted. For long regarded as mere illustrations of written texts, they are increasingly being seen as symbolic statements in their own right, whose significance has, where possible, to be teased out by replacing them within an iconographical series (structuralism and differences again), and within their functional contexts.[11] Finally, the question of *believing* in myths has been highlighted in a stimulating book by Paul Veyne.[12] The issue raised

---

[8] Zeitlin in Euben 1986, pp. 101–41 (Thebes as 'other' to Athens), Hartog 1988, Hall 1989.

[9] Calame 1990a, p. 29 (my translation), following where Detienne 1986 went before. (The author's review of the latter in *JHS* 103 (1983) 193–4 was, I now think, too unwelcoming. But note the criticisms of Detienne in Brisson 1982.)

[10] Among a torrent of publications one may note Pomeroy 1975, Loraux 1981, 1987 and 1989, Cameron and Kuhrt 1983, Halperin, Winkler and Zeitlin 1990.

[11] Examples are Moret 1984, Bérard et al. 1989, Lissarrague 1990, Sourvinou-Inwood 1991.

[12] Veyne 1988.

cannot be dodged, even though the abstruse manner in which Veyne chooses to approach it does not command universal support.

In spite (or because) of the fashionableness and obvious fertility of the topic, there is in some quarters, in Britain at least, a residual feeling that to treat mythology as a distinct area of study, as opposed to either a byway of traditional classical philology or (merely) that from which philosophy and history manfully 'emerged',[13] is a gambit bound up with Theory, Methodology and The Continent, and is thus *not quite sound*.[14] I believe that those who hold this view are misguided (cf. the ostrich), but at the same time they too are touching on a genuine problem: is mythology an autonomous territory, or merely a modern category stuck on to recalcitrant ancient data?

Every book is a product of its time, and mine inevitably reflects the developments just outlined; indeed, part of my purpose has been to incorporate the results of the best contemporary work. But I wanted, in addition, to stress one particular aspect of the subject which seems to me fundamental: the need to interpret myths *in context*. I make no contribution to the quest undertaken by some for the supposed transhistorical or universal meaning of myths, for I suppose such a quest to be aimless; at the very least, its results are unverifiable. But to locate the stories within the largely peasant communities in which they were told; to analyse narrative contexts and social contexts; to chart the distance travelled between narrative fantasy and everyday life – all this seems to me worthwhile and, no less importantly, possible.

My title is designed to reflect these emphases. In 'imaginary' the reader may detect an echo of the French/Italian *imaginaire/immaginario*. But I do not want to associate myself with any one approach which may have appropriated these terms; not, especially, with the

---

13 The negative connotations are sometimes spelled out, as in Barnes 1987, p. 58: 'The other reports of Pherekydes' work [sc. as against 'the two most "philosophical" pieces'] contain nothing but fanciful mythology.' Cf. also p. 60, where the linking of the Presocratic philosopher Thales with Near Eastern mythological parallels is discouraged: 'to me Thales seems to live in a different and *more luminous* world' (my italics – it is the imagery which gives the game away).

14 This is the consistent subtext of Kirk 1970, even if, laudably, it brings in a wide range of comparative material. Cf. the criticisms in B. Vickers 1973, Appendix II.

attempt to classify archetypal symbols, valid *semper et ubique*, advocated by G. Durand and his school.[15] Nor, emphatically, do I wish to suggest that myths are generated by 'the imagination', in the sense of a particular mental faculty, perhaps even to be differentiated from 'reason'; the existence of such a faculty is quite chimerical. What I do want to do is to allude at the outset to one of my central themes: the distance and interplay between the imaginary world of the stories and the (real?) world of the tellers. (The methodological problems raised by this distinction will occupy us later.) As for my subtitle, 'the contexts of mythology' should be taken in two ways. In Part One I deal with narrative contexts, in Part Two with social contexts in the broadest sense. Part Three draws on both the narrower and the wider type of context in order to re-examine the functional aspect of Greek mythology.

I hope that this book will be read by students, and I would like to think that scholars too will find something to interest them in it. But I have an additional aim. Greek mythology remains popular amongst the reading public. Yet some common assumptions (e.g. that the most exciting question to ask about Jason is 'Did he exist?') are badly in need of revision. Moreover, the form in which this readership often gains access to the stories – for example, in the English-speaking world, via H. J. Rose's *A Handbook of Greek Mythology* and Robert Graves' *The Greek Myths* – can give a startlingly distorted view of the sort of interpretation which would be considered persuasive by contemporary scholars working on the tales. Rose, for example, attributes the differences between Greek and Roman mythology to the fact that the imagination of the Greeks was 'active', while that of the ancient Italians was 'narrow and sluggish'; he regards Greek myths of the monstrous as imports ('in all this hideous brood we may safely recognize the influence of non-Greek fancy, chiefly Anatolian, on the Greek mind'); and he persistently devalues the 'obscure' or 'late' or 'purely local' story – truly a history of mythology written from the winners' standpoint.[16] Graves, for his part, follows a Foreword about hallucinatory mushrooms with an Introduction dominated by The

---

[15] Durand 1992, pp. viii and xviii.   [16] Rose 1958, pp. 1 and 31.

Great Goddess ('Early Greek mythology is concerned, above all else, with the changing relations between the queen and her lovers'), and his distinction between 'true myth' and twelve other sorts of tale simply cannot be justified from ancient texts.[17] I hope, in short, that the present book will reach the wider audience too. To that end I have tried to cut down the jargon with which scholars like to armour-plate themselves. Most things worth saying about Greek myths can be expressed clearly.[18]

Finally, a word about chronological limits. The earliest examples of mythological narrative to which I refer are from the eighth century BC, to which Homer and Hesiod may reasonably be dated. Deciding how late to go is more difficult. The poets Oppian and Nonnos are recognisably composing in the same tradition as their predecessors of a thousand years earlier; and Pausanias, writing in the second century AD, is the richest single literary source for Greek ritual and many of its accompanying stories. I shall frequently refer to this later material, but it cannot be denied that the world had greatly changed by the time Pausanias decided to present the Greeks themselves as an object of curiosity.[19] The principal focus of this book, then, is the Archaic, Classical and early Hellenistic periods down to the middle of the third century BC. By that date the growing interest of Romans in using Greek culture had inaugurated a fresh direction in the transmission of myths. By the time that Fabius Pictor and Naevius relate the tale of Aeneas' arrival in Latium, the history of Greek myth-telling has become inseparable from the history of the Romans' approach to Greek civilisation;[20] and that is beyond our scope here.

---

[17] Graves 1960, pp. 16 and 12.
[18] I am aware that to identify obscurity in others is to take a stand – some would say, to adopt a rhetorical ploy. I readily accept the implications of this conscious decision on my part. For a historical perspective on the obscurity/clarity debate see Hurst 1991, pp. 9–17.
[19] Cf. Calame 1990b, pp. 26–7.
[20] See Momigliano 1987, pp. 264–88.

PART ONE

Narrative contexts

1

Telling tales

From accounts of the nature of the world, to gossip about the wife of the man next door, Greek society was characterised by the exchange of stories. The aim of the tellers was to convince. To do this, they had to speak the truth, or something like the truth – the territory annexed for themselves by the Muses who met, mocked and inspired Hesiod on Mount Helikon (*Th.* 26–8).

Our evidence for the convincing tale goes back to the *Odyssey*, that supremely persuasive interweaving of contrasting narrative voices. Apart from the Homeric narrator, the most skilful manipulator of stories is Odysseus himself. The version of the past which he recounts to the swineherd Eumaios in Book 14 overlaps at numerous points with the hero's 'true' adventures: he was courageous, a lover of ships, a wanderer, a fighter in the Trojan War, a captain whose shipmates were disobedient; he was shipwrecked, saved himself by clinging to a mast, was rescued on the shore by a king's child. But *this* wanderer was a Cretan; the shore was that of Thesprotia, not Phaiakia; his saviour was not a princess but a prince; and the sailors instructed to carry him onwards, far from exhibiting extraordinary hospitality, stripped and bound him. Like Scheherazade, Odysseus uses tales in order to survive. They mask, or occasionally reveal, his identity. Above all, they have to be plausible. As the poet sings after another Cretan episode, this time told to Penelope: 'He uttered many false things which he made to seem like true things.'[1]

---

[1] *Od.* 19.203; cf. Rutherford 1992, *ad loc.*, and Introduction pp. 69–73.

From the work of another consummate carpenter of tales, Herodotos, we get an impression of the phenomenal range of material in circulation in the fifth century. There are amazing travellers' tales about werewolves (4.105) and giant ants (3.102); reports of outlandish places such as Scythia and Ethiopia; narratives of the founding of colonies; elegantly constructed anecdotes about charismatic individuals such as Solon, Kroisos and Polykrates; rival versions of the Greeks' political past ('Such is the Argive account of this matter; there is, however, another version current in Greece ...', 7.150). From all these voices the historian fabricates his own plausible tale, accepting here, distancing himself there: 'My business is to record what people say, but I am by no means bound to believe it.'[2] The range of stances adopted by the historian-narrator – from 'I have seen' to 'it is said' – implicitly locates the attentive inquirer within a polyphony of competing voices.[3]

Plato's *Symposion* narrates an episode from the career of Sokrates, when the philosopher attended a drinking party at which the participants spoke in praise of love. The party is distanced from the reader/hearer by a series of framing devices. First, a certain Apollodoros is prompted by an unnamed friend of his to relate what happened. The party took place, according to Apollodoros, some time ago, but he is practised at recounting it because only two days previously he had, he says, told it to Glaukon. To Glaukon, Apollodoros explains to his friend, he had related that he knew about the gathering from one Aristodemos, who had been present. Glaukon, for his part, had heard a version from someone who had learned it from Phoinix, who had had it in turn from Aristodemos. To cap it all, amongst the tales told at the *symposion* was an account of love which Sokrates reports having heard from a woman called Diotima. There is perhaps no piece of extant Greek literature with a more

---

[2] 7.152; cf. the remark of Herodotos' predecessor Hekataios: 'the stories of the Greeks are many and laughable' (*FGrH* F1).

[3] Cf. Hartog 1988, ch. 7. The notion of story penetrates to the core of the events narrated. The Solonian idea that one must above all study the *end* of an action before evaluating it for (un)happiness (1.32) implies that, in everyday life as in a well-rounded tale, one can indeed know where the end is.

syntactically intricate use of indirect speech;[4] there is certainly no clearer illustration of the fabrication of a work of literature from a network of stories.[5]

To get behind literary constructions like Homeric epic, Herodotean history and Platonic dialogue to the world which constituted a context for them is notoriously difficult, not to say methodologically problematic.[6] But at least one characteristic seems to have been shared by fictions and context: plurality of voice. In the society of the Archaic and Classical *polis*, in a range of arenas, story-telling was a competitive enterprise. In political controversy, persuading one's hearers might take the form of narrating the past. In a debate represented by Herodotos as having taken place in Sparta, the Corinthian Sosikles argued against Sparta's pro-tyrant policy by delivering an account of his own city's past sufferings under tyranny (5.92). In the courts, too, rival, plausible versions of the past were of crucial, sometimes life-or-death importance to those who told them. One way of being plausible was to adduce parallels from particular kinds of story like 'history' or 'fable'.[7] But, more generally, everyone who appeared before a jury offered a narrative designed to convince. Sokrates' response to the men whom he regarded as scandalmongers against him consisted, at least according to the compellingly persuasive *Apology* composed by Plato, of a self-justificatory narrative of his past career.

Formalised, public tale-telling was only a part of the picture. There were also the narratives we call gossip, scandal and anecdote. There may be disagreement about the boundaries of these terms, but surely not about their significance for the definition of friendships and enmities in a face-to-face community.[8] Mostly we can do no more than guess about contexts, but an exception is the barber's shop. Comic writers refer to the males who sat and swapped gossip there;[9]

---

[4] See Dover 1980, pp. 80–1.
[5] For the Platonic Sokrates and stories which are 'like the truth', cf. Lloyd 1987, p. 10 n. 26.
[6] Cameron 1989 raises some of the problems.
[7] See Edmunds 1990, pp. 8–10; on fables, see Jedrkiewicz 1987.
[8] See Dover 1988. Trenkner 1958, pp. 16–22, discusses the range of oral narratives circulating in, specifically, Athens.   [9] Ar. *Av.* 1439–45, *Pl.* 337–9, Eupolis fr. 194 *PCG*.

Polybios damningly ranks the work of two rivals 'not with history but with the common gossip of the barber's shop'.[10] But the chat at these 'wineless symposia'[11] could have deadly serious consequences, as in an episode recalled by Plutarch from the period just after Athens' disastrous expedition to Sicily.[12] A stranger lands in Peiraios and goes for a haircut. At the barber's he 'makes *logoi*' about the disaster, news of which has not yet hit Athens. The barber goes up to the city and creates panic: 'he threw the *logos* in the agora'. The originator of the rumour is hauled up before the archons, who decide he is a *logopoios* ('maker(-up) of *logoi*') – and have him tortured.[13]

Amongst the wide range of stories told in Greece, there was one group which recounted the deeds of divinities and heroes. Tales of this type have conventionally been referred to as 'myths', the term 'mythology' being variously reserved for the corpus of myths regarded as a whole, or the study of myths as an academic discipline. There are, however, notorious definitional problems. In spite of its derivation from the Greek word *muthos*, the English term 'myth', like its analogues in other Western European languages, is far from corresponding to a classification about which there was universal agreement in antiquity. It is true that the attempts of, for example, Thucydides, Plutarch, Diodorus Siculus and Sextus Empiricus to differentiate between what is improbable/unverifiable and their opposites are *sometimes* couched in terms of a contrast between that which is *muthos* and that which is not.[14] It is true, too, that Plato takes important steps towards systematising two distinctions between *muthos* and *logos*: that between *muthos* as unverifiable discourse and *logos* as verifiable discourse, and that between *muthos* as story and *logos* as rational argument.[15] However, in a considerable body of passages from the Archaic period onwards *muthos* and *logos* are used with no

---

[10] 3.20.5. Note however D. *Aristog.* 1 52: a man who does *not* spend time at the barber's is unsociable. See Nicolson 1891, p. 42.

[11] Plu. *Quaest. conv.* 679a, quoting Theophrastos.   [12] *Nic.* 30. 1–2.

[13] For Herodotos, his predecessor Hekataios is a *logopoios*; cf. Hartog 1988, p. 297. The eighth of Theophrastos' *Characters* is a *logopoios*.

[14] Th. 1.21, D. S. 4.1, Plu. *Thes.* 1.3, S. E. *Adv. gramm.* 263–4, cf. Str. 11.6.2–4; Veyne 1988, p. 143 n. 99.   [15] Cf. the whole of Part II of Brisson 1982.

such contrast implied.[16] Moreover Plato himself, writing of the tales which should be banned from his ideal republic, calls them not *muthoi* but *logoi*, and includes the *muthoi* told to children under the general heading of *logoi* ('discourse').[17] In short, historians of ideas who read Greek culture as a progress from *muthos* to *logos* can only be using these as honorary English (German, French ...) words; at best, they are taking further a distinction which was *sometimes* made in antiquity.

There is a further problem with the classification 'myth'. It has recently been argued, and with some force, that the deployment of this concept has resulted in the unwarranted constitution of a cross-cultural genus, 'mythology', of which 'Japanese mythology', 'Egyptian mythology', and indeed 'Roman mythology', are taken to be particular species.[18] It is true that, if the terms are so used as to elide cultural differences in the context and content of story-telling, then they are doing more harm than good. Nevertheless it seems to me that, at least in the case of Greece, this conceptual puritanism does not gain us much.[19] We know that some Greeks on some occasions focused on stories of the gods and heroes as a separate class, even if *muthos* was not, or not always, the label for them. In Aristophanes' *Wasps* the old man Philokleon and his son Bdelykleon have a comic

---

[16] Detienne 1986, pp. 44ff., discusses examples in authors as diverse as Homer, Xenophanes, Parmenides, Pindar and Herodotos.

[17] *R.* 376e6–377a8, with Brisson 1982, pp. 111–12. See also Lloyd 1987, p. 181, and 1990, p. 23. Lloyd's emphasis is on the fact that a distinction *could* be made in antiquity between *muthos* and *logos*; but it is none the less true, as Lloyd is well aware, that such a distinction is often ignored.   [18] Cf. Calame 1988, Introduction.

[19] Not, at any rate, as much as the abandonment of 'legend', 'saga' and 'folk-tale', at least in relation to ancient Greece. 'Legend' seems to be typically used to ascribe some vaguely historical reality to the story in question, by comparison with 'pure' invention; but this distinction is in practice virtually unworkable. (Strabo can use it at 1.2.9 because he assumes that the Trojan War really occurred.) 'Saga' has a precise meaning in relation to Icelandic prose narratives; any extension from that only causes pointless territorial disputes (when is an epic a saga? etc.). 'Folk-tale' appears at first sight to have more going for it. Almost all writers on Greek mythology use it, in the sense of 'story transmitted orally at a popular (usually undetectable) level'. But 'the folk' has its conceptual origin in late eighteenth- and early nineteenth-century European history (Burke 1978, Ch. 1), and it is questionable whether its extension to ancient Greece is viable: who, if not 'the folk', were the people who listened to tragedy? For unconvincing attempts to distinguish myth from folk-tale, see Kirk 1970, pp. 31–41, and 1974, pp. 30–7.

argument which turns on the distinction between human stories and stories from a world of mythical fantasy.[20] Quite apart from this, it is convenient for us as observers to have a designation for a group of stories which are of outstanding interest because of their symbolic richness, their centrality to Greek culture, and the authority which they commanded. I propose, then, to retain 'myth' to do what seems to me to be a respectable heuristic job. But I stress two reservations: (1) no automatic equation can be made between Greek myths and apparently similar stories found in other cultures; (2) mythology is not being regarded as constituting an autonomous, hermetically-sealed territory.

To illustrate (1) we may compare Herakles with a closely comparable character from nineteenth-century American 'mythology': Davy Crockett.[21] Crockett lived on the frontier, defending civilisation against varmints of the human or animal kind (Redskins, alligators, rattlesnakes). His closeness to nature was marked by his racoonskin cap, while his violence expressed itself through his rifle Killdevil and his knife Big Butcher (Herakles had a lionskin, a bow and a club). Like Herakles, who was known for bedding fifty sisters in a night, Crockett was a famous lover: among his conquests were Lottie Richers (the Flower of Gum Swamp) and Sal Fungus. But the two heroes differ in one crucial respect: Crockett was not worshipped. For all that he embodied a number of central aspects of American popular feeling – ridicule of sophistication, suspicion of authority, self-reliance, the celebration of violence – the only cult he had was the metaphorical one generated by film and television in the 1950s. Herakles, by contrast, like most of the heroes in Greek religion, retained even after death the power to intervene in human affairs, a fact reasserted with every invocation and sacrifice to him. Thanks to their interfusion with ritual, the Greek heroes had a durability far beyond anything which might be expected of mere characters in stories.[22] An equation between Herakles and Crockett is meaningless

[20] *V.* 1179–80, cf. D. *Aristocr.* 65; Edmunds 1990, pp. 2ff.

[21] On Crockett, see Dorson 1977, esp. pp. 203–14, with refs. at p. 304. For a different comparison (with Tarzan), see Holtsmark 1981, e.g. pp. 93 and 97, and Bérard 1983.

[22] On heroes, see the excellent brief sketch in Rudhardt 1958, pp. 127–35; also Brelich 1958.

without a recognition of the major differences between the social roles of tales in the two cultures.

Examples of (2) – the non-autonomous character of Greek mythology – will recur throughout the book. For the moment it will be enough to mention Hesiod's poem *Works and Days*. In this plausible tale, the narrative persona of a cantankerous Boeotian peasant lends authenticity to diverse material: an animal fable about the nature of power, a self-justifying version of how the poet lost his inheritance to his brother, stories of how the intrigues of divinities and heroes brought the world to its present unforgiving state. Erecting an artificial barrier between the mythical and non-mythical in Hesiod – a barrier between Dike ('Right') and *dikē* ('right'), or between Pandora and womankind – travesties the poet's thought. This is not to deny that attempts *were* made to draw some kind of conceptual boundary around 'myth', for example by those staking a claim to originality in the areas which we designate as natural philosophy and medicine. But such attempts at boundary-drawing themselves demonstrate that the integrity of the territory of 'myth' could not be taken for granted.

Bearing in mind the preceding discussion, we may put forward the following working definition: 'A Greek myth is a narrative about the deeds of gods and heroes and their interrelations with ordinary mortals, handed on as a tradition within the ancient Greek world, and of collective significance to a particular social group or groups.'[23] Three points need clarification.

'Narrative' appears uncontroversial. However, it might be taken to imply that by 'myth' we want to denote something verbal, on the grounds that it is in language alone that we find true narrative. But what of visual art? The sense in which an art form can be said to narrate is debatable.[24] Yet it would be preposterous to deny the importance of visual images in relation to Greek stories. Probably the

---

[23] This definition makes no claim whatever to originality, following as it does in the wake of e.g. Burkert 1979, pp. 1–5, which discussion owes in turn a good deal to Kirk 1970.

[24] See Hanfmann 1957, Schlingloff 1981, Snodgrass 1982 and in Bérard, Bron and Pomari 1987, pp. 11–18, Raeck 1984, Moret 1984, I, pp. 153ff., Brilliant 1984, Bérard in Calame 1988, pp. 187–99. It has even been claimed that for the development of the mythological tradition artistic representations were not merely *as* important as verbal narratives, but *more* important (Moret 1984, I, pp. 156 and 159).

best solution is to retain the notion of narrative, while recognising that it may need to be applied differently to verbal and visual forms of expression. A related issue touches on a major contemporary debate: are we trying to recover a structure of thought, or analysing a type of story with characteristic modes and conventions?[25] The present book rests on the assumption that, while Greek mythology was a set of narratives, it also constituted a body of material whose effects spread far beyond its immediate narrative contexts. 'Mythical thought' is a problematic and misleading notion; but that large areas of Greek mental life were shaped by myths is beyond question.

The idea of myths as 'traditional' has a long history: it was central to the Romantic view that mythology was a form of expression which welled up from and was transmitted by 'the people'.[26] More recently, the definition of a myth as a traditional tale has been advocated by G. S. Kirk and Walter Burkert. Burkert cleverly uses the concept of tradition to sidestep the obsession with origins: in his view a story becomes a myth only when its origins have been forgotten – when, in other words, it has become traditional.[27] But this raises a difficulty. If a version of the sack of Troy is found in only one ancient source, are we to refuse to call it a myth because we cannot be sure that it has been handed down? While it would be possible to limit the term 'myth' to those stories which we are certain were told repeatedly, in view of the patchy nature of our evidence it is unwise to be so restrictive. Greek mythical tradition was dynamic: given the right circumstances an innovation would achieve currency, only to lose it later if other versions were found more persuasive.[28]

'Collective significance to a particular social group or groups' designates a myth as a social phenomenon, not an idiosyncratic, individual one.[29] It is useful to distinguish, say, stories about the Trojan War from the eschatological narrative about Er in Book 10

---

[25] Calame 1988, Introduction.

[26] 'Accordingly the author of the *Nibelungenlied* would be unknown, as normally is and must be the case with all national poems, since they belong to the whole *Volk* ...' (Jacob Grimm, 'Über *das Nibelungen Liet*', in *Kleinere Schriften* (1869; reprinted by Olms in 1965), IV, p. 4 (my translation)).   [27] Burkert 1979, p. 2.

[28] See Bremmer 1984b, p. 128, and 1987, pp. 1–4, for reservations about the extent to which myths are traditional.   [29] Cf. Bremmer 1987, pp. 4–6.

of Plato's *Republic*. The difference is not just that many Greek myth-tellers retold the story of Troy, whereas the Myth of Er is (for us) uniquely Platonic, since, as has just been argued, we may usefully describe as a myth something which exists for us in just one version. The point is, rather, that the Trojan expedition formed part of a web of interrelated tales about figures who were claimed as ancestors by families or cities in historical times and whose actions were recalled in ritual and religious iconography. The story of Er had, as far as we know, no analogous relationship with the fabric of Greek religious and social life: the tale as we have it is a Platonic construction which serves a Platonic philosophical end. The distinction between socially embedded myths and idiosyncratic narratives is not, however, without its problems. How do we define the stories characteristically told by the adherents of Orphism – a *group* whose beliefs were marginal to the more orthodox religion of the *polis*? The answer is that a definition makes a good servant but a bad master: Orphic stories – the tearing of the infant Dionysos by the Titans, or the cosmogonical account involving the world egg – had many, but not all, the characteristics of the stories embedded in the *polis* religion. The distinction between central and marginal traditions is not absolute: pluralism – the simultaneous existence of competing versions of a story – was already a feature of the central tradition; for there to be rival stories told by Orphics or by Plato is merely an extension of the same situation.

2

Myths in performance

From the cradle . . .

The home was where children began to incorporate into their developing construction of the world the perceptions, symbols and values embedded in myths. Who were the tellers? Our most extensive evidence comes from Plato. Once he refers to the narrators as 'old men and old women',[1] but usually he presents the transmission of stories as a female preserve, ascribing it to nurses, mothers or old women.[2] One group of tales centres on bogey figures – again, usually female – such as Gello, Gorgo (Plate 1), Lamia and Mormo.[3] Typical is a story recounted about Lamia. Loved by Zeus, she went mad with grief when her children were killed by a jealous Hera; thereafter she kidnapped and murdered the children of others. Some writers portrayed her as a theriomorphic cave-dweller with a taste for human flesh.[4] Mormo too lost her own offspring and turned ghoulishly on those of others.[5] When Greek women invoked such terrifying stories, their aim was usually to seek to control unruly children by conjuring up an image of what might happen if they continued to misbehave (a

---

[1] *R.* 378d.

[2] *Grg.* 527a, *R.* 377c, *Lg.* 887d, *Lys.* 205d. See J. Bremmer in Blok and Mason 1987, pp. 200–1, and Veyne 1988, pp. 139–40 n. 56.

[3] See Rohde 1966, Appendix VI, Scobie 1979, pp. 244–50. Gello: *RE* VII, cols. 1005–6 (Maas). Gorgo: Vernant 1985, pp. 31–63. Lamia: Scobie, *loc. cit.*, Vermeule 1979, p. 223 n. 21. Mormo: Gow's commentary on Theoc. 15.39–40, Bowra 1953, pp. 158–9. The demon Ephialtes (The Leaper) is a rare male exception.

[4] Schol. Ar. *Pax* 758, D. Chr. *Or.* 5, Ant. Lib. 8, Philostr. *VA* 4.25.

[5] Schol. Theoc. 15.40.

1. The face of the nightmare: Gorgo, under whose arm snuggles her child, the winged horse Pegasos. (From a seventh-century terracotta relief.)

motive explicitly mentioned in our sources).[6] However, some psychologists argue in relation to the nightmarish beings of modern folklore that, whatever the intention, the *effect* is to invest a child's fears with a specific shape and named identity and so diminish those fears by making them more manageable.[7] There is no reason to doubt that the same is true for antiquity.

[6] X. *HG* 4.4.17, Theoc. 15.40, Str. 1.2.8, schol. Aristid. *Or.* 102, 5 (vol. III, p. 42 Dindorf).
[7] Cf. Bettelheim 1976, pp. 120–1. On the role of terror in stories told by British nannies, see Gathorne-Hardy 1985, pp. 282–8.

In addition to relating tales of bogey-figures, women in the house drew on a much wider range of narratives about the exploits of the gods and the heroes. According to Philostratos, the abandonment of the sleeping Ariadne by Theseus is a story which 'you must have heard from your nurse; for those women are skilled in telling such tales, and they weep over them whenever they will'.[8] A funerary inscription from the island of Chios, dated to the early first century BC, quotes the poignant words of two old women from Kos: 'O sweet dawn, to whom by lamplight we sang *muthoi* of the demigods'.[9] Already in Plato's *Lysis* we hear about something dismissed as an old wives' tale, namely an account of how Lysis' ancestor, who claimed descent from Zeus, entertained Herakles.[10] And of course there is Plato's *Republic*. While it is the immoral tales of poets which he famously banishes, tales told to children are also singled out for particular censure (378d–e):

> But we must not admit into our city stories about Hera being tied
> up by her son, or Hephaistos being hurled out of Olympos by his
> father for trying to help his mother when she was getting a beating,
> or any of Homer's Battles of the Gods, whether or not their
> intention is allegorical. The young cannot distinguish between what
> is allegory and what is not, and opinions formed at that age are
> usually difficult to eradicate or change; so we should perhaps do our
> utmost to ensure that the first stories they hear shall be as finely
> composed as possible with a view to instilling moral excellence.

So the stories which we know as Homeric and Hesiodic figured in some form in the domestic repertoire as well – and presumably not *just* the tales of divine violence singled out for criticism by the Platonic Sokrates. Unfortunately, we can only guess about what kinds of occasion might have prompted the telling of stories of the non-Mormo type.[11] What would we not give for a detailed contextual account of a domestic story-telling occasion to compare with the information available to us about the public narrations of poets?

We now confront a revealing paradox. In narrating myths, women

---

[8] *Im.* 1.15.1 (trans. A. Fairbanks, Loeb edn).   [9] Kaibel 1878, no. 232.
[10] *Lys.* 205c–d; cf. Thomas 1989, p. 109.   [11] For a guess, see p. 179 below.

were performing the vital role of preparing children for entry into the symbolic world of the adult community. Yet ancient authors usually refer to female story-tellers only in order to disparage them: 'old wives' tales' is an expression with an impeccable ancient pedigree.[12] It has been suggested that *old* women, in particular, were generally looked down upon because they could no longer fulfil the two main roles expected of women – arousing male desire and producing legitimate children.[13] While Greek attitudes in this matter were doubtless complex and conflicting, the tales told by old women were indeed systematically devalued,[14] in spite of the fact that, as we have seen, at least some of the tales they told were the very ones told in public by poets. But poets – almost always male – were inspired by the gods, and had a central and prestigious social position; their narratives carried far greater authority for the *polis* than those of a nurse or a mother.[15]

The songs of youth

At domestic or local festivals such as the Athenian Amphidromia (when the five-day-old baby was welcomed into the family by being carried round the hearth), the ten-day festival (for naming), and the Apatouria (for the registration of male infants into the hereditary association known as the phratry), the very young began to take a passive role in the community's rites.[16] In due course the growing child would come to understand that such occasions often featured myth-telling, or had associations with mythology. On one of the days of the Apatouria, children took part in a contest as if they were rhapsodes (professional reciters).[17] Children also participated in the Anthesteria, the festival for Dionysos celebrated in Athens and in many parts of Ionian Asia Minor.[18] The second day, known as Choes

[12] See Massaro 1977.   [13] Bremmer in Blok and Mason 1987, p. 191.
[14] Compare the worries of Roman intellectuals about the effects of stories told by nurses and slave childminders (Tac. *Dial.* 29.1, with Wiedemann 1989, p. 144).
[15] Inspiration: P. Murray 1981, Herington 1985, pp. 58–9.
[16] See Garland 1990, pp. 93ff. and 121.   [17] Pl. *Ti.* 21b; cf. Brisson 1982, p. 61.
[18] Burkert 1983, pp. 213–43, Simon 1983, pp. 92–9.

(Pitchers), was grim and solemn: the community gathered together yet remained symbolically apart, individuals sitting at separate tables and drinking wine competitively and in silence. Each child had a tiny pitcher, and in drinking from it had a taste of adult life. As the children grew older they would be told about the myth which 'explained' the rite. When the polluted mother-murderer Orestes arrived at Athens, the outcast was neither turned away nor fully accepted: at the original Choes festival he was made to sit at a separate table and drink from an individual pitcher.[19] In short, myth-telling at festivals was partly 'educational', partly fun:

> and the same stories (as they heard from their nurses and mothers) they heard repeated also in prayers at sacrifices, and they saw spectacles which illustrated them, of the kind which the young delight to see and hear . . .[20]

Impressions gained at first hand were reinforced in school, an institution which can be traced back for several places in Greece to the beginning of the fifth century, and which probably began earlier still.[21] It should not be assumed that only a tiny proportion of the population – the wealthiest – could afford to send its children to receive formal education: when a school on Chios collapsed soon after 500 BC, there were said to have been 120 children inside.[22] In addition to the learning of letters, emphasis was placed on physical training and 'music'; in relation to the latter, poetry was the staple fare.[23] Attitudes varied about the preferred method: some advocated rote learning of the entire output of certain poets, others emphasised the usefulness of

[19] Euripides, *IT* 947–60.

[20] Pl. *Lg.* 887d (trans. R. G. Bury, Loeb edn). See also *Lg.* 658c–d, where it is suggested that infants go for puppet shows, older children for comedies, while most of the rest of the populace prefer tragedies (except the old men, who enjoy recitations from epic).

[21] See Mario Alighiero Manacorda in Vegetti 1983b, pp. 187–209, esp. 190–1, Harris 1989, p. 57.

[22] Hdt. 6.27.2. A sceptical view about the suspiciously 'typical' number 120 is expressed by Fehling 1989, p. 232.

[23] Cf. Ar. *Nu.* 961ff., though for reservations about Aristophanic fantasy, see Harris 1989, pp. 58–9. See also Russell 1981, pp. 84–5, for the suggestion that in later antiquity education in poetry became increasingly confined to children.

memorising anthologies.[24] Exercises might involve fables[25] and mythological poetry, for which a range of major poets was prescribed. One vase shows a child being tested, evidently at school, on the recitation of a piece of poetry; another depicts a boy holding a roll of papyrus, on which are written the opening two words of what we know as *Homeric Hymn* 18.[26] Homer was required study: when the fifth-century politician Alkibiades went to a school and was unable to get a text of part of the poet's work, he left – or so the story ran – after punching the teacher.[27]

Experience of mythology gained in childhood was developed and enriched in adolescence through participation in choral singing, a form of socialisation which long predates the introduction of formal schooling. As Claude Calame stresses in his detailed study of girls' choirs, choral performance was not merely associated with traditional education, it could be virtually synonymous with it.[28] In Plato's *Laws* the Athenian remarks: 'If, then, we three understand what constitutes goodness in respect of song and dance, we also know who is and who is not rightly educated . . .'[29] For the Dorians, a school might be called a *choros*; in Aristophanes' *Frogs* the chorus praises good old Athenians as 'brought up in wrestling-grounds, in choruses and in the practice of the arts (*mousikē*)'.[30]

In view of the contrasting life-patterns in store for Greek youths and girls, it is not surprising that they usually sang in separate choirs.[31] Evidence about males comes from Polybios, in a chapter about the deep influence of music on the culture of his native Arkadia:

> not only boys, but young men up to the age of thirty were
> compelled to study [music] constantly . . . the boys from their
> earliest childhood are trained to sing in measure the hymns and

[24] Pl. *Lg.* 810e–811a.

[25] Cf. Easterling and Knox 1985, pp. 27 and 702–3, on the Hellenistic period (fables figured in the preparatory exercises known as *progymnasmata*). For fables in the context of Roman education, see Wiedemann 1989, pp. 145–6.

[26] School test: Berlin 2285 = *ARV*² 431, 48 (illustration in Boardman 1975a, pl. 289). Hymn: Beazley 1948, pl. XXXIV.   [27] Plu. *Mor.* 186e; same story in Ael. *VH* 13.38.

[28] Calame 1977, I, pp. 386ff.   [29] Pl. *Lg.* 654d (trans. adapted from R. G. Bury, Loeb edn).

[30] Poll. 9.41; Ar. *Ra.* 729, cf. *Nu.* 964 (on which, however, NB n. 23 above).

[31] See Calame 1977, I, p. 63 n. 29, for a few known cases of mixed choirs.

paeans in which by traditional usage they celebrate the heroes and gods of each particular place: later they learn the measures of Philoxenos and Timotheos, and every year in the theatre they compete keenly in choral singing to the accompaniment of professional flute-players, the boys in the contest proper to them and the young men in what is called the men's contest.[32] And not only this, but through their whole life they entertain themselves at banquets not by listening to hired musicians but by their own efforts, calling for a song from each in turn ... Besides this the young men practise military parades to the music of the flute and perfect themselves in dances and give annual performances in the theatres, all under state supervision and at the public expense ...[33]

Although the author makes it clear that his homeland was in his own day (second century BC) not typical, there can be no doubt that in Archaic and Classical times the participation of young males in choral song was a widespread custom. Alkman apparently composed for them at Sparta;[34] the dithyrambic event at Athens was for ten choirs of fifty boys as well as ten of fifty men;[35] at the Spartan Gymnopaidiai there were probably three different age-groups of males, young, adult and old;[36] we hear of a choir of thirty-five boys sent from Messina to a festival at Rhegion, and as many as a hundred youths in the choir sent from Chios to perform at Delphi.[37]

Was there anything 'masculine' about the content of the songs of

---

[32] There is nothing rigid about Greek perceptions of age-classes. Xenophon (*Cyr.* 1.2.4) speaks (with reference to Persia) of four male groups, namely boys, ephebes, mature adults, and those past military service; in another of his works 'the young' are defined as those under 30 (*Mem.* 1.2.35). Plato's *Laws* (666a–c) discriminate between boys under 18 (no wine allowed), young men under 30 (moderate amounts) and the over-40s (drink allowed to soften 'old age') (B. E. Richardson 1933, p. 29). Aristotle distinguished youth, full adulthood and old age, but without giving numbers (*Rh.* 2 1389a). In spite of these variations, there was widespread recognition of a category of 'the young', not yet married. In addition to forming the implicit basis for the choirs, this category was fundamental to institutionalised male homosexuality, the structure of which depended on an age difference between the partners (lover : beloved :: mentor : pupil).   [33] Plb. 4.20 (trans. W. R. Paton, Loeb edn).

[34] Alkman fr. 10 *PMG*; see Herington 1985, pp. 24–5 and 228 nn. 41 and 50, for a discussion of some of the uncertainties in the fragment.   [35] Pickard–Cambridge 1988, pp. 66 and 75.

[36] Brelich 1969, pp. 139–40, Calame 1977, I, p. 352 n. 350, Herington 1985, pp. 25 and 230 n. 56, R. Parker in Powell 1989, pp. 149–50.   [37] Messina: Paus. 5.25.2–4. Chios: Hdt. 6.27.

young males? Surely yes. Corroboration comes from the victory ode, a genre which generated mythological narratives of astonishing complexity and richness. Athletic victors in one of the great Games would in the first instance be celebrated by friends and supporters in the place of victory,[38] but later there would follow, in the victor's own city or household,[39] a performance of a commissioned ode, sung by males who are sometimes said specifically to be young.[40] Their praise set the deeds of the mortal winner among the eternally shining exploits of the gods and heroes. Untypical only in its length is Pindar's elaborate fourth Pythian ode, which presents Jason as a paradigm for a returning chariot-victor. For an ordinary mortal, returning home with new glory entails making a difficult transition back into his own community – envy and big-headedness are twin dangers. Jason is the perfect model: formidable, handsome, modest in the face of arrogance: 'In my twenty years of life I have done and said nothing shameful' (104–5). He 'returns' twice: from childhood in Cheiron's cave to claim his just inheritance, then from Kolchis with the Golden Fleece courageously won. Amid the brightness and clarity of the Argonauts' adventures there is no hint of Medea's murderous quarrel with Jason. The young men gladly follow their heroic leader, preferring the quest for prowess to a life without danger beside mother (186). The human athlete is modelled on the mythical hero, yet stands at the same time as a beacon of achievement for his fellows, whose voices are raised in his praise.

Girls, too, sang. At Trozen, young girls recalled the story of Phaidra's love for Hippolytos.[41] The Homeric Hymn to Delian Apollo refers to maidens of Delos who praise first Apollo, then his mother Leto and his sister Artemis, and go on to sing of 'men and women of olden days'. This may be an allusion to the identity of those

[38] Pi. *Ol.* 10.72–7; Bacch. 2, with Burnett 1985, p. 39; Gentili 1988, p. 20.
[39] The specific location varied. Pindar's 11th *Pythian*, in honour of a Theban boy who won a foot-race, was apparently sung at Apollo's Theban shrine and treasure-house, the Ismenion (lines 5–6); the choir of youths praising the boy pankratiast Kleandros of Aigina seems to have sung outside his father's house (opening of *Isthm.* 8); *Nem.* 1 seems to imply a banquet as the likely context (line 20; cf. *Nem.* 9.48–52).
[40] See Herington 1985, pp. 28 and 183 n. 3. (Lefkowitz 1988 doubts that victory odes were always chorally performed.)   [41] E. *Hipp.* 1423–30.

who performed the hymn: a choir of girls at Apollo's sanctuary on Delos.[42] The Spartan poet Alkman's First Maiden-Song records the words sung by a choir of girls whose individual experiences were explored against a backdrop of local Spartan mythology. A narrative about Herakles' foes the murderous sons of Hippokoon (a Spartan king) gives way to this:

> Such a thing there is as the Gods' revenge: blessed is he who
> merrily weaves the day's pattern to its end, without a tear. And so I
> sing the radiance of Agido: I see her like the sun ... on the tresses of
> my cousin, Hagesichora, is the bloom of purest gold ... not even
> Nanno's tresses will suffice, nor Areta divinely fair, nor Thylakis,
> nor Kleesithera; nor would you go to Ainesimbrota's and say, 'Let
> Astaphis be mine, let Philylla look my way, or Damareta, or lovely
> Vianthemis' – it is Hagesichora for whom we pine.[43]

The occasion for which this was originally designed – perhaps one on the same scale as a Derbyshire Well Dressing – is as doubtful as the identity of Hagesichora.[44] But what is unmistakable is the distinctive manner in which the beauty of girls is evoked. Such songs celebrated qualities which were most admired by the peer-group – that is, qualities which made girls seem nubile.[45] For their eventual, socially prescribed goal was to leave the solidarity of the same-sex group and marry. For young men, heroic prowess in the outside world, tempered with restraint; for young women, beauty and marriageability. Aristotle was echoing a common Greek (at least, male Greek) attitude when he maintained that the aim of individuals and communities should be to promote in young men 'stature, beauty, strength, fitness for athletics contests, ... self-control and courage', and in young women 'beauty, stature, self-control and industriousness without meanness'.[46] What was ideally expected of the young of both sexes was expressed in their songs.

---

[42] *H. Ap.* 156–61; cf. a hymn to Apollo sung by Boeotian girls (Proklos ap. Photios *Bibl.* 321a-b = Herington 1985, pp. 186–7 no. 14).

[43] Fr. 1, 36–77 (trans. slightly adapted from Page 1951).

[44] On the local immediacy of Alkman's *partheneia*, see R. Kannicht in Haug and Warning 1989, pp. 50–1.   [45] See Calame 1977, I, ch. 4.   [46] *Rh.* 1.5.6.

Stories for citizens

At no point in the period with which this book is concerned were Greek myths marginalised as of interest only to the young. Adults recounted and listened to myths in a variety of contexts. We may begin with certain social rituals of conviviality[47] which constituted settings for the exchange, between adult males, of songs and stories, including those evoking the deeds of gods and heroes.

The Homeric poems include a number of references to poetic performances during or after a banquet (*dais*), when the poet held his noble audience rapt with tales of the past.[48] When Menelaos laid on festivities in his palace to celebrate the marriages of his son and daughter to the children of fellow nobles, the proceedings were crowned with a song:

> So these neighbours and townsmen of glorious Menelaos
> were at their feasting all about the great house with the high roof
> and taking their ease, and among them stepped an inspired singer
> playing his lyre...[49]

Such songs were based on tales of heroic endeavour: after a banquet in Odysseus' house the bard Phemios sang to his audience of young aristocrats about 'the Achaeans' bitter homecoming from Troy'; in Alkinoos' palace the meal was followed by Demodokos' songs about the deeds of noble heroes – the quarrel between Odysseus and Achilles, the ruse of the Trojan horse.[50]

The Homeric accounts of the transmission of myths are fictions; the aristocratic households evoked by the epic poet are the construct of a poetic tradition. When we eventually have definite information about recitations of Homer, the contexts are different from anything described in the *Iliad* or *Odyssey*: the setting is usually a public festival or a *leschē*.[51] However, the Homeric image of poetic performance may represent in idealised form an actual situation in which heroic poems were once sung in Archaic Greece. There is nothing absurd

---

[47] I borrow the phrase from P. Schmitt Pantel in O. Murray 1990, p. 24.
[48] E.g. *Od.* 8.98–9, 9.5ff., 17.359. On the *dais*, see Bielohlawek 1940, Nagy 1979, pp. 127ff.
[49] *Od.* 4.15ff. [50] *Od.* 1.325–7, 8.72ff., 8.499ff. [51] See below, p. 40.

about the idea that epic poetry was sung in noblemen's houses, as later poets would regularly perform at the courts of rulers.

An institution which in some ways represents a real-life continuation of the Homeric image of the feast is the *symposion* of Archaic times. But there are differences amid the similarities.[52] Like the Homeric *dais*, the *symposion* affirmed solidarity between aristocratic males.[53] It was a place for mingling and exchange: for the mingling of wine and water, and for the exchange of stories. But at the *symposion* song was passed on from symposiast to symposiast like a filled cup;[54] the Homeric situation of the singing or reciting bard had changed in the direction of, on the one hand, choral performance and, on the other, participation by the guests themselves.[55]

Drinking songs figured prominently,[56] and so did patriotic and other political verses; in addition, we know that some of the poetry performed, elegiac as well as lyric, had a mythological content.[57] Indeed, it has been persuasively claimed that a significant proportion of the lyric and elegiac poetry surviving from the Archaic period was performed or reperformed at *symposia*.[58] While such an attempt to reconstruct a context of performance is entirely justified, a reservation needs to be entered about the notion that what we have is a private setting, as opposed to the public gatherings characteristic of the later Classical *polis*. The vast banquet said to have been laid on by Kleisthenes for the wedding of his daughter illustrates how a display of aristocratic largesse could embrace virtually the whole of the public domain.[59] The same point is suggested by a consideration of the victory ode which, as we saw earlier, might be performed within the household of the victor's family, yet might at the same time retain civic importance, in that victory brought honour to the city as well as

---

[52] Cf. J. Latacz in Kullmann and Reichel 1990, p. 228.

[53] See O. Murray in Hägg 1983a, p. 196.

[54] Cf. Lissarrague 1990, pp. 123–4, where Pindaric and other references are cited.

[55] Lissarrague 1990, p. 124.   [56] On these *skolia*, see Reitzenstein 1893, pp. 3–44.

[57] Mythical allusions as paradigms for valour: Tyrt. fr. 12, 3–8 (West 1989–92, II, p. 177). Xenophanes implies that myths involving violent dissension (Titans, Giants, Centaurs) are inappropriate at *symposia* (ap. Ath. 462f = West 1989–92, II, fr. B1, 20ff.).

[58] Herington 1985, pp. 49–50, Bowie 1986.

[59] Hdt. 6.126–31. See P. Schmitt-Pantel in O. Murray 1990, pp. 20–1.

to the winner's own relatives.[60] However, we must not go to the opposite extreme of over-emphasising the civic dimension. This becomes clear as soon as we ask how the poetry of Sappho, Bacchylides and Pindar was preserved until it was eventually codified and edited in Hellenistic Alexandria. The answer must be that its survival was above all in the interests of the families of those celebrated in the poems. Whether we imagine the existence of written family archives,[61] or, as seems very much more likely, a continuous tradition of performance, above all in aristocratic milieux,[62] we must conclude that the function of the victory ode in harking back to a glorious and exemplary past continued long after its most famous poets were dead. In the *symposion*, as in the Homeric feast, we see myths acting as a symbolic focus for the values of an aristocracy.

In the fifth century the *symposion* continued to operate as a focus for aristocratic self-definition, as can be inferred from Aristophanic mockery of the behaviour of sophisticated symposiasts.[63] But as the centrality of the *symposion* waned in face of the growth of other arenas for social intercourse in the developing *polis*, so its role as a stage for the exchange of stories and poetry, and for the mythology on which they so often drew, gave ground to new arenas for expression offered by the city-state, arenas which unambiguously deserve the descriptions 'public' and 'civic'. From local ceremonies in tiny communities to grand events at the Panhellenic sanctuaries, there took place performances, frequently competitive, involving the retelling of myths.

Often the narrator was a single individual, either a rhapsode (reciter) or a citharode (lyre-singer).[64] Although rhapsodes delivered

---

[60] 'When the Eratidai rejoice, the city too holds feasts' (Pi. *Ol.* 7.93–4; cf. *Isthm.* 6.65–6).

[61] Herington 1985, p. 203.

[62] Herington 1985, pp. 55–6, and see p. 28 on reperformance of an epinician ode at a *symposion* (Ar. *Nu.* 1354–8; cf. Pavese 1972, pp. 71–2). On the connection between epinician poetry and the aristocracy, cf. Gentili 1988, p. 116: 'mythology ... provided the aristocracies of archaic Greece with both an inherited set of precedents and an inherited claim to power'. Thomas 1989, p. 100, is convincingly sceptical about the role of writing in preserving family history even in the fifth century.

[63] *V.* 1208ff., with Murray in O. Murray 1990, p. 150. Note too Kimon's reputation for lavishness at table (Plu. *Cim.* 3.3, with M. Vickers in O. Murray 1990, p. 111).

[64] Herington 1985, pp. 10–20.

other poetry than epic, and although we hear of them composing
their own verses, the commonest role in which they appear is that of
reciters of Homer.[65] Examples of the purple passages they might
select are those featuring Odysseus scattering the suitors, the show-
down between Hektor and Achilles, and the pathos of Andromache,
Hekabe and Priam.[66] There is evidence of rhapsodic performance at
Brauron, Olympia, Sikyon and Syracuse,[67] and we know that Ion,
whom Plato describes in the dialogue named after him, has just
carried off the first prize at the festival of Asklepios at Epidauros, and
will soon be taking part in the Panathenaia at Athens.[68]

Lyre-singers such as Arion, whose artistry and dearness to the gods
are the subject of a memorable Herodotean anecdote,[69] look like
lineal descendants of the bards depicted in Homer.[70] They had a
major competition at Delphi, for which we have the names of many
poets traditionally regarded as victors; the great Terpander of Lesbos
was said to have won there four times in succession.[71] Terpander's
fellow-countryman Perikleitos carried off the prize at the Karneian
festival in Sparta.[72] As well as setting to music and singing Homeric
verses,[73] lyre-singers may also have composed their own narratives,
on epic themes but in metres which, in spite of a dactylic flavour, were
not identical with the hexameters of Homeric and Hesiodic poetry.[74]
This may be how we should regard the West Greek poet Stesichoros.
His work has been almost obliterated by time, but we know it
included numerous poems on mythological themes: Helen, the
Oresteia story, the sack of Troy, the returns of the heroes from Troy,
the funeral games of Pelias.[75]

---

[65] Poetry other than epic: Gentili 1988, p. 7, with p. 238 n. 19. Composing as well as reciting:
Gentili 1988, p. 7 (*re* Kynaithos). More on rhapsodes: Patzer 1952, Sealey 1957, Ritoók 1962,
Pavese 1972, pp. 215–30.   [66] Pl. *Ion* 535b.

[67] See the references collected in Herington 1985, pp. 167–76.   [68] *Ion* 530a–b.

[69] Hdt. 1.23–4. Arion is a human analogue of Dionysos – surrounded by dolphins.

[70] Plu. *De mus.* 1131f–1133d, schol. Hom. *Od.* 3.267; Brelich 1969, p. 404, Pavese 1972, p. 247.

[71] Paus. 10.7, Plu. *De mus.* 1132e.   [72] Plu. *De mus.* 1133d.

[73] Herington 1985, p. 19, cf. Pavese 1972, pp. 230ff.

[74] Perhaps this should be regarded as a parallel tradition to that of Homeric/Hesiodic hexameter
poetry, rather than as a tradition *descended* from Homer; cf. Gentili 1988, p. 125.

[75] See West 1971 and 1981, p. 125.

The importance of these solo performers is threefold. First, their extensive travelling illustrates how the language of mythology transcended local boundaries. Secondly, in spite of the dangers of over-simplifying the public/private distinction, it is clear that the narrations of rhapsodes and citharodes were public in a way that performances at banquets of the aristocracy were not: in principle, they stood before the whole community. Thirdly – and here we have an element of continuity rather than contrast between the Archaic and Classical periods – the *contest* is a fundamental feature of the transmission of myths.[76] At a time when story-telling was poet-led and still predominantly oral, competition provided a mechanism for keeping the tradition within bounds acceptable to the community's expectations.

We have seen how considerable and socially significant was the participation of adolescents in choral singing. Such participation by adults was rarer. For males, cases like the Spartan Gymnopaidiai and the Athenian dithyrambic competition are exceptional, while the choruses of adult women who sang at Eleusis and on Aigina have characteristics which mark them too as atypical.[77] But in the late sixth century there developed a mode of representing myths which not only included choral performance by adults, but combined with it features of rhapsodic declamation to produce a form of myth-telling unprecedented in its involvement of the whole *polis*.

Athenian tragedy, a genre which decisively affected the course of

[76] Between bards: Hes. *Op.* 650ff. (Chalkis); Hom. *H. Ap.* 150, cf. 173, Th. 3.104.5 (Delos). Between rhapsodes: Pl. *Ion* 530a–b (Athens, Epidauros). *Humnos* competitively sung: Thgn. 993–6. For elegiac competitions at Pythia/Panathenaia see Bowie 1986, pp. 27ff. More on contests in Càssola 1975, pp. xv–xvi, Humphreys 1978, p. 215, Wiseman 1979, p. 144, Graf 1985a, pp. 10–11, Henderson 1989. See also Lloyd 1987, pp. 85ff.: archaic contests, including contests in 'wisdom', are to be seen as the antecedents of more formalised public argumentation by sophists, doctors and other enquirers into 'nature'.

[77] At Eleusis, women 'formed a chorus and sang for the goddess' (Paus. 1.38.6). For Aigina, Herodotos (5.83) records a custom of 'mocking' choruses of women, led by male *chorēgoi*, in honour of the goddesses Damia and Auxesia (see How and Wells' commentary on Hdt. 82.1 and 83.3, N. J. Richardson 1974, pp. 213ff.). The two ceremonies have close similarities, being linked by the notion of scurrilous joking which was prominent in the Eleusinian festival as in the Aiginetan (cf. Calame 1977, I, p. 247).

Greek mythological narration, was put on competitively at the festival of the Great Dionysia. At the smaller, winter festival of the Lenaia, a local event apparently attended by few outside visitors, non-citizens could take part in the dramas staged; but on the greater occasion, where the city and its values and priorities were on show to the Greek world, the citizen group publicly expressed its exclusive-ness: it was the citizens alone who put the tragedies on at the Dionysia.[78] Tragic myths were passed through the filter of the democratic *polis*.

Athens appears prominently. Theseus' democratic city is con-trasted with Kreon's autocratic Thebes (*Oidipous at Kolonos*); it is a haven for the oppressed and the stateless (*Children of Herakles, Medea, Oidipous at Kolonos*) as, earlier, it had been the champion of Greek freedom (*Persians*) and the city where goddess and people together relied on persuasion in order to settle an impossible dilemma (*Eumenides*). But tragedy's roots in the *polis* go deeper than mere Athenian self-definition or propagandistic self-assertion. Debates about the sources and authority of law (*Antigone*), about the best political constitution (Euripides' *Suppliants*), about the contrasting roles of persuasion and violence in a state – all this signals the influence upon drama of the argumentative, word-driven city which fostered it.

While there is a sense in which it is true to say that Athenian ideology – for example, the emphasis on the fundamental role of persuasive debate – is not just implicit in tragedy but often explicitly justified, this is barely half the story: and the less interesting half. Much more remarkable is the extent to which tragedy asks uncomfortable questions. Questions, for instance, about the *fairness* of the gods: how can Apollo's behaviour towards Kreousa, as represented in Euripides' *Ion* – rape and desertion – be defended? Questions about the *uncanniness* of the gods: what is to be made of the monstrous bull from the sea which kills Hippolytos in Euripides' play? Questions about the *incomprehensibility* of the gods: what is Zeus's attitude towards the

---

[78] Ar. *Ach.* 504–5 ('*no* foreigners at the Lenaia'), schol. Ar. *Pl.* 953, Plu. *Phoc.* 30.3; Pickard-Cambridge 1988, p. 41.

fates of Herakles (*Women of Trachis*) and Oidipous (*Oidipous Tyrannos*)? Even more than Greek mythology in general, tragedy concentrates on extremes: dislocations within a family, intensified to a degree rarely or never experienced in real life; hopeless dilemmas which had to be solved, yet could not be, like Agamemnon's at Aulis, or Orestes' at Argos. Tension, disruption, questioning: it has been suggested that the very structure of tragedy – with the deeds of heroes being played out before and examined by a collective group, the chorus – mirrors what is distinctive in the genre's narrative stance, as the city-state confronts the mythical past and questions it anew.[79]

Most radical of all – a paradox which, paradoxically, makes perfect sense – is the fact that even the values of the dominant ideology (Greekness, Athenianness, democracy, the very values which license tragic questioning) are themselves subjected to critical exploration.[80] When the inadequacy and shallowness of the Greek husband Jason are set beside the passion and suffering of his 'barbarian' wife Medea; when the haste and authoritarianism of the Athenian hero Theseus are tragically exposed in *Hippolytos*; when Odysseus' claims to be acting on democratic orders ring so hollow in *Hekabe*; then the authentic voice of tragedy resounds with all its disconcerting power.

How could the *polis* tolerate such self-doubt? Perhaps because, when it came down to it, the whole enterprise was impossible to mistake for anything other than 'play'. The citizens who took the roles of actors and chorus were transformed by masks: that their identities were changed corresponded to the fact that they performed in the precinct of Dionysos, god of the dissolution of boundaries. For all its political dimension, the tragic theatre is not the democratic assembly. The debates and arguments represented are in all kinds of ways displacements or ironic inversions of the political context. Choruses, those apparent embodiments of society's traditional wisdom, are socially marginal, as are those other 'neutrals', the

---

[79] Vernant and Vidal-Naquet 1981 is the classic exposition, e.g. pp. 1–5.

[80] Cf. Goldhill 1986, p. 78: 'The drama festival offers not just the powers and profundity of a great literature but also the extraordinary process of the developing city putting its own developing language and structures of thought at risk under the sway of the smiling and dangerous Dionysos.'

newsbringers ('messengers'); male actors play women who act with more-than-male aggression; gods appear side-by-side with mortals, while being morally incommensurate with them. In spite of, but also because of, its concentrated, fantastical exaggeration, tragedy demonstrates, with a force equalled only by the *Iliad*, that 'mere stories' can open up areas of experience more strange and profound than any touched elsewhere in Greek culture.

Comedy was less homogeneous than tragedy. Not only did it undergo a long and complex development (as against the domination of the great fifth-century tragic trio over the entire subsequent ancient tradition), but it also exhibited greater geographical diversity. There is some evidence for a sixth-century Peloponnesian farce which the Syracusan Epicharmos is credited with having formalised; the apparent importance of Odysseus and Herakles in his works suggests the presence of mythological spoof, a major strand in Greek comedy until the late fourth century. Similar dramatised travesties of mythology seem to lie behind the so-called Kabeirion vases of Thebes, while the broad humour of the vases often seen as reflecting the *phlyakes* (perhaps 'Gossips') comedies of Southern Italy show what fun we have missed by the loss of the plays themselves (Plate 2).[81]

Fifth- and early fourth-century Attic comedies often presented or alluded to mythical characters.[82] They might appear in person, as with Dionysos, Aiakos, Charon and Herakles in Aristophanes' *Frogs*; or their stories might provide a point of reference for parody, as with Perseus and Menelaos-in-Egypt in his *Thesmophoriazousai*. But always the scene is contemporary, not 'the time of myth'. The *Birds* features Tereus, the mythical king of Thrace who turned into a hoopoe after raping and mutilating his wife's sister and then being horribly punished by the two women, who fed him his son Itys. The myth is explicitly alluded to, yet the fantastic plot is rooted right in the middle of the Peloponnesian War, so that a character talking to the

---

81 Kabeirion vases: Demand 1982, p. 121. *Phlyakes*: Trendall 1967, with Long 1986, p. 181 n. 1 for bibliography. Taplin 1993, contrary to received opinion, argues that so-called *phlyakes* vases preserve evidence for Athenian Old Comedy.   82 *RE* XI, cols. 1239–42 (Körte).

2. One of the tonal possibilities on offer in Greek mythology is broad farce. Here Helen emerges from the egg in what looks like a re-creation or parody of a theatrical performance. The axe-wielder could be playing Hephaistos; the identity of the fellow on the right ('Enough!'?) is unknown. Leda, Helen's mother, looks on anxiously. (Fourth-century Apulian bell-*kratēr*.)

transmogrified Tereus can refer to the dilly-dallying of the Athenian general Nikias.[83] Such fantasies are in no ordinary sense 'retellings' of myths. Rather, various aspects of experience go into their outrageous melting-pot: contemporary celebrities, men and women in the street, excrement, sex, prejudice of every kind – *and* mythology.

The mythology of Middle Comedy is characterised by appetite. The gluttony of Herakles and the promiscuity of Zeus (as in the Ganymede episode) illustrate the humorous reductionism apparently exploited here.[84] But dramatists found potential in a wide range of

[83] *Av.* 209ff., 640.
[84] Herakles: cf. Antiphanes' *Omphale* (PCG 174). Ganymede: plays by Euboulos and Antiphanes.

tales, from the Judgement of Paris and Aiolos' interesting family (his fifty sons married his fifty daughters) to Adonis and the blind bard Thamyras.[85] The popularity of this mythological drama may have been partly due to the increasing export of comedy: myths travelled better than domestic Athenian politics.[86]

In later fourth-century Athens, comedy developed into the un-Rabelaisian art-form of which the greatest exponent was Menander. In this genre the world of mythology recedes. While it is true that certain themes (e.g. the chance survival of foundlings) bear an obvious and hardly accidental resemblance to motifs familiar from mythology – once more, no autonomous territory – they were worked out through the fates not of heroes but of ordinary men and women. Religion remained one dimension of the plot, and the gods might appear in a Prologue in order to give an overview of the story (Pan in *Dyskolos*, Tyche (Chance/Fortune) in *Aspis*, Agnoia (Ignorance) in *Perikeiromene*), but when an old man came on stage he was called Demeas or Nikeratos, not Amphitryon or Kadmos.

At virtually the same moment at the end of the fifth century, two plays were put on depicting Dionysos: Euripides' *Bakchai* and Aristophanes' *Frogs*. It would be hard to overstate the contrast between the smiling–menacing god in the tragedy and the richly comic figure who bears the same name. Plurality is a fundamental characteristic of Greek mythology, a characteristic which may well be causally linked with, and which was certainly nourished by, the more general pluralism built into the Greek *polis*. It is at least symbolically appropriate that the perfect illustration of this plurality – the twin portrayals of Dionysos – should belong to the *democratic* city of Athens. To answer the question, 'How did the Greeks perceive Dionysos (Herakles, Jason . . .)?', it is necessary first of all to specify the context.[87]

At most festivals it was the poet whose voice was heard, either directly or through the performance of others. Responsive though they had to

---

[85] Long 1986, pp. 55–60.   [86] Cf. Dover 1987, p. 213.

[87] Even without going outside fifth-century drama, the picture is further complicated by the genre of the satyr-play. For a speculative but convincing reconstruction of its development, see the Introduction to Seaford 1984.

be to the expectations of the community, poets were set apart, inspired by the Muse (*Od.* 1.1), the 'goddess' (*Il.* 1.1), the Muses who spoke to them (Hes. *Th.* 22ff.), the Muse who is present to swell the wind of song (Pi. *Pyth.* 4.3).[88] Yet there were certain occasions at which the language of myth–telling was prose; and here, for once, the authority of the speaker was not conferred by the Muse.

The best–known example is the *epitaphios logos* or funeral speech, another Athenian phenomenon. We know something of the context thanks to Thucydides, who described the ceremonial burial of the first Athenians to perish in the Peloponnesian War:

> Anyone who wishes, whether citizen or stranger, may take part in the funeral procession, and the women who are related to the deceased are present at the burial and make lamentation ... But when the remains have been laid away in the earth, a man chosen by the state, who is regarded as best endowed with wisdom and is foremost in public esteem, delivers over them an appropriate eulogy. After this the people depart.[89]

The evidence about the genre poses many problems, but it is clear that the oration was an encomium of the Athenian *polis* by a representative of itself.[90] Specifically, it is the praise of men's deeds by a man; lamentation belongs to women.[91] As is clear from Plato's *Menexenos* (235b), these speeches were delivered before foreigners as well as Athenians; as at the Great Dionysia, the city's self-image was turned outwards as well as towards the home audience.

The role of mythology was modest, and this very limitation is significant. A small group of heroic exploits by Athenians recurs in several of the speeches: the defeat of invasions by the Amazons and by Eumolpos (a Thracian who helped the Eleusinians in their fight against the Athenian king Erechtheus); Athens' piety in securing burial for the Argive dead after the expedition of the Seven against Thebes, and in accepting the suppliant children of Herakles. In addition, individual speeches invoke mythology to praise the dead: Athens has been so loved by the gods that Athene and Poseidon

---

[88] See P. Murray 1981.   [89] Th. 2.34 (trans. C. F. Smith, Loeb edn).
[90] See Colin 1938, Jacoby 1944, Pohlenz 1948, Vollgraff 1952, Collard 1975, II, p. 323, Loraux 1986, Thomas 1989, ch. 4.   [91] Th. 2.34.4; cf. Loraux 1986, p. 45.

fought over who should be patron deity; the tribe of the Aigeidai were unwilling to disgrace the democratic principles espoused by their ancestor Theseus, while the Aiantidai were true to the glorious memory of Ajax, who preferred suicide to dishonour.[92] The tales serve merely to introduce the exploits of Athenians in more recent times, above all in the Persian Wars.[93] Indeed these later Athenians could be seen as actually superior to their heroic predecessors: great as they were, the demi-gods of old were *less* impressive than the contemporary general Leosthenes who lies among the dead.[94] Significantly, the role of the gods, and even the leadership of individual, named heroes, pale beside the collective valour of the ancestors.[95] Lacking what is perceived to be the poet's directly inspired access to the past, the prose orator is a human representative of the *polis*. He works within a perspective which differs fundamentally from those of epic and victory poetry; no less striking is the contrast with tragedy, a form of discourse exactly coincident in time and place.

The *epitaphios logos* forms part of a wider genre, the *epideixis* or display speech. In the *Greater Hippias* Plato's Sokrates is in conversation with the sophist whose name the work bears. Sokrates alludes to the private performances given by Gorgias and Prodikos in addition to their official speeches (282b–c). Hippias too has travelled the world giving verbal recitals. Like any prudent lecturer he tailors his material to his audience. In Sparta, it seems, tastes did not favour new-fangled astronomy or mathematics, but mythology:

> They are very fond of hearing about the genealogies of heroes and
> men, Sokrates, and the foundations of cities in ancient times and, in
> short, about antiquity in general, so that for their sake I have been

---

[92] *Mx.* 237c–d, D. *Fun. Or.* 29ff.

[93] Cf. Th. 1.73, where Athenian ambassadors in Sparta explicitly refrain from referring to 'very old matters' (glossed by a scholiast as 'the events concerning Amazons, Thracians and the children of Herakles') in favour of 'the Persian War and all the other events of which you have personal knowledge'.

[94] Hyp. *Fun. Or.* 35; cf. D. *Fun. Or.* 10, Lys. *Fun. Or.* 20.

[95] See Loraux 1986, pp. 53–4.

obliged to learn all that sort of thing by heart and practise it
thoroughly.[96]

Sokrates mischievously observes that the Spartans use Hippias 'as
children make use of old women, to tell stories agreeably' (285e–
286a). Hippias rejoins that he has a very beautiful *logos* prepared,
which has already brought him acclaim in Sparta, and which he is
going to repeat in Athens in Pheidostratos' schoolroom, the subject
being Nestor's advice to Achilles' son Neoptolemos, after the fall of
Troy, about how a young man should behave. This passage tells us
several things: that travelling lecturers in the fifth century had
inherited the role of rhapsodes and lyric poets, moving from city to
city, instructing and entertaining audiences;[97] that mythology was
one option within a repertoire which embraced (in Hippias' case)
astronomy, geometry, arithmetic and euphony (285); that a possible
context for performance was a schoolroom – to which we may add
private houses and (for Prodikos) the Lyceum at Athens;[98] that
mythology might go down better in some places than others (though
Hippias' words refer to what was *perceived* to be typically Spartan
behaviour). As a guide to the kind of material which might have been
performed, we need probably look no further than the myth about
the origins of human society ascribed by Plato to the sophist
Protagoras. The role of prose myths as vehicles for conveying that
which cannot be conveyed otherwise – the role developed by Plato
himself with such eloquent sophistication – surely has its origin in
performances of this kind.

Prose and poetic performances share two important features: both
were put on at festivals, and both might be competitive. Hippias
recited at the Olympic Games, having in his repertoire pieces from
epic, tragedy and dithyramb as well as prose; Gorgias spoke at
Olympia and at Delphi, Lysias at Olympia, while other panhellenic
occasions such as the Isthmian Games afforded the same kind of

---

[96] *Hp. Ma.* 285d (trans. H. N. Fowler, Loeb edn).

[97] See Guthrie 1962–81, III, p. 42, Lloyd 1987, pp. 83ff., esp. 90–1.

[98] Guthrie 1962–81, III, p. 41, for refs.

arena.[99] As for competition, we may return to Plato's portrait of a vainglorious Hippias: '... since I began to contend at the Olympic Games, I have never met anyone better than myself in anything'.[100] The differences between a Hippias and a Sophokles (or even a Euripides) were wide, but both aimed at retaining an audience by telling tales. For all Sokrates' irony in the *Greater Hippias*, it is clear that it was not just in Sparta that listening to stories was a serious, grown-up business.

... to the grave

When Odysseus' swineherd Eumaios lists the types of wandering strangers who are invited into people's houses and communities because of what they can contribute, along with prophets, healers and skilled workmen he mentions the *thespin aoidon*, 'inspired singer'.[101] While the *Iliad* and *Odyssey* may perhaps owe their monumental length and complexity to special recitals at a religious festival,[102] epic poetry will doubtless also have been sung (in addition to performances at the noble feast) in smaller, local contexts like the ones envisaged by Eumaios. The Herodotean *Life of Homer* depicts the great bard singing in, among other places, a cobbler's shop and 'the *leschai* of the old men' (99, 141). The latter may have been a more significant location than is usually realised.

Leschē (plural *leschai*) means both a public place where people could sit and converse, and the conversation which occurred there.[103] The *leschē* best known to us is the sumptuous one built by the Knidians at Delphi, perhaps in gratitude for the conclusive defeat of the Persians at Eurymedon.[104] Pausanias dwelt at length on this hall because of its huge murals of the fall of Troy and Odysseus' visit to the Underworld

---

[99] Hippias: Pl. *Hp. Mi.* 363, 368c–d. Gorgias: Philostr. *VS* 1.9. Lysias: *Or.* 33. For specific locations at Olympia where verbal recitals were given, cf. Luc. *Herod.* 1 (inner chamber of the temple of Zeus), Paus. 6.23.5 (council chamber within a gymnasium). Antisthenes at Isthmian games: D. L. 6.2.   [100] *Hp. Mi.* 364a.

[101] *Od.* 17.382ff.

[102] See *Certamen Homeri et Hesiodi* (OCT Allen) 315–21, where Homer performs the Hymn to Apollo at Delos (and the Delians write it down and dedicate it to Artemis).

[103] Refs. at *RE* xii, cols. 2133–4 (Öhler).   [104] Cf. Kebric 1983.

(10.25–31). Of special interest in Pausanias' account is a passage in which he mentions another connection between the *leschē* and stories:

> It is called by the Delphians *leschē*, because in former times they used to meet there to discuss matters which were more serious and those which were fanciful/mythical/legendary (*muthōdē*). That there used to be many such places all over Greece is shown by Homer's words in the passage where Melantho reviles Odysseus: 'And you are unwilling to go to a smithy to sleep or to a *leschē*, but you talk too much here [sc. in the palace of Odysseus].'[105]

Melantho, daughter of Dolios (Tricky), repays Penelope's kindness to her by becoming the lover of one of the suitors; she is unlikely to mince her insults towards Odysseus. The attribute of the *leschē* which makes it suitable for her scorn is that, being a place where one can drop in and find others, it can be perceived as a resort of idlers. Melantho's words find an echo in Hesiod, where the parallel with the forge is repeated, and the opposition between *leschē* and agricultural work is made explicit:

> Pass by the smithy and the warm *leschē* in winter, when the cold keeps men from work in the fields ... The idle man, who waits on empty hope, lacking a livelihood, lays mischief-making to his heart; it is not a wholesome hope that accompanies a needy man, sitting in a *leschē*, while he has insufficient livelihood.[106]

A *leschē* was a place to sit for men who were not working; it might either attract criticism ('idle') or be viewed more constructively (cf. 'more serious' matters in the Pausanias quotation above). Sometimes our sources make a connection between *leschai* and communally taken meals,[107] but it is clear that the activities generally regarded as characteristic of the *leschē* differ from those associated with banquets and *symposia*. The essential ingredient was, not eating and drinking,

---

[105] Paus. 10.25, quoting *Od.* 18.328–9.

[106] *Op.* 493ff. (trans. based on that of H. G. Evelyn-White, Loeb edn). For 'warm' see West's commentary *ad loc.*

[107] Hsch. *s.v. leschē*, *Et. magn. s.v. leschē* (the latter referring specifically to Boeotia); see Bremmer in O. Murray 1990, pp. 136–7.

but talk.[108] The *leschē* was a context for 'gossip' or for 'important debate': at Sparta, for example, the *leschē* was where decisions were taken about which infants should be allowed to grow up and which exposed to die.[109] Gossip and important debate are two sides of the same coin, depending on whether talk is seen negatively as contrasted with work or positively as the desirable preliminary to decision-making. In general the *leschē* seems to have functioned, above all in winter, as a place of informal resort which might from time to time be the scene of more formal events involving all those males who dropped in. The parochial and class-oriented English analogy of the club is less helpful than the 'men's house' familiar to anthropologists, a parallel buttressed by the fact that in a number of societies the smithy fulfils, as in Greece, just such a focal role.[110]

For evidence about myth-telling in the *leschē* we are reduced to the anecdote in the *Life of Homer* and Pausanias' word *muthōdē*, plus guesswork. *Muthōdē* (plural of *muthōdēs*) is hard to translate. Sometimes it refers to old stories on what we should describe as mythical themes, as in a speech by Demosthenes where accounts of the court of the Areopagos are divided into traditional, *muthōdē* tales and later stories about matters 'of which we are witnesses'.[111] Plato could use the word to distinguish between fabulous stories and truer ones, Thucydides to characterise the fanciful tale-telling element which he purports to be excluding.[112] The *leschē* was evidently a setting in which traditional stories, far from being discredited as opposites to the true or the verifiable, were *de rigueur*.

Not only is the *leschē* a place for men: it is more than once linked

---

[108] A relevant passage occurs in Kallimachos' legendary epigram on the death of Herakleitos. 'I remembered', says the poet, 'how many times the two of us made the sun go down [*en*] *leschēi*.' It is widely assumed that the meaning is 'in conversation'; thus Hopkinson 1988 *ad loc.* writes: '*leschēi*: a Homeric *hapax* (*Od.* 18.329), = "lounging-place". Here, however, the later meaning "conversation" is more suitable.' But (1) to *translate* the word as 'lounging-place' is to replace meaning with (possible) implication; (2) when, a little later in his commentary, H. explains how the poem draws freely on 'the Homeric lexicon', it is fair to ask why the same cannot apply to *leschē*. On the Kallimachos poem, see further Macqueen 1982, esp. n. 15.

[109] Gossip: Hsch. *s.v. leschē*, Suid. *s.v. leschē*. Important debate: Plu. *Lyc.* 16.

[110] Cf. Brelich 1969, p. 424 n. 269 (an important note), and in general Eliade 1977 (cited by Brelich).   [111] *Aristocr.* 65.   [112] *R.* 522a, Th. 1.22.

specifically with *old* men. The *Life of Homer* refers to the great bard sitting down 'in the *leschai* of the old men' (141), while the Spartans who deliberated over the fate of their babies are described as 'the oldest men'. Does this preserve a clue to the working of tradition in an oral culture? In order to survive, did a version of a tale have to earn the approval of the most respected, because senior, members of the community? The hypothesis sounds attractive, but it is unconvincing. The attitude of the Greeks towards old age is multiple, and certainly cannot be boiled down to the catch-all 'respect'.[113] True, various institutions and customs did involve priority for the old, for instance the Spartan Gerousia, and the practice of 'eldest speaks first' on Aeschines' legation to Macedon.[114] But individual old people are often presented as surly or cantankerous in our literary sources, and it is far commoner to come across praise of people who repay the care of their elderly *parents* than to find the elderly as a class singled out as worthy of deference.[115] What of the idea that once upon a time (perhaps 'in the Dark Ages') the old *were* more greatly respected, this respect being enshrined in the *leschē*? There is no evidence for this; and there can be few riskier historical procedures than the hypothetical derivation of a complex and heterogeneous present from a past conceived in simplistic and naively rosy terms.[116] It is true that we have sporadic information about the role of old men as preservers of tradition, as when Pausanias cites as his informants 'the old man whom I questioned' and 'the oldest man';[117] but it is a big step from this to drawing conclusions about the *leschē* as an institution. It is safest to regard the *leschē* as something about which we know tantalisingly

[113] Evidence collected in B. E. Richardson 1933, Falkner and de Luce 1989.

[114] Aeschin. *De legat.* 22.

[115] Cf. B. E. Richardson 1933, pp. 48–58, Lacey 1968, pp. 116–17, Dover 1974, pp. 273–5, Parker 1983, pp. 196–7.

[116] Cf. Momigliano 1987, p. 313, on Dumézil's speculations about Indo-European civilisation: 'By assuming that what is at best a partial organization in known societies must be explained by a total organization of the same kind in an unknown, more ancient, society we are perhaps going beyond the limits of legitimate conjecture' – an understatement. 'The refinement of our historical sense chiefly means that we keep it properly complicated' (Trilling 1951, p. 188).

[117] 6.24.9; 8.42.13. Cf. Palaeph. p. 2 Festa (Teubner edn): 'I found out from the oldest inhabitants what they had heard about each of these stories . . .'

little – but that little suggests there are interesting things which escape us. What we do know is that the *leschē* was a context within which itinerant singers, like Homer in the *Life*, could find an audience. It would be a nice piece of calculated humour if Hesiod's lines in reproach of idlers were originally intended for singing precisely in the *leschē*. There is about his poetry a strong whiff of the modern Greek village coffee-shop ('First of all, get a house, and a woman, and an ox for ploughing ...').[118]

[118] *Op.* 405. The Greeks were not the only peasant farmers to hold such no-nonsense views. 'A big wife and a big barn will never do a man any harm' runs the Pennsylvania German proverb (Dorson 1977, p. 79); cf. the Italian proverbial advice, 'Moglie e buoi dei paesi tuoi'.
    On the *leschē*, see now Burkert 1993, an important comparative and linguistic study which came to my attention when the present book was in proof.

3
Performance into text

The Tuscan custom of the *veglia* is a story-telling event with complex rules. Time (a particular period of winter; 'at dark') and place (round the fire in the farmhouse) are prescribed. So are many of the conditions of performance: the story-teller is old, reluctant to begin, and affects grumpiness if people appear to know the stories already. Sometimes the sessions take place in silence, sometimes the audience will interrupt, 'correcting the narrator and then telling the story in competition with the story-teller to see who could tell the best stories ... (each person [is] convinced that his or hers [is] the only true version ...)'. Too great a departure from what was expected will soon be censured: 'It's not that one!', 'It does not go like this!', 'You don't know it!' Interruptions are governed by implicit rules about what is acceptable, the teller's hesitation and false starts being all part of the game:

> It is [the tale of] Genoveffa, then but ... I remember very little, eh then! This girl, I don't remember if she is a king's daughter or if she is of a ... but anyway, yea, of Brabante; I think Genoveffa was of the house of Brabante. She marries this king, this prince. This very young girl, Genoveffa ...[1]

A far cry, this, from the neat, aesthetically rounded narratives which we find in the Grimms' *Kinder- und Hausmärchen* or Italo Calvino's compilation of Italian folk-tales. As recorded by Alessandro Falassi, the *veglia* stories give a flavour of one possible mode of interaction

[1] Falassi 1980, pp. 4, 30ff., 53, 67, 148, 263.

45

between audience and oral narrator. Falassi's description is not complete – such a thing is inconceivable. (For a start, it concentrates on the sort of things which interest contemporary anthropologists.) But it does pack in a lot of circumstantial detail about performance conditions: exactly what we would like to know about antiquity, but virtually never do.[2]

That Greek epics continued to be reperformed orally in a living tradition of controlled improvisation is strongly suggested by the very existence of what were in later antiquity perceived as interpolations; for us, by contrast, the epics have become fixed words on a page. The works of the tragedians may contain clues which enable us to speculate with some plausibility about stagecraft; but the plays are preserved in writing. The same goes for Pindar's victory songs, and for all the surviving hymns and prose displays. Every extant mythical narrative, whatever its putative origin in oral story-telling, has achieved the status which Thucydides claimed for his history: a possession for all time.

Let us assume that one of our objectives in investigating the contexts of mythology is to reconstruct the oral performance 'behind' the written text. The problems involved are immense; nowhere more so than with epic. It is enough to envisage the time required to write down one of the Homeric poems to realise that the conditions of performance in the *leschē* or at a festival will have been replaced by a laborious process of transcription, with consequences for the text which are bound to have been considerable.[3] Furthermore, the very idea of an authoritative version of the *Iliad* and *Odyssey* only makes sense if what is meant is an authoritative *written* version, since the

---

[2] Even Apuleius' *Golden Ass*, which evokes some of the techniques of oral story-telling ('Well now! I'm going to string together in the well-known Milesian manner tales of various kinds, and I'll soothe your well-wishing ears with a witty whisper . . . But perhaps, critical reader, you will criticize my story . . .', 1.1; 9.30), remains obstinately a text: there is no video-recording of actual interruptions or of the narrator's reaction to them. See further Scobie 1979, pp. 256–7, from whom I borrow the translation. The importance of recovering the performance conditions of a text is emphasised by B. Malinowski in Dundes 1984, p. 206: '. . . the functional, cultural and pragmatic aspect of any native tale is manifested as much in its enactment, embodiment and contextual relations as in the text'.

[3] M. L. West argues for dictation at the prompting of a patron as the likeliest scenario for this transcription (in Kullmann and Reichel 1990, pp. 33–50, at p. 47).

work done in this century on oral poetic composition has shown that
oral poets produce different versions of their works at different
performances, according to the requirements of the audience. Does
the writing down of an epic mark a decisive turning-point in its
development? Up to a point: but it is easy to exaggerate. Even if it is
true that a text of the Homeric poems was assembled in sixth-century
Athens, there is no reason to suppose that this version would have
been accepted everywhere.[4] Indeed, there is every reason to suppose it
would not: when Athens and Megara quarrelled over possession of
Salamis in the sixth century, each side quoted a different version of the
Homeric 'Catalogue of Ships' to support its claim.[5] For centuries after
a written text of Homer had been established, the epics continued to
be recited, and, as the editorial scholarship done in Hellenistic
Alexandria showed, such performances were by no means free from
'interpolation': the living tradition continued. The texts of Homer
which we possess are the amalgamation of many performances and
many rewritings. That there is no uniquely authentic version which is
the Homer is a reflection both of the centrality of Homeric epic to
Greek society and of the conditions in which such poetry was handed
on.

With lyric poetry, too, getting from writing back to performance
is rendered problematic by the prior question: which performance?
While we know of cases of the preservation of poems in written form
(e.g. as dedications),[6] we have much more evidence for an ongoing
tradition of reperformance of lyric poetry, for example at *symposia*
and festivals.[7] As Herington has persuasively suggested, we must
imagine Greece, at least in the Archaic period, as a thriving song-
culture in which poems would not survive unless they were thought
worthy of reperformance.[8]

---

[4] On the so-called 'Peisistratean recension', see Merkelbach 1952, Davison 1955, S. West in
Heubeck, West and Hainsworth 1988, pp. 36ff., Janko 1992, pp. 29–32.

[5] Aristot. *Rh.* 1375b, Plu. *Sol.* 10, D.L. 1.48; Nilsson 1951, pp. 28–9, Janko 1992, pp. 29–30.

[6] Schol. Pi. *Ol.* 7; cf. Pavese 1972, p. 115 n. 2. Herakleitos' book was deposited in the temple of
Artemis at Ephesos (D.L. 9.6).

[7] *Symposia*: Herington 1985, p. 208 (ii), cf. p. 151. Festivals: ibid. pp. 25 and 207 no. 6
(Gymnopaidiai).

[8] Herington 1985, pp. 62–3, followed by Latacz in Kullmann and Reichel 1990, p. 241.

So far as drama is concerned, the question, 'Which performance?' is hardly simpler. In the fifth century each tragedy put on at the Dionysia was a new play, with a sole exception: such was the fame of Aischylos that after his death others might re-present his plays in the competition.[9] As for productions outside Athens, a handful are known from the fifth century,[10] and some reperformance of works staged first in Athens cannot be excluded. But only in 386 was a non-Aischylean 'old play' put on for the first time by an Athenian tragedian.[11] From then on there was an increasing tendency towards reperformance of old plays, in Athens and elsewhere. Before the end of the fourth century it was necessary to establish at Athens official texts of Aischylos, Sophokles and Euripides, further testimony to a living tradition of reperformance.[12] Comedies also were reperformed. Old Comedy, such as that of Aristophanes, seems to have been a wine which travelled poorly in time as well as space, but there is plenty of evidence for re-presentations of New Comedy.[13] If we take the two major dramatic genres together, the question of how widespread were *written* texts probably needs to be answered differently for the fifth and fourth centuries. Although Aristophanes' Dionysos read the *Andromeda* (sc. of Euripides) to himself,[14] and although poets presumably needed a text in order to train actors and chorus, myth-telling in the fifth-century theatre was essentially an oral phenomenon. Aristotle's opinion that tragedy will produce its effect irrespective of whether it is acted or read belongs to a period when the written word was growing in importance.[15]

Prose too involves interpretative complexities at the intersection of text and oral performance.[16] Of the funeral orations, that by Hypereides may be close to an oral original; so, perhaps, may those

---

9   *TrGF* III Test. Gm 72–7. A tragedian might modify an unsuccessful play and put it on again, as with Euripides' *Hippolytos*: Pickard-Cambridge 1988, p. 99.

10   *TrGF* I DID B (p. 17).   11   *TrGF* I DID A I (p. 24).

12   On the whole question of interpolation, see Page 1934.

13   Dover 1972, p. 223, Pickard-Cambridge 1988, pp. 100–1. 'What truly is the point of an educated man going to the theatre', wrote Plutarch, 'if not to see Menander?' (*Mor.* 854b).

14   *Ra.* 52–3; cf. Havelock 1980, p. 89.   15   *Poet.* 1462a11–18, cf. 1450b18 and 1453b4.

16   See L. Canfora in Detienne 1988, pp. 211–20, in relation to the far-from-linear progression from oral to written in Attic oratory.

ascribed to Lysias and Demosthenes. But the attribution of the speech in Plato's *Menexenos* to Perikles' mistress Aspasia makes it uncertain whether what we have is transcribed from life, while the Periklean oration has to be seen in the light of Thucydides' remark that he has recorded that which he thought it *appropriate* for his speakers to say, keeping as close as he could to the general purport of what was really said (1.22).[17] Other prose displays are equally difficult to place. Was Isokrates' *Panegyrikos* ever presented at the type of panhellenic gathering which it seems to presuppose? Did the genealogical studies of Pherekydes, so influential in later compilations of mythology, circulate already in the fifth century as a book, or were they too presented orally?

There is clearly movement in the late fifth and early fourth centuries towards a greater importance for the written word; equally, we should not underestimate the degree to which communication remained oral.[18] But it is in any case misleading to posit a rigid distinction between written and oral means of communication since, in Greece as in many story–telling societies, there is constant interplay between the modes of transmission.[19] A corollary is that it is quite arbitrary to confine the term 'myth' to orally transmitted stories. A definition which glues myth indissolubly to oral performance will generate all kinds of terminological side-issues (e.g.: Is there an essential difference between 'primary' (= oral) and 'secondary' (= written) myths?), instead of allowing us to look at the tales as what they actually were: a continuum of narratives weaving an enormously complex path between speech and writing.

The years following the conquests of Alexander saw two important developments in the nature of this interface; their combined effect ensured the survival of the tales by providing contexts for their

[17] I am drawing on Hornblower 1987, p. 45, for the paraphrase.

[18] Even in the Hellenistic period, with its intense concentration of effort into the editing of written texts, Apollonios of Rhodes gave oral *epideixeis* of his work in Alexandria and Rhodes; see Hunter 1989, pp. 1–2, on ancient *Lives* of the poet. Rohde 1914, pp. 327–9, has a valuable collection of references to oral performances in later antiquity.

[19] Finnegan 1977, pp. 160–8, Detienne 1988, pp. 10–11. Fehling 1972 takes a sideways look at unjustified assumptions about oral/written traditions.

narration at both a popular and a sophisticated level – a distinction which it becomes for the first time appropriate to make.

The epigraphical work of Margherita Guarducci has revealed how widespread were the phenomena of travelling rhapsodes, citharodes, display-lecturers and theatrical troupes in the Hellenistic period.[20] Rhapsodes still recited the works of Homer and many other poets.[21] Theatres were to be found all over the Hellenised world, and were the setting for a rich variety and a huge number of popular entertainments.[22] Prose displays remained popular, frequently being held under competitive rules: the contest held in 352, at which three distinguished orators each gave an *epitaphios logos* for the deceased ruler Mausolos, can be paralleled by numerous comparable events from the years after Alexander.[23] Then there were the popular reciters, whose festival performances of local mythological stories exploited the insatiable interest of residents of Hellenistic cities in their own mythical past.[24]

Public recitals depended on and maintained an awareness of the traditional stories amongst a wide range of the population. But a new direction in myth-telling was developed by an elite group of literati whose poetic and scholarly activities were fostered in the urban sophistication of Alexandria. The city was a new foundation, its original inhabitants lacking any unifying tradition or common, inherited festivals. The ruling Ptolemies patronised a library-based literary culture, one of whose objectives was to conserve the great days of the Hellenic past by codifying its writings. Yet the conservers were also creators.[25] By examining what they created we can observe a new inflection in the relationship between performance and text.

Alexandrian poets often incorporated the circumstances of oral performance into their literary works. When Kallimachos wrote his

---

20 Guarducci 1927–9, pp. 629–65; see also Sifakis 1967, Gentili 1988, pp. 174–6; more references in Falivene 1990, p. 105 n. 10.   21 Ath. 14.620b.

22 Cf. Webster 1964, pp. 8–21, Sifakis 1967.

23 A. Gell. 10.18.5–6; *RE s.v.* 'Epideixis', col. 55 (W. Schmid).

24 See nos. XVII and XXXI in Guarducci 1927–9, Gentili 1988, p. 176. Weiss 1984 discusses the role of mythological traditions in the Graeco-Roman East.

25 For an excellent characterisation of Hellenistic literature, see A. W. Bulloch in Easterling and Knox 1985, pp. 541–4.

hymn for Athene ('The Bath of Pallas'), he included a number of circumstantial details about the Argive ritual which the work is designed to recall. But these are details ('The mares just now began to neigh', 2) which no hymn designed to have been performed at the festival would conceivably have mentioned.[26] The poem is evidently aimed at a learned audience, assumed to be knowledgeable about details of the Teiresias story and the festival of Athene at Argos, but no less certainly assumed to be *reading* (or, conceivably, hearing) about the festival instead of participating in it. Again, Theokritos' 18th *Idyll* consists almost entirely of a song imagined to have been sung by twelve Lakonian maidens outside the marriage chamber of Helen and Menelaos. The girls' praise of one who was once one of their number recalls the kind of song sung in Alkman's Sparta four hundred years earlier. Yet, for all its Doric dialect, Theokritos' poem is not a composition for performance by a choir of local Spartan girls, but a highly conscious literary adaptation of a traditional song-type.[27]

Such sophisticated blendings of myth and ritual imply a complex relationship with the world of ceremony and story. On the one hand, the poets lovingly evoke a religious context; on the other, everything about the evocations – particularly the need evidently felt for precise circumstantial detail – suggests a change in the relationship between mythological poetry and its context. Poetry of all kinds continues to narrate and allude to mythology, and poets remain crucial for the preservation and renewal of mythical tradition. But their focal position as the authors of communally performed stories is beginning to be eroded in favour of a situation in which written poetry creates and constitutes its own context for a non-local audience. While it is true that even the performance-oriented poetry of Archaic Greece contains its share of the extra-contextual and should not be reduced to the status of a libretto,[28] there is still a crucial difference between a

---

[26] See Bulloch 1985, p. 5, Falivene 1990. Cf. the opening of Kallimachos' hymn to Apollo ('How Apollo's laurel branch trembles!').

[27] It is possible that by this time the performance of ritual wedding songs was becoming a thing of the past. According to Philodemos, *De musica* (p. 68 Teubner edn, 37ff.), wedding songs were virtually all literary by the first century BC; cf. Muth 1954, p. 34.

[28] Cf. W. Rösler in Kullmann and Reichel 1990, pp. 271–87, on *Realitätsbezug* and *Imagination* in Sappho.

work conceived for oral performance and one which *imitates* such a performance *in writing*.[29] The decontextualisation of Greek mythology, a process which will gather momentum in Rome and become definitively exemplified in Ovid's *Metamorphoses*, is already embryonic in Alexandria.

Two characteristics of Alexandrianism – the will to preserve the now classical past, and the tendency to rework orally performed narratives in written form – come together in the genre of mythography.[30] Mythographers were collectors and classifiers: not performer-poets but writer-scholars. One major mythographical enterprise was the assembling of background material to facilitate the understanding of great authors of the past; some of this information has come down to us in the form of marginal comments in medieval manuscripts. Since many of the classic authors came from Athens, there was a noticeably greater proportion of Athenian stories in such compendia (e.g. the 'Library' ascribed to Apollodoros) than in, say, Homer or Hesiod.[31] Rather different in scope was thematic mythography, the aggregation of stories sharing a common narrative pattern. This was not an exclusively Hellenistic phenomenon. Ordering of myths by genealogy, as in Apollodoros, goes back at least to Hesiod's *Catalogue of Women*, and is a well-known feature of other traditions, such as that represented by the Old Testament,[32] while the gathering of information on the foundation of cities and the origins of local cults, typically Alexandrian though such antiquarianism is,[33] has a precedent in the work of fifth- and fourth-century local historians. But the idea of grouping and retelling tales about metamorphosis (Nikandros) and the constellations (Eratosthenes) illustrates the academic and text-governed orientation of the mythographers. Whereas the thriving world of Hellenistic festivals shows the continuing importance of public narration, mythography promotes the centrality of the text.

[29] Cf. Falivene 1990, pp. 105–8.
[30] See A. Henrichs in Bremmer 1987, pp. 242–77.
[31] See R. Parker in Bremmer 1987, p. 187.
[32] West 1985 collects a range of comparative material. On the Old Testament, see Rogerson and Davies 1989, pp. 51ff. See also ch. 5 of Goody 1977, on lists.
[33] Cf. Cairns 1979, p. 13.

4

Images in context

Archaic and Classical Greece

We have been listening to voices: nurses and old men, youths and girls, bards and orators. But myths could be seen as well as heard.[1] Coins often bore images evoking a local story: Herakles and the lion at Herakleia in southern Italy, Pegasos at Corinth, the Minotaur and its labyrinth at Knossos.[2] Precious rings might figure scenes from mythology, such as Danae under her golden shower, or Phrixos on his magic ram.[3] Shield-bands drew their images from the heroic past.[4] Textiles too were embroidered with mythical representations, as with the sacred robe offered to Athene depicting the battle between Gods and Giants.[5] To illustrate the character and range of possible relationships between context and mythological image, we shall look at three media, beginning with the small-scale but richly exemplified genre of vase-painting.

Pottery contained substances practically and symbolically central to Greek life: water, wine, oil, perfume. Hence vases were used in a number of important social contexts: the *symposion* (cups, mixing bowls, perfume containers),[6] athletic competition (vessels holding oil

---

[1] The range of pre-Hellenistic artistic contexts for myth-narration is summarised in Carpenter 1991, pp. 7–12.   [2] Kraay 1966, pls. 88, 89; 152, 153; 165.

[3] Danae: Boston, Mus. of Fine Arts, 99.437 = Boardman 1970, pl. 667. Phrixos: Syracuse 42251 = Boardman 1970, pl. 785.   [4] Kunze 1950.

[5] Pl. *Euthphr.* 6b–c, cf. *R.* 378; Ath. 196f.

[6] For perfume, see Long 1986, pp. 75–82, with refs. at p. 185 n. 32 (add Detienne 1977). Perfume at the *symposion* (men anointed their hair with it): Long 1986, pp. 77–8.

or awarded for victory in the games, as with Panathenaic prize amphorae), the lives of women, predominantly within the house (water-jars, containers for cooking oil or for perfume and unguent), the wedding ceremony (the vessels known as the *loutrophoros* and the *lebēs gamikos*),[7] death (vases used as grave-markers or as offerings to the deceased),[8] and other ritual contexts.[9]

Fine vases of all these types were regularly embellished with images: images of *situations*. There are combats, abductions, pursuits, meetings – not stories, but scenes encapsulating them, usually linking several figures in a meaningful way through a series of significant gestures.[10] In hundreds of cases there can be no doubt about the mythical status of what is represented, either because of the presence of inscriptions or because of the unmistakable particularity of the scene. But often, and far more interestingly, there is no way of telling whether a mythical allusion is intended. Or rather: it is impossible *because meaningless* to distinguish between the mythical and the everyday (Plate 3).[11] A shepherd pursued by an erect Pan could be either the legendary hero Daphnis, or just any herdsman.[12] The figures on a *pyxis* (a small box used to contain jewels or cosmetics) may bear the names of Helen, Klytaimestra, Danae, Iphigeneia and

---

7 *Loutrophoros*: Richter and Milne 1935, pp. 5–6, Ginouvès 1962, p. 257, L. Ghali-Kahil in *Festschrift Schefold* 1967, p. 150 n. 35, Kurtz and Boardman 1971, pp. 151–61. *Lebēs gamikos*: Richter and Milne 1935, p. 11, Robinson 1936, Kurtz and Boardman 1971, p. 151.

8 (Geometric) pottery and death: bibliography in Vermeule 1979, pp. 213–14 n. 16; see also Hyatt 1981, figs. 34 and 35, with discussions. Absence of bottom to a vase, as in many S. Italian products, suggests that the purpose was funerary, since libations could pass directly into the grave; see M. Schmidt in Mayo 1982, p. 24. Also funerary are fifth-century white *lekythoi*: cf. Ar. *Eccl.* 996; Kurtz and Boardman 1971, pp. 102–5, Kurtz 1975. Vases with no original funerary significance were often re-employed in a funerary context, as with four Panathenaic prize-amphorae buried with an athlete at Tarentum: Kurtz and Boardman 1971, p. 313, with fig. 84.

9 E.g. miniature *oinochoai* for use at the Anthesteria, *kernoi* at Eleusis, and Theban 'Kabeirion vases'.

10 Combat, etc: Metzger 1951, pp. 414ff. On significant gestures, one may note the observation by D. Metzler that Greek vases depict not so much figures who act, as figures who *represent* (or perhaps re-present) actions ('Gestalten, die Aktionen darstellen'), (in Bérard, Bron and Pomari 1987, p. 74).   11 Snodgrass 1980, pp. 69ff., Bažant 1981, pp. 13–22.

12 See Himmelmann 1980, pp. 65–7, discussing a *kratēr* by the Pan Painter (Boston 10.185 = *ARV*² 550, 1).

3. A youth/hero makes his departure. Myth, or life 'as' myth? The question, posed by this late-fifth-century Apulian volute-*kratēr*, is unanswerable. (Cf. Williams 1985, pl. 63.)

4(*a*) and (*b*). Imagery in a funerary context. The vessel known as a *lekythos* held oil,
and was often used as an offering to the dead. Picture (*a*) shows one such container
placed on the steps of a tomb. (The vessel on which the image appears is itself a
lekythos.)

Kassandra, but they are involved in no known mythical exploit:
rather, these women, who are deploying objects of adornment just
like those kept in the trinket box on which they are painted, inhabit
the space between the mythical and the everyday.[13] The imagery of
vases is not a photographic record of ordinary life, but a selective
representation of it, located in a world where the ordinary and the
mythical interfuse.[14]

[13] London Brit. Mus. E 773, discussed by F. Lissarrague in Schmitt Pantel 1991, pp. 215–16.
[14] On the problems involved in the idea of a photographic record of life, it is enough to
mention the work of E. H. Gombrich, especially Gombrich 1977.

Picture (*b*), again on a *lekythos*, represents Charon, boatman of the dead; to his right is Hermes, leading a (dead) woman.

Often there is an intimate connection between image and context, as in the case of the abundant use of Dionysiac imagery on wine-vessels. Again *alabastra* (small containers for perfume), which were 'associated with making beautiful, [with] the world of women, and with weddings',[15] bore scenes taken from the life of women. Similar links exist between the *lebēs gamikos* and the imagery of the wedding, and the white-ground *lekythos* and the imagery of the funeral (Plates 4a, b). As for the *hydria* (water-jar), a vase now in Bari evokes the fate of one mythical water-carrier. Amymone, a daughter of Danaos, is

[15] Sourvinou-Inwood 1985, p. 128.

shown drawing water at a spring, observed by a seated Poseidon and a bouncy satyr. Amymone did not scorn her divine lover, but her sisters, whose reaction to their own grooms was to kill them, became eternally futile bearers of leaking water-jars in the Underworld.[16]

As well as the large number of function-related images, there are innumerable vase-paintings which do not in any obvious sense 'refer' to their functional setting. Cups, mixing-bowls and amphorae carry a huge repertoire of non-Dionysiac mythological imagery; the formal delicacy of a sixth-century *pyxis* is belied by its depiction of the gruesome death of Hektor's young son Astyanax.[17] Yet it may be that such images corresponded in a more general way to their function. Perhaps to own and display artefacts depicting the gods and heroes – or (to reverse matters) to be surrounded by works depicting situations from everyday life as if they were mythical – implied, at some level and to some degree, a claim to status.[18] However, certainty is as yet unattainable in view of the still unresolved debate about the social register of painted pottery: was it a luxury or a poor man's imitation of precious metalware?[19] In any case, the role of mythical images on different types of object will not necessarily have been the same.[20] This is the more true in view of the phenomenal variety of emotional tone to be found on Greek painted pottery. No other vehicle for the narration of myths leaves the interpreter so often forced to end with a question mark. Mobile themselves, these objects demand from their viewers extreme openness of mind and a readiness to concede multiplicity and fluidity of meaning.

In comparison with decorated vases, public sculpture had a spatially fixed, ideologically central thrust, making it correspond more nearly to a 'voice of the *polis*'.[21]

Suitable architectural spaces were often filled with variations on the theme of conflict between two contrasting groups. The frieze of the

---

[16] For the vase, see Cambitoglou and Trendall 1961, pp. 29–30, with pl. x. For the myth of the Danaid water-carriers, see Keuls 1974.   [17] Schefold 1966, pp. 93–4, with pl. 78b.

[18] This is argued strongly by Bažant 1981, pp. 4–12.

[19] Bažant 1981, p. 4, is sure it was a luxury: 'These vases served mainly to show others the wealth of their owners and to indicate their high position in society as a result of it.' Poor man's imitation: see M. Vickers 1985.   [20] A point made by Schefold 1985, pp. 4–5.

[21] L. Burn in Mackenzie and Roueché 1989, p. 62.

5. A favourite motif of architectural sculpture is the combat between that which is 'other' and its opposite. Here a Centaur fights with a Lapith hero. The imagined scene is the wedding feast for King Peirithoos of Thessaly. The Centaurs were kinsmen of the groom; hence they received invitations, despite their monstrous pedigree and inclinations. (Parthenon metope.)

Siphnian treasury at Delphi includes combats between Gods and Giants and between Greeks and Trojans; Greeks and Amazons, and Lapith youths and their adversaries the Centaurs, appear on the frieze of Apollo's sanctuary at Bassai; Lapiths and Centaurs, Greeks and Amazons, Gods and Giants fight it out again on the Parthenon metopes (Plate 5), the Lapith/Centaur motif even being picked up around the soles of the sandals of Pheidias' Athene Parthenos.[22] Such representations of conflict have been understood in various ways: as tedious repetition; as political–allegorical propaganda of a specific

[22] Plin. *NH* 36.18.

kind; as expressing equivalent versions of the general opposition between order (human, male, Greek) and chaos (bestial, (half)-female, barbarian).[23] It is of course possible to be bored by anything if one tries, but tedium seems a peculiarly shallow response. Readings-in of precise political allegories are usually impossible to disprove if their proponents dig their toes in, but such an approach frequently has an impoverishing effect on the material it is designed to illuminate. The most plausible approach is the third, or a rephrasing of it. These combats are exercises in self-definition: human against beast, Greek against non-Greek, civilised against wild. In the case of the Periklean buildings, this extends to *Athenian* self-definition: the west pediment of the Parthenon depicted Athene and Poseidon struggling for the right to be patron of Athens; the east pediment showed the birth of Athene.

There is a surprising degree of uncertainty about the details of even some of the most well-known architectural sculptures, such as the friezes of the temple of Athene Nike and of the Erechtheion on the Athenian Acropolis. It is true, too, that some of the largest commissions – the throne by Bathykles at Amyklai, Pheidias' throne of Zeus at Olympia, the 'chest of Kypselos' dedicated at the same site – depicted an enormous range of mythological narratives about whose treatment we remain largely in the dark. Yet, regarding architectural sculpture as a whole, we can hardly avoid registering a strong link between image and context. On the east pediment of Zeus's temple at Olympia competitors and tourists saw the preparations for the mythical chariot-race between Pelops and Oinomaos; the metopes illustrated the Twelve Labours of Herakles, founder of the Games. Beside the freedom and fluidity of vase-painting, sculptural iconography had a resonantly public voice.

In terms of its contexts, painting was akin to architectural sculpture. Sometimes the two were inextricable, as with the painted metopes on Apollo's temple at Thermon in Aitolia, or the mythological scenes

[23] 'Tedious', 'tiresome', 'exasperating': Ashmole 1972, p. 164. Propaganda: Podlecki 1966, pp. 13–14. Order/chaos: Snell 1960, p. 35.

painted on the throne of Zeus at Olympia.[24] Religious sanctuaries were typical locations for mythological painting. The temple of Athene Areia at Plataiai had an account of Odysseus after his killing of the suitors, and a *Seven against Thebes*; the Propylaia, gateway to the Athenian Acropolis, housed a gallery of masterpieces; Zeuxis' legendary *Helen*, in which the heroine allegedly blended the best features of the five prettiest women in Kroton, was to be found there in the shrine of Hera Lakinia.[25] Direct relevance to context is exemplified in the Athenian sanctuaries to Theseus and to the Dioskouroi (Kastor and Polydeukes). The former displayed paintings of battles between Athenians and Amazons, and between Lapiths and Centaurs, in both of which struggles Theseus participated. There was also a picture of Theseus' descent to the kingdom of Poseidon to assert his divine parentage by recovering the ring which Minos had cast into the sea.[26] The shrine of the Dioskouroi had a work by Polygnotos depicting the abduction of Leukippos' daughters by the divine twins, together with Mikon's painting of an episode from the Argonautic expedition, another adventure featuring the twins.[27]

Paintings could also be found in *leschai*. From Pausanias' description of the *leschē* of the Knidians at Delphi we get an idea of the scale and detail of the two compositions by Polygnotos on its walls.[28] In the representations of the Fall of Troy and of Odysseus in the Underworld, the characters who appeared constituted a high proportion of the better-known figures in Greek mythology, drawn, in keeping with the panhellenic context, from a broad range of cities in the Greek world.

A comparable building, the Athenian Stoa Poikile, incorporated imagery with a stronger local flavour.[29] This columned hall along the north side of the Agora was called after the murals which adorned it (*poikilos* = 'many-hued'). Once more Polygnotos was involved: the various commissions of this Thasian master in Athens, Delphi, Plataiai

---

[24] Thermon: see Koch 1914 and 1915, A. Rumpf 1953, p. 34, with pl. 8, 1–2. Olympia: Paus. 5.11.4–6, with Swindler 1929, pp. 221–2.

[25] Plataiai: Paus. 9.4.2. Propylaia: Paus. 1.22.6–7. Kroton: Cic. *De inv.* 2.1.1–3, Plin. *NH* 35.64; Pollitt 1990, pp. 149–51.

[26] Paus. 1.17.2–3.   [27] Paus. 1.18.1.   [28] Paus. 10.25–31.   [29] Paus. 1.15.

and Thespiai suggest a comparison with the travelling bard. The scenes represented evoked different, violent stages in the Greek, more particularly the Athenian, past. Alongside representations of the fifth-century battle between Athenians and Spartans at Oinoe, and the earlier battle between Athenians and Persians at Marathon, there appeared the conflict between Theseus' Athenians and the Amazons, and the aftermath of the sack of Troy.[30] In this prominent location, one of the foci of public life, the contrast between Athenian and non-Athenian received strong visual affirmation. At the same time, recent conflicts were assimilated to mighty combats of the heroic past, so that an implicit link emerged between various examples of the 'other' – Spartans, Amazons, barbarians.[31]

Three general observations may be made about the iconographical contexts. First, there are significant correspondences between verbal and visual mythology. The *symposion* typically centred on vessels sporting images of Dionysos, satyrs, and other inhabitants of a liberated but ambiguously aggressive world; the room itself might have an elaborate décor, including mythological representations.[32] *Leschai* and sanctuaries were enriched with visible reminders of narrative traditions relevant to the location or deity. Weddings and funerals deployed vessels whose imagery corresponded to the ceremony. Words and images were mutually reinforcing. A hymn gained new vitality and imaginative precision if the audience could look up at a painting or sculpture of the god being praised; images ceased to be 'mere' when echoed by the poet's authoritative voice and embedded in the practices of social life.

Secondly, in none of the contexts reviewed is the iconography exclusively mythical. Many cups and bowls used at *symposia* had no overt mythological reference. On the walls of the Stoa Poikile Amazons rubbed shoulders with the Athenians and Spartans of the Oinoe campaign. Even the Parthenon incorporated the frieze of the

---

[30] See Hinks 1939, pp. 64–7, and especially Hölscher 1973, pp. 50–84.

[31] See DuBois 1982.

[32] Lissarrague 1990, pp. 93–4, discusses the iconography of the *symposion*. For satyrs, cf. A. Collinge in Mackenzie and Roueché 1989, pp. 82–103.

Panathenaic procession, in which the participants are not identifiable figures from mythology but anonymous, albeit idealised, Athenian citizens and their sons and daughters.[33] It is the modern observer who creates the categories here. In the original context the two types of representation, far from existing in hermetic isolation, blend into one another. Since mythology does not control an autonomous territory, perceiving life *as myth* becomes that much more natural.

Thirdly, we should notice a paradox analogous to that concerning the systematic devaluation of women story-tellers in the home. The producers of mythological imagery were regarded as *banausoi*, mere artisans.[34] Makers of art which would be bought or admired by citizen-peasants, they could nevertheless themselves be looked down on by their customers. Poets were inspired, craftsmen merely expert in *technē*, technical skill.[35] In their role as narrators, craftsmen-artists, like tellers of old wives' tales, were marginalised; poets were central.[36] But the belittling of the *products* of story-tellers within the home does not seem to be paralleled in relation to craftsmen. What craftsmen produced emerged into the public world, to be treasured and gazed on by citizens, the arbiters of tradition.

Collection and domestication

In the hundred years after Alexander, developments in iconography paralleled what was happening in verbal myth-narration.

Conservatism towards past masterpieces, such a feature of Alexandrianism in textual study, is exemplified in the phenomenon of art collecting. Aratos, the third-century ruler of Sikyon, assembled works by earlier Sikyonian artists. The rulers of Pergamon bought up and displayed sculptures and paintings by past masters. Where it was impractical to remove originals, they had copies made, as in the case of Pheidias' Athene Parthenos.[37] By this means new dynasties used the

[33] For a balanced account, see Simon 1983, pp. 55–72.

[34] Cf. X. *Oec.* 4.2–3.   [35] Burford 1972, p. 207.

[36] The position of *female* poets is shot through with ambiguities, some of which can be heard in the complex voice adopted by Sappho to publicise women's privacy.

[37] Aratos: Plu. *Ar.* 12. Athene Parthenos: see Winter 1908, no. 24. Cf. also Webster 1967, pp. 16–17, and, on copies, Bieber 1977.

conspicuous assertion of cultural continuity with the great Greek past to bolster their claims to political legitimacy.

To be thus effective, collections needed to be displayed. In Archaic and Classical times sanctuaries had been the principal location where sculpture and painting could be publicly viewed. Usually such works were inseparable from their architectural settings, but already in the fifth century the Propylaia on the Athenian Acropolis housed a gallery of masterpieces on mythological themes. This situation becomes much commoner in the Hellenistic period. The temple of Asklepios on Kos housed a fine collection of sculpture and painting, including works by Apelles and the sons of Praxiteles.[38] Even through the medium of the copy, even transported far from its original context, Greek mythological imagery carried formidable cultural authority.

Nowhere is this clearer than at Pergamon.[39] Its chief military achievement was the defeat of marauding Gauls, a group no less 'barbarian' than the Persians or Etruscans or Phoenicians with whom earlier Greeks had variously perceived themselves to be contrasted.[40] One monument in particular shows how iconographical tradition was harnessed to celebrate Pergamene glory. Dedicated in Athens, it included four sets of opponents: Gods and Giants, Athenians and Amazons, Greeks and Persians (Marathon), Pergamenes and Gauls.[41] The ruler of Pergamon thus symbolically linked his own city with the traditional cultural capital of Greece, setting the victory over the Gauls in the kind of company enjoyed in the Stoa Poikile by Athens' own triumphs.[42]

Conserving and renewing the Greek heritage is one major strand in Hellenistic mythological art. Another is the domestication of death and life.

In Archaic and Classical times Greek funerary iconography consisted mainly of vases and stone monuments put up as grave-

---

[38] Kos: Herondas, *Mim.* 4.   [39] Bieber 1955, pp. 106–22.

[40] On this theme in Pergamene art, see Plin. *NH* 34.84.

[41] Paus. 1.25.2, on which see Ridgway 1990, pp. 284ff.

[42] For a setting of this monument within the wider context of Helleno-Celtic relations, see Momigliano 1975, pp. 62–3.

markers along roads leading from towns.[43] But in the Hellenistic period a new form of conspicuous *post mortem* existence began to be favoured by those who could afford it. The rich and powerful now marked their demise in monumentally imposing form, with chamber tombs below ground or mausolea above it.[44] In these constructions, façades and interior walls were sometimes painted with scenes from mythology. Famous examples are the façade at Lefkadia in Macedonia, with Hermes, Aiakos and Rhadamanthos (the two judges of the dead), and Vergina Tomb 1 (a magnificent representation of Pluto's abduction of Persephone).[45]

The adornment of private dwellings for the dead reflects what was happening to the houses of the living. In pre-Hellenistic times private houses might contain works of art such as decorated vases or engraved mirror-cases, but, even amongst the rich, wall-paintings were rarely to be found outside public contexts, while floor mosaics were relatively rare.[46] A house in an Archaic or Classical Greek city-state was not self-sufficient. It needed to be complemented by the outside world of public intercourse, and it was there, in temple and *leschē*, that the shared iconography of mythology found expression. In Hellenistic times the public dimension continued, of course, to be of importance, as exemplified by the focal splendour of royal palaces.[47] But it also seems possible to detect, even amid the huge cultural diversity of the period, a greater sense of domestic self-sufficiency: windows on one kind of Hellenistic house are too high for outsiders to be able to peer in, since 'Hellenistic man wanted to be truly "at home" in his private dwelling.'[48] At all events, domestic art became more lavish and more widespread.[49] The villas of Pompeii demonstrate eloquently that, by the time Hellenistic civilisation was ingested into Roman, private individuals in a provincial town of modest size might, if they could afford it, have their floors and walls richly embellished

---

[43] Exceptions did occur, such as the decorated sarcophagus; cf. Kurtz and Boardman 1971, ch. 15.   [44] Kurtz and Boardman 1971, ch. 16.

[45] Kurtz and Boardman 1971, pl. 75 (Lefkadia); Pollitt 1986, p. 191, with pl. 204 (Vergina).

[46] Mirrors: Züchner 1942. Mosaics: A. Rumpf 1953, p. 123.

[47] Cf. Theoc. *Idyll* 15, about the celebration of the Adonia at the royal palace.

[48] Schneider 1967–9, II, p. 9.   [49] Bieber 1955, p. 5.

with graceful evocations of the Greek mythological past. The imagery of Greek mythology would eventually be appropriated into the sphere of *otium*, that leisured, extra-political realm set apart from the ruthless world of public political conflict.[50]

While analysis of this enthralling process (and process of enthralling) is indispensable to the study of a whole range of new contexts for the Greek tales, the additional, Roman dimensions which it involves are beyond our scope. It is time to retrace our steps. Having sketched the principal narrative contexts of Greek mythology from the Archaic period to the mid-third century BC, we now alter our perspective. In Part Two we shall investigate the fabric of social life within which the narrative contexts had their setting. We shall consider how this wider, social context shaped myths and was in turn refashioned by them. A recurrent concern will be the distinction – real or apparent – between myth and life.

[50] Zanker 1988, pp. 27–31.

PART TWO

Re-imagining the world

5

Cookery and recipes

In his *Works and Days* Hesiod recounts the stages through which
humanity passed before arriving at the gloomy present. It all began
with the Race of Gold. 'They were in the time of Kronos, when he
was king in heaven; and they lived like gods, with carefree heart,
remote from toil and misery' (111–13). In the same poet's *Theogony*,
Kronos' rule is again located between the sovereignty of Ouranos and
the present dispensation under Zeus, but this time the age of Kronos –
castrator of his father, swallower of his sons – is neither idyllic nor
Golden. The contrast with the present is emphatic in both narratives,
but it is worked out quite differently. In the *Theogony* it would have
made no narrative sense to give a positive characterisation of Kronos'
reign, since the story centres on the strengths of the present order, not
its drawbacks; in *Works and Days*, on the other hand, Kronos' old
world appears desirable, because the point of *this* story is that life now
is hard.[1] This is not a matter of inconsistency, but of contextual
cookery. Differences between works, between different narrators
within a genre, between the 'same' story told in different genres, are a
standard feature of the pluralism of Greek mythology.

Visual representations too vary with context, but the significance
of iconographical variation is hard to recover, being located in the
spaces between images. A natural reaction is to look around for words
to fill the silence, relating images to texts which they in some way
resemble. The tendency (which used to be almost universal) to see
images as *illustrations* of literary versions reflected the imperialism of

---

[1] Cf. Rowe 1978, p. 122. Ambiguity of Kronos: H. S. Versnel in Bremmer 1987, pp. 121–52.

philology within classical studies. But a reaction has set in, as iconographers have begun to prise art away from texts and to study visual traditions in their own right. A valuable model is J.-M. Moret's analysis of the Oidipous story.[2] Anyone coming to the topic fresh from Sophokles, Freud or Lévi-Strauss would expect the parricide and the marriage with Jocasta to be frequent in artistic representation. On the contrary: except for one vase-painting of the parricide, and one of Oidipous' childhood, the rest of the surviving images focus on the Sphinx.[3] There are all kinds of nuanced differences between versions according to the bearing of the Sphinx (on a column / on a rock; position of claws, etc.) and the demeanour of Oidipous; for artists, like poets, were ready to vary the inherited schemata of their medium. But why did artists concentrate on just these features of the story, while poets took a quite different line? Moret's confession of ignorance is remarkably frank: 'The motives which led artists to represent one episode and not to represent another, completely escape us.'[4]

The trickiness of interpreting visual variants is especially evident in relation to differences of historical context. Sometimes a strong case can be made for a historical component to the explanation. A well-known example is the rapid growth in importance of Theseus in Athenian art from the late sixth century onwards, particularly in scenes where his civilising role (e.g. in defeating the anti-social Sinis and Prokrustes on the way from Trozen to Athens) comes to the fore. This development can hardly be divorced from the Athenians' increasing power and political self-confidence during the period, represented symbolically by an idealised ancestral leader combining physical prowess with moral and political fairness.[5] Or one may cite the common motif in Hellenistic art of the return of Dionysos from India. Why this image at this period? The key is Alexander. We have

[2] Moret 1984.

[3] At the time of writing, the *LIMC* article on Oidipous has not yet appeared.

[4] Moret 1984, p. 2 n. 4 (my translation). The only alternative to such caution is educated guesswork: 'Despite its popularity with the poets the Oresteia aroused surprisingly little interest among the artists. Perhaps its implications were too disturbing, and better studied by poets than painters' (Prag 1985, p. xi).

[5] W. R. Connor in Ward 1970, pp. 143–74, Graf 1985a, pp. 130–5, cf. Herter 1936 and 1939.

textual evidence that he saw himself as a second Dionysos, the mortal's victorious return from the East re-enacting that of the god.[6]

When such proposed historical links convince, it is because there is documentary evidence to support the idea that the symbolism could actually have been available to its audience. This is not the same as reducing art to the status of illustration, but it *is* a recognition of the fact that documents are our best hope of deciphering meanings. Without such confirmation, historical readings-in often look arbitrary, as with the speculation that Herakles' importance in pre-510 Athenian art is due to an identification between the hero and the Peisistratid régime, or the view that Thebes' mid-fifth-century recovery after the trauma of her Medism was reflected in coinage bearing assertive images of Theban-born Herakles.[7]

These iconographical issues are part of the general question of the relationship between mythology and historical context; which brings us back to texts. It is not often that we can observe the interaction at close quarters, but there are exceptions. One of the best known is Aischylos' *Eumenides*. It seems clear that this play contains at least two direct allusions to recent political events. The first involves Orestes' emphatic support for an Athens/Argos alliance: one had actually been struck in 462/1, three years before the staging of the trilogy.[8] The second is Athene's establishment of the Areopagos as a lawcourt, the role to which, again in 462/1, it had been pruned back by the reformer Ephialtes. It is always difficult to say what constitutes an allusion (how many members of the audience – and which audience? – have to pick it up before it is deemed to be present?); and in any case the two passages are explicable in internal dramatic terms.[9] But what is evident is that, at a more general level, the unrolling of the action is deeply influenced by Athens' contemporary historical situation. The attempt to find an answer to Orestes' unanswerable dilemma is conducted by a group of ordinary Athenian citizens, and the impression of an idealised, democratic *polis* is confirmed as Athene

---

[6] Arr. *An.* 5.2, 6.28.2; cf. Pollitt 1986, p. 148.

[7] Peisistratid Herakles: Boardman 1972, 1975b and 1978, criticised in R. M. Cook 1987. Thebes: Demand 1982, pp. 2–3.

[8] Thuc. 1.102.4, cf. A. *Eum.* 762ff., with 289–91 and 669–73.   [9] Macleod 1983, pp. 22ff.

extols the virtues of persuasion as opposed to, though backed up with, force, reflecting a central part of the self-image of the Athenian citizen body.[10]

But the relationship between mythology and historical situation can rarely be demonstrated with this degree of certainty. Usually we are in the position of being able to identify conflicting versions within the mythological tradition without being able to go beyond possibilities and likelihoods in specifying a historical context. Skiron, the bandit who enjoyed throwing travellers off the cliffs near Megara and, fatally for himself, tried to do the same to Theseus, was said *by the Megarians* to have been not an outlaw but a sheriff. Unfortunately our source, Plutarch's 'biography' of Theseus (10.2), does not permit us to locate the Megarian counter-myth chronologically. The attempt to connect it with the sixth-century Athens/Megara feud can command no more than qualified assent: after all, this was not the only period when the two states were at each other's throats.[11]

So contexts generate differences. But myths also exhibit cross-contextual *recurrences*. How, though, are these to be described? And what counts as a recurrence? The terms used – theme, pattern, motif, structure, narrative programme, programme of action, mytheme (to confine oneself to English) – carry bulky methodological luggage deriving from earlier scholarship. In speaking of a 'structure', one may reasonably be taken to refer to a feature that is regarded as fundamental, or underlying, or hidden; 'motif' may suggest that the element isolated is thought to lie at the 'surface' of the narrative;[12] 'pattern' or 'programme' typically emphasise the linear quality of a story, its having a direction. Giving a name to a recurrence involves making a judgement about what is significant.

To provide a full account of the differences of approach built into these divergences in terminology would be to retell the history of reflection on mythology from antiquity to the present. The question of whether the meaning of a myth lies on its surface or beneath it is raised as soon as Theagenes of Rhegion, Metrodoros of Lampsakos and Plato investigate the sense *underlying* certain narratives about the

[10] Cf. Buxton 1982, pp. 109–13.   [11] The attempt is that of Nilsson 1951, pp. 54–6.
[12] On 'motif', see Bremond 1980.

gods and heroes.[13] It persists through the Middle Ages and the Renaissance, as with Boccaccio's reading of the punishment of the Danaids as a warning against female vanity (pointless expenditure of effort) or against male sexual indulgence (endless and futile pouring out of liquid);[14] continues through Vico's interpretation of Kadmos' Theban Sown Men as protagonists in an early class struggle,[15] and Max Müller's theory that the Greek myths are disguised accounts of celestial phenomena; and it is still going strong in the Jungian theory of psychic archetypes, and in some versions of structuralism.

The stressing of the narrative linearity of myths also has excellent classical credentials, for instance in the person of Aristotle, who in *Poetics* gave a massively influential analysis of the recognition- and reversal-based story-pattern which in his view made for the best tragedy. In the present century the linear approach is represented in the work of Vladimir Propp, the Russian folklorist who claimed to have detected a limited number of features ('functions') recurring in the same order in the actions of characters in certain Russian fairy tales. Propp's writings have been resuscitated and used to counteract some of the excessively anti-linear and algebraic absurdities of extreme structuralism.[16] Concentration on the ordering of mythical actions is also central to the work of Walter Burkert, for whom the 'programs of action' exhibited by some myths and rituals correspond to basic socio-biological patterns fundamental to human and even primate behaviour.[17] For example, the comedy of innocence, the drama which expresses man's attempt to absolve himself of the guilt of killing the hunted animal upon which he depends, is seen as constituting a model for many Greek rituals and myths.[18] But there has not been general agreement here, any more than there has been over allegorical readings, or over the universality of Propp's functions.[19]

---

[13] The term *huponoia* (e.g. Pl. *R.* 378d) is earlier than *allēgoria*; cf. Lanata 1963, pp. 106–11.

[14] *Genealogie deorum gentilium libri* 2.23. See in general Seznec 1953.

[15] *The New Science*, para. 679; see below, pp. 186–7.

[16] The central work is Propp 1969, on which see Burkert 1979 (index *s.v.* 'Propp').

[17] Since one is talking of *basic* patterns, one might argue that for Burkert the recurrences have *both* an essential linearity *and* an 'underlying' quality.

[18] This is a major theme of Burkert 1983.

[19] A sensible account of Burkert's work is given in Graf 1985a, pp. 53–7.

How are we to proceed in the face of this diversity? I believe we can make progress if we bear in mind two principles. (1) If *both* underlying *and* surface recurrences seem to be detectable, we should welcome the fact in a spirit of pragmatic eclecticism; there is no advantage in being doctrinaire. (2) Recurrences should not be interpreted only within the narrative. Against the puritanically anti-referential trend of some temporarily modish literary criticism, it must be stressed that a text has meaning only within a context – and that includes the social context.[20]

We may begin with principle (1). Greek mythology is full of different kinds of recurrence. First, there are many instances where what appear to be contrasting narrative variants function as equivalents. In particular, motivation and chronology vary while other elements remain stable.[21]

How does Agamemnon offend Artemis at Aulis? By killing a deer in her sacred grove, or by boasting that he is the better hunter.[22] But in both cases Agamemnon infringes the goddess's territory. How does Thetis propose to make Achilles invulnerable? By exposing him to fire, or to water (the Styx), or to a combination of the two (a cauldron of boiling water).[23] But all the variants have in common the notion of fatal incompleteness, since to call into question the boundary between divinity and mortality is perilous and usually catastrophic. Does Helen elope willingly or unwillingly with Paris? The matter was controversial, and engaged the forensic talents of writers as diverse as Stesichoros, Gorgias and Euripides. But on either view the elopement broke the sacred custom of hospitality. The willing/unwilling and persuasion/force equivalences are, incidentally, extremely common, as with Polyneikes (did he leave the kingdom voluntarily, or was he pushed?) and Theseus (did he *want* to abandon Ariadne?).[24]

---

[20] On this modish view, The Reader is All, enjoying a godlike freedom to ascribe meaning at will. Among the adherents of this belief is a small group of classicists whose trademark is exhibitionist ranting. They should be unreservedly pardoned. As Confucius might have put it: a man who has just sawn through the branch he is sitting on will naturally start to whistle very loudly.   [21] Cf. Buxton 1980, p. 27.

[22] For the variants, see Fraenkel 1950, II, pp. 97–8.

[23] Fire: A. R. 4.869ff., Apollod. 3.13.6. Styx (a late variant, as far as we know): e.g. Stat. *Ach.* 1.269–70. Cauldron: e.g. schol. on A. R. 4.816. See *RE s.v.* 'Achilleus', col. 225 (Escher).

[24] Polyneikes: e.g. Pherekydes, *FGrH* 3 F 96, Hellanikos, *FGrH* 4 F 98. Theseus: Hom. *Od.* 11.321–5, Hes. fr. 298 MW, Plu. *Thes.* 20.

Chronological variants are no less frequent than motivational ones. Did Io's union with Zeus occur before or after her wanderings?[25] Who is the older, Achilles or Patroklos? Zeus or Poseidon?[26] In each case, different versions follow different chronologies (incidentally undermining Proppian assumptions about the recurrence of functions *in the same order*). Often chronological and motivational variants interlock. Did Herakles commit infanticide before or after his Labours? According to Euripides in *Herakles* (17ff.), after: the Labours were performed out of filial piety, a motive which fits the dramatist's strategy of raising Herakles to the heights in order to explore what happened when he fell. According to Diodoros (4.10.6–11.2), before: the hero, depressed with the news that he must endure the Labours, went mad and slew his family.[27] But either way the hero shows his ambiguous relationship with his own capacity for violence, using it now for the good of humanity, now in self- and other-destruction. Whichever the narrative order, the ambivalence persists. It seems not unreasonable to describe all these equivalences as 'underlying'; whether or not we call them 'structural' depends on how far we are willing to push the analogy with the 'deep structure' of linguistics.

There is another, broader type of recurrence. Different and ostensibly unrelated myths frequently incorporate similar themes or patterns of action – terms which I adopt in order to suggest that the features identified are this time deployed explicitly in the narrative as opposed to being concealed beneath it.

The story of the Argonauts provides a useful illustration. (1) Jason is a young man who threatens the authority of a ruler and is therefore sent away to execute a seemingly impossible task. (The role of ruler is taken first by Pelias of Iolkos and then by Aietes of Kolchis.) The same pattern occurs in relation to Herakles (obliged to undertake Labours for Eurystheus), Bellerophon (sent away by Proitos and then by Iobates) and Perseus (packed off by Polydektes).[28] (2) The quest for the Golden Fleece is a heroic expedition by young men to win

---

[25] Burkert 1979, p. 147 n. 20, discusses the variants (e.g. Hes. fr. 124 MW, A. *PV* 848–9).

[26] Achilles/Patroklos: Hom. *Il.* 11.786–7, Pl. *Smp.* 180a (= A. fr. 134a Radt). Zeus/Poseidon: Hom. *Il.* 15.182, Hes. *Th.* 453–8, 468ff.   [27] See Bond 1981, pp. xxviii–xxx.

[28] While Bellerophon leaves Argos never to return, Perseus' progress brings him full circle; see Dillon 1989, p. 6.

honour: obvious parallels are the Trojan War and the campaign of the
Seven against Thebes. (3) Medea defies her father to help a stranger,
leaves home for a new life across the sea, and is then abandoned. We
may compare Theseus' relationship with Minos' daughter Ariadne.
(4) Grown mature after adventures in the outside world, Jason returns
to a household disrupted through usurpation. So Odysseus returns to
Ithaka, Orestes to Argos, Perseus to Seriphos, Herakles to Thebes (in
Euripides' *Herakles*). (5) Medea uses subterfuge (*dolos*) to gain revenge
over Jason. Similarly, from the daughters of Danaos to Klytaimestra
and Deianeira, women cunningly destroy their husbands.[29] (6)
Finally we may note how successive episodes of the story replicate and
so reinforce a central aspect of the narrative. One repeated theme is
Medea's responsibility for the disruption of a household. She destroys
her own family in Kolchis, killing and dismembering her brother and
scattering his limbs in the sea to delay pursuit by her father;[30] there
follow the catastrophes of the households of Pelias in Iolkos and Jason
and Kreon in Corinth; in Athens Medea precipitates a domestic crisis
between Aigeus and Theseus. Similarly Eriphyle, bribed on two
different occasions, first with a necklace and then with a robe, betrays
first her husband and then her sons by persuading them to embark on
(for them) doomed military expeditions.

These different kinds of recurrence point to the social dimension of
Greek stories: for it is hardly being excessively positivistic to claim
that the most potentially revealing features of the tales are precisely
those which *recur*. In the contemporary West, the folklore of the city
clusters round a limited group of themes: the dangers of technology
(microwave ovens which incinerate pets), the alienating remoteness-
from-the-consumer of mass-produced goods (ghastly finds in tinned
food), hideous threats from impersonal urban living-systems (motor-
way killers; giant alligators roaming the sewers).[31] What student of
modern tales could refrain from asking: why just *these* motifs?
Similarly, if Greek myths return again and again to certain themes,
the matter cries out for an analysis with a sociological dimension.

[29] Unwittingly in Deianeira's case (at least in Sophokles' version).
[30] Apollod. 1.9.24. There are variants: see Frazer 1921, I, pp. 112–13 n. 2.
[31] The classic work is Brunvand 1981.

Here we rejoin principle (2). A necessary part of any contextual analysis should be the setting up of a confrontation between the world of story and the world of ordinary experience. (Adapting the term 'homology' so much favoured by structuralists, we might speak of an *allological* relationship.) To return to Jason and Medea: it is impossible to know how to interpret the deceitfulness-of-women theme without replacing it within the context of the role of women in Greek life; nor can we understand a myth about young men going out to Troy or Kolchis without some awareness of ordinary Greek patterns of adolescence.[32] By constantly switching our gaze from narratives to the life of the community in which they were told, we give ourselves the best chance of recognising the social dimension of meaning.

By no means everyone accepts the validity of this procedure, however. In *The Mirror of Herodotus*, in which an analysis of the historian's account of Scythia leads to the investigation of a cluster of problems about how to read Greek stories, François Hartog rejects attempts to measure the veracity of the narrative against external referents such as the findings of archaeology or native Scythian records. Hartog's own reading consists of locating Herodotos' Scythian *logos* in relation to *other* Herodotean *logoi*. Now it is true that Hartog has enormously enriched our sense of the complexity of Herodotos' text. It is also true that to mark Herodotos out of 10 by confronting him with the real truth, whencesoever it may be invoked, is a simplistic procedure which risks missing many points in, perhaps even the point of, the narrative. Yet to refuse to consider extra-textual material *alongside* the internal evidence is to take purism too far. If we interest ourselves, as we certainly should, in the gaps between different Herodotean *logoi*, why should we refuse to look also at the gaps between one of those *logoi* and *other* types of evidence outside the text? *Mutatis mutandis*, the same goes for the *logoi* which are the focus of the present book. The meanings of Greek stories about the gods and heroes are constituted by two types of difference: differences from other narratives, and differences from the world of everyday experience.

[32] See Bremmer 1978.

Nevertheless, the separation of the everyday from the imaginary is surprisingly controversial. That such a separation is actually impossible is argued by Pauline Schmitt Pantel in relation to the representation of women in antiquity. 'To describe as "models of the feminine" certain approaches embedded in the discourses of antiquity obviously does not mean that we think it possible to separate representations from reality, or discourse from practice. We have known for some time that such a separation is an illusion, and that every social institution has its own representation, every discourse its own practical outcome in real life.'[33] Here again, however, things are being carried too far. Take first the distinction between discourse and practice. That X weaves a robe, that Y attends a funeral, are events whose reality does not depend on who describes them; and this truth is not undermined by the obvious fact that the *significance* of weaving or funerals will vary from culture to culture. Secondly, the difference between representation and reality. A woman may see herself 'as' Antigone or Penelope, but that does not mean that she can detect *no* difference between herself and those heroines – otherwise, the phenomenon is not so much social as psycho-pathological. In short, while not denying that perception and behaviour interrelate in an extremely complex manner, I am convinced that the best starting-point for an analysis of the fantastic is to be found in an analysis of the ordinary.

A straightforward illustration of this may be found in Greek myths which refer to agriculture. Most of the male hearers/readers of the tales had as their main economic activity the tilling of the soil and the growing and harvesting of crops. Yet it is rare for the major figures in Greek myths to be shown performing these basic peasant tasks.[34] Nevertheless, amid the vengeance-killings, warfare, wanderings, erotic encounters and monster-slaying, the theme of agricultural work does recur from time to time. First, as an *explanandum*, as in Hesiod's *Works and Days*, where the myth of Pandora is invoked to

---

[33] Schmitt Pantel 1991, p. 26 (my translation).
[34] Cf. Lacoste-Dujardin 1970, p. 155: 'Le paysan kabyle est rarement mis lui-même en scène dans les contes alors que la culture est, dans la réalité, la principale activité économique des hommes.'

account for the tough conditions of human life nowadays. Then, as a foil for the life of the fighting hero: in numerous Homeric similes, as well as in the Iliadic description of the imagery on Achilles' shield, the work of the peasant offsets and provides a context for the pursuit of honour in battle.[35] Again, tilling occurs *in displaced form* in Odysseus' attempt to avoid going to war: he feigns madness by yoking together an ox and a horse (or donkey).[36] The myths of Kadmos and Jason, which share the theme of sowing a serpent's teeth (in Jason's case after ploughing with fire-breathing bulls), once more represent agriculture *obliquely*, as if a socially central activity is being shifted in fantasy onto the margin or into the wild. When a hero *is* directly involved in agriculture, it is characteristically such a figure as Odysseus' father Laertes (*Od.* 24.205ff.), marginalised both in virtue of his age and of his ambiguous status (his son being absent and possibly dead). Agriculture, then, is almost never the *focus* of a mythical narrative, yet it provides a constant, implicit norm for heroic endeavour. The otherness of the marvellous world of adventure has little time to dwell on this central feature of peasant existence; but, at the same time, the presence of agriculture as a metaphorical reference-point establishes a direct and significant bond between the myths and their audience. Virtual absence and metaphorical presence; sameness within otherness. There could be no clearer illustration of the distance between the fantastic and the ordinary and, simultaneously, of the permeating of the fantastic *by* the ordinary.

All this is not to deny that the categories 'fantasy' and 'everyday life' – not to mention '*real* life' – need handling with care.[37] The distinction is a working hypothesis, to be tested and, if necessary, revised, as our account proceeds.

[35] Shield: *Il.* 18.541ff.

[36] Variants discussed in *RE s.v.* 'Odysseus', cols. 1921–2 (Wüst), cf. Pearson 1917, II, pp. 115–16. Roman commentators add the detail that Odysseus sowed salt.

[37] 'The everyday' corresponds to some extent to the German *Alltag*, as in the contrast between *Alltag* and *Fest* (cf. C. Meier in Haug and Warning 1989, pp. 569–91). But that distinction is less ticklish than the one involving myth. In any event, although we shall sometimes speak of a distinction between real life and mythology, this should not be taken as implying that the perceptions of mythology were *un*real, in the sense of illusory. The existence of a mythical tradition within a community is just as real a fact about that community as the plumbing it uses.

6

Landscape

Singing of the origin of the world, Hesiod told how Earth produced Heaven, Mountains and Sea (*Th.* 126ff.). But neither Earth nor any other deity gave birth to City, Village or Household. These, fashioned by mortals not gods, had to be hewn by them out of the natural landscape. The contrast between Nature and Culture has become a cliché of modern anthropological thought, but for many Greeks, especially those involved in the founding of colonies overseas, some such contrast must have had immediate relevance to the business of living. City-founders had to choose from the raw land before them sites for the immigrants' basic requirements: walls, houses, temples and ploughland. These items, singled out in the *Odyssey* in a passage relating to the establishment of the Phaiakians' territory, constituted the cultural framework for every Greek settlement, whether newly-founded or long-established.[1] But beyond and interfused with them was the setting of mountain, sea, river, cave, plain, meadow and spring, natural features complementing, contrasting with and partially defined by the constructions of human society: a world to be exploited, avoided, revered.[2]

Assessing ancient Greek perceptions of the landscape is not without its difficulties. The island Rhodian's attitude towards the sea will not have coincided with that of the landlocked Arkadian; folk dwelling in the mountain fastnesses of Taygetos will have had a different

[1] *Od.* 6.9–10; cf. Malkin 1987, p. 138.
[2] For a quite different symbolic landscape explored in another corpus of tales, see Lacoste-Dujardin 1970, pp. 112–41.

perspective from that of Thessalian plainsmen; and of course we cannot assume that *all* Rhodians and *all* Thessalians thought alike. More fundamentally, the way the environment impinges on a given individual is not simply a question of that individual's passively absorbing what is 'there'. Human beings create an image of their surroundings through their interaction with them, so that perception of a landscape is inevitably mediated by cultural factors.[3] Thus our enquiry into the real-life aspect of the landscape must involve, in addition to a review of what people did, some sense of what they perceived themselves to be doing; indeed it is impossible to give a meaningful account of the former without the latter. This is not to deny that there are such things as real landscapes 'out there', with real differences between them. Only a very determined epistemological sceptic will refuse to accept that Holland really is flatter than Switzerland.

We begin by analysing in some detail one feature of the landscape. Afterwards we shall consider how far our conclusions can be extended to cover other parts of the natural environment.

To the mountain

At the outset we have a terminological problem.[4] A mountain is in the eye of the beholder. The Greeks were agreed that, for example, Olympos, Cretan Ida, Parnassos, Helikon, Pelion, Kithairon and Lykaion – which on our reckoning range from about 2,900 metres to about 1,400 metres – were *orē* (plural of *oros*). But so, according for instance to the geographer Strabo, was 'Mount' Kynthos on Delos – a stiff walk on a hot day if you have only limited time before catching the ferry, but with the best will in the world only 113 metres above sea level; while at Olympia 'the *oros* of Kronos', as Pausanias calls it, can manage a mere 123 metres.[5] An *oros* is not, then, to be defined simply

---

[3] Bloch 1989, ch. 5, raises issues relevant to the conflict between 'passive acceptance' and 'active construction' views of cognition.

[4] A more complete analysis of imaginary Greek mountains can be found in Buxton 1992a.

[5] Kynthos: Str. 10.5.2. *Oros* of Kronos: Paus. 5.21.2, 6.20.1 (altitudes taken from Philippson 1950–9). On the fluid meaning of *oros*, see Buck 1949, p. 23, Pritchett 1965, p. 66. For *oros* in Strabo, see Baladié 1980, pp. 124ff.

6. The landscape of the *oros*. (The glen of Ávgo, looking E. from Kavousi Kastro, Crete.)

in terms of physical height. Instead we should look to what, in our sources, is contrasted with an *oros*. An *oros* is not the plain (where you grow corn and fight in phalanx), nor is it the city or the village (where you live);[6] but neither is it the acropolis, that fortified height, often also religious centre and symbol of political power, *within* the city.[7] An *oros* is a height outside inhabited and cultivated space – outside the *polis*, the *astu* ('town'), and the *kōmai* ('villages') (Plate 6).

What was an *oros* used for?[8] First, for pasturage, particularly (bearing in mind the practice of transhumance) during the summer heat.[9] Although direct evidence about herding is mostly confined to

---

[6] Cf. Arr. *An.* 7.9.2, Thphr. *HP* 1.8.1 and 3.11.2. For plain/non-plain contrasted in warfare, see Osborne 1987, p. 144, with ref. to Plb. 18.31. 'Plainsmen' and 'men from beyond the hills' form two political constituencies in the time of Peisistratos: Hdt. 1.59, Aristot. *Ath. pol.* 13.4 (with Rhodes' commentary *ad loc.*).

[7] Cf. Martin 1974, p. 32. Like the *oros*, the acropolis may be contrasted with the plain: Aristot. *Pol.* 1330b (an acropolis is 'oligarchic' and 'monarchical'; level ground is 'democratic').

[8] See Pease 1961, Fehling 1974, ch. 2 ('Fernsicht').

[9] See Georgoudi 1974, J. E. Skydsgaard in Whittaker 1988, pp. 75–86.

cases where it impinged on the interests of the *polis*, it was clearly the principal activity which drew men to stay in the mountains for long periods.[10] Next, mountains were a source of raw materials. Sometimes this is stone or metal (Hymettos and Pentelikon; Pangaion); usually it is wood. Scholars have differed over just how much afforestation of mountains there was in ancient times,[11] but that one of the reasons for going to an *oros* was to get timber is not in doubt: a man mentioned in one of Demosthenes' private orations had a farm in an outlying deme and kept six donkeys permanently busy sending wood down to the city.[12] Wood, hence charcoal: like shepherds, charcoal-burners might, from the city-dweller's perspective, be felt to be outsiders. Such an attitude is implicit in a fragment of Andokides: 'May we never again see the charcoal-burners and their waggons arriving in the city [of Athens] from the mountains' – apparently a reference to the consequences of the occupation of Attica during the Peloponnesian War.[13]

Shepherds, woodcutters and charcoal-burners dwelt on or regularly visited mountains out of economic necessity. Others visited the *oros* more occasionally, in order to hunt. Not all hunting was done on mountains, but most of it was.[14] Xenophon notes that traps for deer and boar are set in the mountains; up there, as opposed to in the plain, you can catch deer by day as well as by night.[15] The *oros* was where groups of men went out to pit themselves against beasts, and then return to the city.

Another use of mountains was for travel. In spite of steep gradients

---

[10] The data are reviewed in Robert 1949, 1955 and 1966; see also Georgoudi 1974, pp. 180–1, Sartre 1979, Whittaker 1988.

[11] See Georgoudi 1974, Halstead 1987, pp. 79–80, O. Rackham in O. Murray and Price 1990, pp. 85–111.

[12] D. 42.5–7; Theoc. 13.25, with Gow's commentary. Woodcutters: Thphr. *HP* 3.3.7, 3.12.4, etc. For wood-cutting on Mount Ida, see Theoc. 17.9–10, with Gow.

[13] And. fr. 4 Blass. See further Lacey 1968, pp. 53 and 256 n. 13. For a modern example of the charcoal-burner's marginality one may compare the dissident, radical charcoal-burners of the Mount Pelion area in 1921–2. (I owe this information to M. Llewellyn Smith.) Note also the clandestine movement in nineteenth-century Italy whose members styled themselves *i carbonari*.

[14] On the 'space' in which hunting was conducted, see Schnapp 1973.

[15] X. *Cyn.* 9.11, 9.17, 10.22; cf. Paus. 3.20.4.

and narrow passes, mountain paths were used by both individuals and armies;[16] Pausanias tells us often enough of routes that take a direct line across mountains.[17] It might be risky: a simile in the *Iliad* begins,

> As when upon the peaks of a mountain the South Wind
> scatters thick mist, no friend to the shepherd,
> but better than night for the robber...

and a millennium later Lucian reports the story of a wealthy Theban murdered by brigands on Kithairon.[18]

Mountains played various roles in warfare. In time of extreme need the *oros* could function as a kind of temporary acropolis, a refuge for those with no prospect of winning a pitched battle and no safe settlement to which to withdraw.[19] We hear too about reconnaissance ascents, and about the ingenious use of fire-signalling from mountain-top beacons.[20] Clearly, though, this is all peripheral to the main issue: fighting. The *oros* was a territory which could be exploited by light-armed troops, but which was wholly unsuited to the hoplite phalanx. Given the strong ideological component in the divide between hoplite and non-hoplite,[21] and given the pervasive rules of appropriateness underpinning Greek warfare,[22] it is surely comprehensible that mountain warfare is as relatively infrequent as it is.[23] It is comprehensible, too – indeed, it is part of the same framework of ideas – that the *oros*, a space which is simultaneously not the city and not the plain, should in some parts of Greece form the backdrop to the military education of the adolescent male, at the stage when he was neither (yet) a full member of the community nor (yet) a hoplite.[24] The *oros* could be an initiatory space (one may compare the wolf-men of Lykaion).[25]

[16] Cf. Burn 1949, p. 322. This and Burn 1951 are described by W. K. Pritchett as 'the two best articles ever published on Greek mountain terrain' (Pritchett 1982, p. 207).

[17] Paus. 8.12.8, 10.22.8, 10.33.3.   [18] *Il.* 3.10–11, Lucian, *D. mort.* 22.2.

[19] Hdt. 8.32, cf. 8.27, Paus. 4.17.10, 4.24.6.   [20] Livy 40.21–2, Plb. 10.43–7.

[21] Cf. Ducrey 1985, pp. 110–11.

[22] This has been repeatedly shown by Pritchett in his great study (Pritchett 1974 and its companion volumes).

[23] The absence of a developed mountain strategy in Greek warfare is discussed in Gomme 1945, pp. 10–15; cf. Pritchett 1974, pp. 173–4.

[24] Cf. Vidal-Naquet 1986, p. 108, with particular reference to Crete.

[25] Cf. my remarks in Bremmer 1987, pp. 60–79.

We hear also of 'touristic' ascents, as at Etna;[26] and of those who climbed in order to find plants[27] or observe the heavens.[28] But to the average Greek village- or city-dweller such eccentricity was irrelevant. What was far more important was the final use of mountains which I want to mention: their role as locations for sanctuaries of the gods.

Zeus was pre-eminent. In A. B. Cook's monumental study of the god there are references to nearly one hundred mountain cults.[29] More recently, in a review of the evidence for mountain-*tops* as locations for sanctuaries of Zeus, Merle K. Langdon has concluded that, while occasionally these are explicitly dedicated to Zeus as god of rain (e.g. Zeus Ombrios on Hymettos), in most cases no specific divine function of this or any other kind can be identified with certainty.[30] Nevertheless the association between Zeus and the *peak* is worth noting as an example of differentiation in the religious topography of the *oros*.[31] May one go on from this to posit a structuralising opposition between Zeus, god of the summit of the *oros*, and Athene, goddess of the Acropolis, Athene as Polias or Poliouchos, in which role she appears in many cities?[32] I think the answer is yes, provided we acknowledge certain facts which soften the rigidity of the schema. For example, Athene herself may be worshipped on the *oros*.[33] Nor is Zeus a stranger to the acropolis: he had temples on the citadels of Argos and Akragas, and an altar at the highest point of the Athenian Acropolis.[34] Again, Zeus is not the

---

[26] Paus. 3.23.9. (In his commentary *ad loc.* Frazer's comparatist approach is at its most beguiling: he turns up the flinging of tufts of grass (amongst the Masai) and the hurling of 'vast numbers of hogs' (Hawaii) into the relevant volcano.) For Etna one may compare the anecdotal 'death' of Empedokles, 'luckily' accepted by the crater (D.L. 8.69).

[27] Plin. *NH* 25.3. Much plant-gathering, however, will have had more to do with everyday needs than with research: Thphr. *HP* 9.10.2–4 (black hellebore best from Helikon, white from Oita).

[28] Thphr. *Sign.* 4, Philo, *Prov.* 2.27, Philostr. *VA* 2.5, Petron. *Sat.* 88, Iamb. *VP* 3.14–15. NB also Hadrian's ascent of Etna 'ut solis ortum videret arcus specie, ut dicitur, varium' (*Scriptores Historiae Augustae, Vit. Hadr.* 13).

[29] A. B. Cook 1914–40, I, p. 165.

[30] Langdon 1976, esp. p. 81, to be looked at in conjunction with Lauter 1985, esp. pp. 134ff.

[31] Cf. also Graf 1985b, pp. 202–3.   [32] Cf. Burkert 1985, p. 140.

[33] Paus. 1.32.2, 2.36.8, 8.21.4.

[34] Paus. 2.24.3, Polyain. 5.1.1; see A. B. Cook 1914–40, I, pp. 122–3, Burkert 1983, p. 136 with n. 2.

dominant power on every *oros*: Helios, Artemis, Dionysos, Demeter, Pan, Apollo, Hermes and the variously-named 'Mother' goddess of Asia Minor all have mountain sanctuaries.[35] However, notwithstanding these qualifications, Zeus's statistical pre-eminence on the *oros* looks unchallengeable.

Turning to mythical narratives, we may begin with a partial truth: myth reflects.

Mythical herdsmen, like real ones, live on mountains. The Euripidean Cyclops had his home on Etna; Paris and Anchises dwelt on Trojan Ida; Apollo was out on the slopes of Pieria when Hermes came to rustle.[36] Herdsmen in myth practise transhumance, like the two in *Oidipous Tyrannos*: 'We herded as neighbours three times', recalls the Corinthian, 'for six months from spring to the rise of Arktouros.'[37] A myth ascribed by Antoninus Liberalis to Nikandros tells of a herdsman who, when helpfully advised by Pan to take his flocks down from Mount Othrys on account of the impending onset of a harsh winter, declined the advice, and for good measure insulted the Nymphs. The flock disappeared in the snow, and the rash herdsman turned into a beetle.[38]

Mythical mountains are a source of wood: again myth reflects the ordinary world. Timber for the *Argo* came from Pelion; the Trojan horse is of mountain pine; wood for Patroklos' pyre came from the spurs of Ida.[39] Lykos sent servants out from Thebes to gather wood on Helikon and even Parnassos in order to incinerate Herakles' family.[40] Woodcutters put in rare appearances in myths, as in the oracle recorded by Eusebios about nine woodcutters who were stunned near Miletos when they heard Pan singing.[41]

As in life, so in myth, men hunt on mountains. Teiresias was hunting on Kithairon when he saw Athene; so was Aktaion when he

---

35 Some examples noted by Pausanias: 3.20.4 (Helios), 2.24.5, 2.25.3, 8.13.1 (Artemis), 3.22.2 (Dionysos), 8.10.1 (Demeter), 8.24.4, 8.36.8 (Pan), 9.23.6 (Apollo), 8.17.1 (Hermes). For the 'Mother' cf. Hdt. 1.80, Paus. 5.13.7; *Der kleine Pauly s.v.* 'Kybele' (Fauth).

36 E. *Cyc.* 114, Apollod. 3.12.5, Hom. *H. Ven.* 53–5, Hom. *H. Merc.* 69ff.

37 S. *OT* 1133ff.   38 Ant. Lib. 22; cf. Borgeaud 1988, pp. 61–2.

39 E. *Med.* 3–4, *Tro.* 534, Hom. *Il.* 23.117.   40 E. *HF* 240ff.

41 *Praepar. evang.* (in *Sources Chrétiennes* vol. CCLXII) 5.6.1.; cf. Lane Fox 1986, pp. 131–2.

made an analogous mistake; Endymion hunted by moonlight on Latmos, and was loved by Selene; Peleus and Akastos hunted on Pelion.[42] In Bion's *Lament for Adonis*, the crying of the young man's hounds was echoed by the Oreads (18–19).

Mythical mountains could be used for travel, as when one of Ida's shepherds describes the march of Rhesos.[43] Where there are lonely travellers, there you find robbers: the mythical brigand Autolykos lived on Parnassos.[44] Mythical mountains also provided a refuge. Megaros escaped Deukalion's flood by taking refuge on Mount Gerania; the better-known refuge on the same occasion was Parnassos.[45] In Aratos' *Phainomena*, when Dike (Justice, Right) abandoned humanity after rebuking it during the Silver Age, she too sought refuge in the mountains.[46] Even the use of fire-beacons is reflected in myth, in the famous account of the mountain-to-mountain relaying of signifying flame from Troy to Argos in Aischylos' *Agamemnon* (281ff.).

Lastly, the presence of sanctuaries has its mythical counterpart, since many of the gods in the traditional tales can be found on mountains. Zeus's birth and upbringing, his functions as god of rain and lightning, and his supremacy on Olympos all focus his power on the *oros*.[47] The Olympians' foes the Titans fought from Mount Othrys.[48] You find the Muses on Helikon, Pan on mountains everywhere, especially Arkadia; likewise the Nymphs.[49] Artemis loved the heights: the simile in *Iliad* Book 6 depicts her on Taygetos and Erymanthos; in *Trojan Women* she is 'of the mountain'.[50] And in the *Bakchai* Dionysos, god of Nysa and Tmolos, sharer of Parnassos with Apollo, comes at last to Kithairon.

Myths, then, reflect. But they also refract, transforming the world

---

[42] Call. *Hymn* 5.75 (Teiresias), Apollod. 3.4.4 (Aktaion), schol. A. R. 4.57–8 Wendel (Endymion), Apollod. 3.13.3 (Peleus, Akastos).

[43] E. *Rh.* 282ff.   [44] Paus. 8.4.6.

[45] Paus. 1.40.1 (Megaros), Apollod. 1.7.1, Paus. 10.6.2 (Parnassos), cf. Paus. 4.34.10 *re* Asine.

[46] Arat. *Ph.* 127.   [47] Cf. Burkert 1985, p. 126.

[48] Hes. *Th.* 632. Cf. Apollod. 1.6: the combat between Zeus and Typhon moves from Kasios to Nysa to Haimos to Etna.

[49] Hes. *Th.* 1 (Muses), Hom. *H. Pan* 6–7, D. Hal. *Ant. Rom.* 1.38.1 (Pan), Hom. *Il.* 24.614ff., Hom. *H. Ven.* 257–8 (Nymphs).   [50] *Od.* 6.102–3, E. *Tro.* 551.

by a process of selective emphasis and clarification and exaggeration. Myths present an image of mountains which is both more extreme and more consistent than that of everyday life, paring down that wide range of uses which men actually made of the *oros*, and coming back again and again to the same few, symbolically productive characteristics.

For the Lele of Central Africa, the forest (opposed both to the village and to the grassland) is the location of spirits, a place of good luck and danger; for the Asante, a visit to the bush (opposed to the village) risks encounters with uncanny powers, and necessitates rituals of transition on one's return; for the Dinka, the homestead (*bai*) is opposed to the wilds (*roor*), which contains harmful antisocial powers; Lienhardt speaks of a 'distinction between the uncontrolled life of the wilds, without human order and reason, and the orderly and rational domesticated life of men and beasts in society'.[51] Such anthropological 'parallels' could be multiplied almost indefinitely.[52] They do not prove anything, but they may at least encourage us to look with new attention at existing data, provided we recognise that each individual cultural situation will have its own configuration.

In Greece there are three main aspects to the mythical image of the *oros*. First and most obvious: mountains were outside and wild. Centaurs lived on mountains, as indicated by Nestor's words in the *Iliad* about an earlier generation of heroes: 'They were strong, and fought against the strongest, the beast men living in the mountains.'[53] The Sphinx lived on a mountain near Onchestos.[54] An *oros* was a place of wild violence too: on Pangaion, Lykourgos was done to death by wild horses;[55] on Kithairon, Aktaion was torn by wild dogs, Pentheus by wild aunts. Being outside, mountains are for outsiders. In the discussion of correct naming in Plato's *Kratylos*, Sokrates praises the name Orestes as appropriate to a 'wild and mountainous nature'. One who commits matricide belongs outside.[56] It is revealing that

---

[51] Douglas 1954, pp. 1–26, esp. 4–6, McLeod 1981, pp. 20–40, Lienhardt 1961, p. 63.

[52] For some Biblical material, see Dozeman 1989, p. 13 n. 48.

[53] *Il.* 1.267–8. Cf. Apollod. 2.5.4 (Centaurs on Mounts Pelion and Malea).

[54] E. *Ph.* 806, Paus. 9.26.2. Apollodoros locates the Sphinx on Mount Phikion (3.5.8); cf. Moret 1984, p. 69 with n. 1.   [55] Apollod. 3.5.1.   [56] Pl. *Crat.* 394e.

Menander's *Dyskolos* (*Bad-Tempered Man*), whose prologue is spoken by Pan, should be set in a mountainous area of Attica on the slopes of Mount Parnes. The misanthrope withdraws up-country.

Being perceived as wild, mythical mountains are the ideal place to expose unwanted offspring: Oidipous on Kithairon, Amphion and Zethos near the same mountain, Asklepios on Titthion, Paris on Ida, Telephos on Parthenion.[57] But exactly what sort and degree of refraction is taking place here? The reality of abandonment is an enormously problematic subject. One starting-point for discussion is now John Boswell's study, which has implications for classical Greece even though it focuses on late Roman antiquity and the Middle Ages.[58] Boswell raises the central issue of how far the *topos* of abandonment − rightly distinguished by him from infanticide − was like the modern cinematic motif of death by quicksand, i.e. basically a fictional ploy.[59] Asking the same question about ancient Greece is no less legitimate and important, but the matter is unlikely to be settled while there is so much controversy about what constitutes proper comparative demographic evidence.[60] In spite of this uncertainty, we can, I think, maintain the following: in depicting abandoned infants as male,[61] as always found, and as always surviving to experience some notable fate,[62] Greek myths were selecting from the real world in

---

[57] S. *OT* (Oidipous), Paus. 1.38.9 (Amphion/Zethos), Paus. 2.26.4 (Asklepios; Hom. *H. Aesc.* 3 gives another version: '... in the Dotian plain'), Apollod. 3.12.5 (Paris), Apollod. 2.7.4, 3.9.1 (Telephos).   [58] Boswell 1988.

[59] Boswell 1988, pp. 6–7. Along the way B. makes some fascinating observations, as when he questions the fictionality of the *topos* of being saved by a shepherd: 'it is worth noting that there was actually legislation in the later empire prohibiting the upper classes from "handing their children over to shepherds"' (p. 97, with refs. in n. 9).

[60] Cf. the disagreement between Engels 1980 and Golden 1981; see also Patterson 1985. Boswell himself reviews discussions of the Greek evidence, from Glotz onwards, at pp. 40–1 n. 96. Garland 1990, p. 86, goes over the ground again, but is rather simplistic over life/myth ('Myths telling of the exposure of royal infants as well as the comedies of Menander suggest that the practice was in fact prevalent or at least tolerated at all levels of society.')

[61] This applies to foundlings in mythology, but not to those in romance (compare Chloe in *Daphnis and Chloe* and the Queen of Ethiopia's daughter in *Aithiopika*) or New Comedy. If it is true, as is usually taken for granted, that abandonment of female infants was in real life commoner than that of males, it may be that we should see romance and New Comedy as extending mythical patterns in realistic directions (though in each case within a highly artificial framework).   [62] Cf. Binder 1964, p. 120.

order to construct an *extreme* image of abandonment; in particular, they were representing the *oros* as a place for extraordinary luck (which is not, of course, necessarily to say *good* luck).[63]

Secondly, mountains are before. They were believed to be humanity's place of first habitation. In the *Laws* (677b–c) Plato's Athenian speculates about a time after a prehistoric flood, when life was preserved on the tops of mountains among herdsmen, since the cities near the sea and in the plains had been destroyed. The same story-pattern applies to Deukalion and Pyrrha on Parnassos, and to the Trojan ancestral hero Dardanos, who left Samothrace to avoid the flood, drifted in a leather bag, and landed on Mount Ida.[64] Before also, in that they are the location of the early lives of gods: Hermes (born on Kyllene); the Muses (born in Pieria, a little below Olympos); not to mention Zeus (born on Cretan Ida or Dikte, reared on Lykaion and Ithome, etc.).[65] If birth is before, so in a different way is adolescence. Jason was brought up on Pelion by Cheiron, before descending, aged twenty and clad in a leopardskin, to claim his rights in Iolkos (Pindar, *Pyth.* 4). Also socialised by Cheiron on the same mountain were Achilles, Asklepios, Aktaion and Aristaios.[66] Paris was a young herdsman on Ida before being recognised and accorded his true name and status in Troy.[67] These pairings of Pelion-and-Iolkos and Ida-and-Troy – to which may be added Kithairon-and-Thebes and Oita-and-Trachis – illustrate a common motif, the symbiosis of city and neighbouring mountain. In tragedy in particular, *oros* and *polis* often constitute two of the significant spaces in terms of which the action is oriented: later we shall mention some examples.

---

[63] More remarks on exposure in Dillon 1989, ch. 2; he stresses the role played in such stories by a breakdown in the father/daughter relationship.

[64] Apollod. 1.7.2 (Deukalion), schol. Hom. *Il.* 20.215–16 (Dardanos).

[65] Hom. *H. Merc.* (Hermes), Hes. *Th.* 53–62 (Muses). For Zeus's Cretan birth see Frazer 1921, I, pp. 6–7 n. 2, A. B. Cook 1914–40, I, pp. 148–54. Paus. 8.38.2 (Lykaion), 4.33.1 (Ithome). Kallimachos' *Hymn to Zeus* attempts a compromise version.

[66] Apollod. 3.13.6 (Achilles), Pi. *Pyth.* 3, Apollod. 3.10.3 (Asklepios), Apollod. 3.4.4 (Aktaion), A. R. 2.509–10 (Aristaios). On Cheiron ('l'antique chamane du Pélion'), see Jeanmaire 1939, pp. 290–1.

[67] Ida/Troy: E. *IA* 1283ff., with Stinton 1990, pp. 40–4; Apollod. 3.12.5. On Ida, see Elliger 1975, pp. 263ff.

7. Mortal meets god on the *oros*. On this *stamnos*, Paris, greeted by Hermes (r.), sits on a rock populated by a delightful array of wildlife.

Thirdly, a mountain is a place for reversals. Things normally separate are brought together, as the distinctions of the city are collapsed.

The divine and the human come together on mountains (Plate 7). Hesiod meets the Muses on Helikon; Philippides meets Pan on Parthenion.[68] Any hunter or herdsman on an imaginary Greek mountain will probably meet a god. Sometimes such an encounter is momentary and disastrous (Aktaion, Teiresias), sometimes it is briefly prolonged in sexual union (Endymion and Selene, Anchises and

[68] Hes. *Th.* 22ff., Hdt. 6.105.

Aphrodite). Occasionally, there is the prospect of an extended relationship: Thetis and Peleus *marry* on Pelion.[69] But the distance is unbridgeable: in the *Iliad* they are living apart.

Metamorphosis entails a collapsing of distinctions: and metamorphoses often take place on mountains. Teiresias saw two snakes copulating on Mount Kyllene, struck them, and turned into a woman.[70] On Mount Thornax near Hermione in the Argolid, Zeus turned into a cuckoo and fluttered into Hera's affections;[71] the changing of Aktaion into a stag on Kithairon, and Lykaon into a wolf on Lykaion, are familiar enough.

Social relationships and normal social behaviour may be reversed on imaginary mountains. In everyday life, hunting is for men. Although Xenophon, in his treatise on hunting, praises in an afterthought the virtues of the chase as applying to women as well as men, nowhere does he mention real-life female hunters.[72] Yet myths regularly speak of female hunting, both individual (Atalanta, Prokris, Kallisto; Kyrene in Pindar's 9th *Pythian*) and collective (maenads hunt down Orpheus on Pangaion[73] and Pentheus on Kithairon). For real-life women to be out on a mountain at all – let alone out hunting – is anyway unusual: observing three striking females, Lucian's Paris remarks to Hermes that 'being so beautiful they are not suitable to go on the *oros*'.[74] The presence of women on the *oros* can even be seen as a symptom of madness. Euripides portrays Phaidra's wish to follow Hippolytos out onto the mountain as the very essence of her mania;[75] the maddened daughters of Proitos run out into the Aroanian mountains of Arkadia.[76] To behave outside the norm, or outside oneself, is to belong on the *oros*, and in a way to belong to it. Here as elsewhere myth sharpens the boundary between *oros* and settlement, a boundary which in everyday life will have been blurred; the livelihood of shepherds and charcoal-burners depended, after all, on the constant crossing of the divide. Such sharpening is an example of the selective emphasis and clarification of which we spoke.

---

[69] Apollod. 3.13.5.   [70] Apollod. 3.6.7.   [71] Paus. 2.36.1–2.

[72] The afterthought is the concluding sentence of *Cyn.* (= 3.18).

[73] Cf. *TrGF* III (Radt) pp. 138–40, West 1983a, pp. 63–71.   [74] *Dearum iudic.* 7.

[75] Cf. the Nurse's reaction at *Hipp.* 232–8.   [76] Paus. 8.18.7.

So far I have assumed that it is meaningful to separate life from myth. However, it is clear that myths feed back into the perceptions of everyday life, even if the level and extent of this process are hard to pin down and virtually impossible to quantify. In the case of Greece, however, there is one aspect of social behaviour into which myths fed back in an unmistakable and literally dramatic way.

In many regions, on certain ritual occasions, the city came to the mountain. The manner of the approach was various: the Plataeans carried wooden images to the top of Kithairon and burnt them for Zeus and Hera; there was a werewolf cult on Lykaion; the Muses received sacrifice on Helikon; and so on.[77] From this variety − for there is no single pattern − I want to pick out two rituals, which will enable me to develop points already made about mythical mountains and to highlight characteristic similarities and contrasts between myth and ritual.

> On the peak of the *oros* there is the so-called 'cave of Cheiron', and a shrine of Zeus Aktaios. At the rising of the Dog Star, the time of greatest heat, those among the citizens who are most notable and in the prime of their lives, having been chosen in the presence of the priest, climb up to the cave, clad in thick new fleeces − so cold is it on the mountain.

The mountain is Pelion; the source, the Hellenistic geographer Herakleides.[78] His comment about the cold hardly squares with the time of year: the wearing of fleeces has symbolic rather than practical significance. But what is the nature of the symbolism? Are the participants assimilating themselves to Zeus the Ram God?[79] Or to 'fleecy' clouds in a weather ceremony?[80] Or to the sacrificial *victims* of Zeus?[81] Or is this 'an ancient religious custom whose real meaning we may never know'?[82] The first two guesses embody assumptions

---

[77] Paus. 9.3 (*daidala* on Kithairon); for Lykaion, cf. n. 25; Paus. 9.29.6 (Muses).

[78] The fragment from which the passage comes is listed under Dikaiarchos in *FHG* II, p. 262; for the attribution to Herakleides see *RE* VIII (1913) col. 484, and Pfister 1951, at fr. 2.8 (p. 208).

[79] A. B. Cook 1914–40, I, pp. 420–1.

[80] A. B. Cook 1914–40, III, pp. 31–2, qualifying his scepticism expressed *loc. cit.* (n. 79).

[81] Burkert 1983, pp. 113–14. [82] Langdon 1976, p. 83.

which have ceased to be as persuasive as they once were; the third is currently more fashionable, with its emphasis on sacrifice as the semantic heart of the drama; the fourth is clearly the safest. But there is perhaps an alternative.

To wear animal skins, whether from cow, goat or sheep, can be a mark of outsiderdom. Arrian's Alexander addressed his troops as follows: 'Philip gave you cloaks to wear instead of hides, brought you down from the mountains to the plains..., made you into *polis*-dwellers, and equipped you with good laws and customs.'[83] With this we may compare Pausanias' remark about Pelasgos, 'who invented sheepskin tunics, which poor people still wear around Euboea and in Phokis'; only at a subsequent stage of civilisation do spinning and weaving make an appearance, thanks to Arkas.[84] But, more specifically, the use of animal skins for clothing is associated with herdsmen. Eumaios puts on a hairy goatskin to keep out the North Wind, and at Odysseus' prompting gives him some extra sheep- and goat-fleeces;[85] in Theokritos' 5th *Idyll* a goatherd and a shepherd argue about the respective merits of the fleeces of their own animals. I believe, then, that the Pelion ritual may be read as follows. Once a year the citizen-group turns, through its representatives, into a community of shepherds, which practises what may be described as a one-day ritual transhumance. The highest turn into the lowest, the most prominent citizens into shepherds: for this is the *oros*, where, in ritual as in myth, metamorphoses and reversals take place. And yet this is ritual, not myth: the reversal of the everyday is itself reversible. After the ceremony, the sheepskins are doffed, herding retires from centre-stage to the periphery, and from Outside and Before (shepherds; Cheiron's cave) a return is made to the Here-and-Now.

A still more striking ritual is repeated with variations in many places. The women of certain cities ran 'raving' on the *oros* for Dionysos either at an annual festival, or at the trieteric festival every second year; best known is the case of the Thyiades, Athenian women who went out onto Parnassos with their Delphic counterparts.[86] A good deal of research has been done in recent years on the ritual

---

[83] Arr. *An.* 7.9.2.   [84] Paus. 8.1.5, 8.4.1.   [85] *Od.* 14.530–3, 518–19.   [86] Paus. 10.4.3.

aspects of Dionysiac *oros*-cults.[87] Here we need add only that in the mountain-dance for Dionysos the *oros* once more stages a reversal of normal values, as the women wander free, thanks to a temporary legitimation of 'madness'. But this is ritual not myth: the women commit no crime, tear no nephew, behead no poet; and return afterwards to their looms. Through ritual the wildness of the mountain (and of women) is both acknowledged and controlled.

The ritual for Zeus on Pelion and the mountain-dance for Dionysos exploit as part of their symbolic drama the contrast between mountain and community. Both, as part of that drama, promote to a focal position social groups which are normally marginalised: herdsmen (on my reading) and women.[88] (It is not without interest that in the symbolism of Greek religion we occasionally find an overt equivalence between these two groups.)[89] Of course the ceremonies for Zeus and Dionysos differ in that, whereas on Pelion a marginal social group is only *symbolically* central to the ceremony, in the *oreibasia* women *in fact* play the central role. But there is also a fundamental similarity: during the ceremonies, normal social relations are inverted; afterwards, when pseudo-shepherds and women have descended from the *oros*, herding and femaleness resume the marginal positions which they occupied before, and from the perspective of the city the *oros* itself recedes into the distance for a year or two.

The largely synchronic account which we have given obviously needs modifying to fit specific contexts. Not all mountains are always perceived as wild: Pausanias reports that 'the people who live near Helikon say that no herb or root on the mountain can harm human life' (9.28.1). Plain and mountain are not always opposed: in Euripides' *Helen* (1301ff.) the Mountain Mother is assimilated to the figure of the grieving Demeter to give a picture of all nature – cornfield and mountain – mourning together. Pasturage may take

---

[87] Henrichs 1978 and 1982, Seaford 1981, Bremmer 1984a, Vernant 1986.

[88] Let us admit that, although marginality is a useful analytical tool, it can be (and has been) overdone. See the wise remarks of H. S. Versnel in Edmunds 1990, pp. 25–90.

[89] Sokolowski 1969, no. 181, discussed by Henrichs 1978, pp. 155–6. See Dodds' commentary on E. *Ba.* 654–5; also Nonnos, *Dion.* 47.117.

place in the plain as well as on the mountain, in myth as in the real landscape.[90] Then there are differences according to genre. Homer's landscape is not the landscape of Theokritos.[91] Even within one genre, and at one historical moment, the language of Greek mythology can make subtly different statements about the 'same' matters. A striking example is the contrast between Sophokles' *Women of Trachis* and Euripides' *Bakchai*: while the latter depicts the dangerousness of the *oros*, which invades, seduces and threatens to overturn the *polis*, the former – a play under the shadow of Zeus rather than Dionysos – creates a sense of the *separation* of mountain and city.[92]

Mindful of this important reservation, we may still make some provisional generalisations about our hypothetical myth/life distinction: (1) Myths rework, pare down, clarify and exaggerate experience; to say that they 'reflect' experience is quite inadequate. (2) Clarification is not only not incompatible with ambiguity, but can actually bring it into sharper relief (cf. mountain 'luck'). (3) Perceptions reworked in mythology feed back into ordinary life, even if the way in which this happens can be hard to specify. (4) In ritual, behaviour is articulated through symbols with a comparable selectivity to that found in myths. The two symbolic languages contrast with and complement each other. (5) Overwhelmingly, our evidence, both mythological and non-mythological, bears the stamp of the city or village. Mountains are unsettling, for those in settlements; they are to be viewed from afar, visited only to be left again. To this extent, at least, the structuralists are right: we should investigate *contrasts* between the symbolic terms deployed in myths. The *oros* needs to be seen in the light of that which is not the *oros*. (6) Useful as oppositional analysis may be, it must not be allowed to override the nuances of individual texts. Greek mythology speaks with an astonishing range of voices; reductivism is the surest way of muffling them.

[90] Hom. *H. Merc.* 491–2; S. Hodkinson in Whittaker 1988, pp. 35–74.

[91] On the Homeric landscape ('espace de nulle-part, poussiéreux et désertique'), see Bouvier 1986, p. 257. For a sophisticated account of space(s) in Theokritos, *Idyll* 1, see Calame 1992.

[92] Tragic mountains: Buxton 1992a, pp. 12–14.

Other territories: sea, cave and spring

We now look, more briefly, at three other features of the landscape in order to test the conclusions just reached. It will be seen that the relationship between myth and ordinary life continues to raise complex problems.

We begin with an element which in Greek perception has much in common with mountains. The sea was a place for fishing, travelling, trading; and the ways in which these human activities were perceived influenced perceptions of the sea itself. In view of the tendency throughout our period for agriculture to be regarded as ideologically central, any mode of livelihood which diverged from that of the grain-growing peasant-farmer risked being seen as inferior. Fishing and the sea-borne importation of grain both fell into this category.[93] Like the shepherd, the fisherman (Plate 8a) is little talked of; both prayed to Pan, god of the wild outside.[94] Usually the fisherman's viewpoint is either passed over in silence, or at best enigmatic. How one would love to know the background to the question put to the oracle at Dodona in the fourth century BC: 'Does the god give an oracle to Phainylos to work at his father's trade of fisherman, thus to become more prosperous and to fare better?'[95] (Was the less conventional alternative to become a mercenary?) As for the sea-trader, an extreme example of the peasant's grumpiness is audible in the words of the Athenian in Plato's *Laws*: '[The sea] fills the land with wholesaling and retailing, breeds shifty and deceitful habits in a man's soul, and makes the citizens distrustful and hostile...'[96] Such an attitude would not be out of place in Hesiod's *leschē*, with its talk of hard earth and hard work.

But this was not the only tone of voice to be heard. Another echoed

---

[93] Imported grain seen as ideologically inferior: Osborne 1987, p. 103. For a possible pastoral period in eleventh- to ninth-century Greece, when grain-production was allegedly *not* dominant, see Snodgrass 1980, pp. 35–6; but note the criticisms of J. F. Cherry in Whittaker 1988, pp. 26–30.

[94] Theoc. 5.14, with Gow's commentary *ad loc.*, *Anth. Pal.* 10.10. Hesiod too implies a parallel between fishing and herding, in that Hekate helps both groups (*Th.* 440–7). On Hellenistic fishermen, see Schneider 1967–9, II, pp. 97–8.

[95] Parke 1967, p. 269.   [96] 705a (trans. T. J. Saunders).

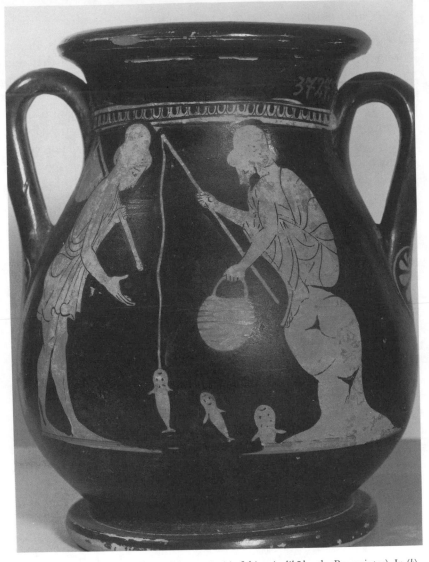

8(*a*) and (*b*). Two faces of the sea. In (*a*), fishing (*pelikē* by the Pan painter). In (*b*), Europa and the bull, surrounded by creatures of the deep (Panathenaic amphora).

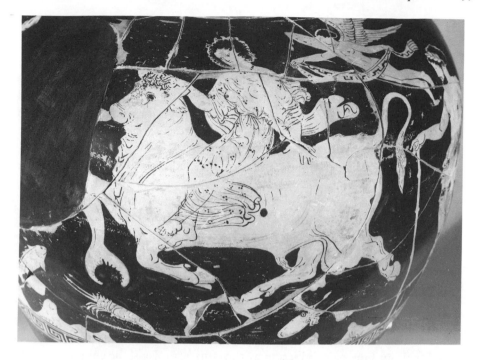

in the cry of Xenophon's men, for so long confined inland: *Thalassa, thalassa.* Without the sea there would have been no colonisation, no victory at Salamis. The sea made things possible. Like all friends, however, it was potentially false. Greeks talked often of the sea's ambiguity. The poet Semonides compared the ocean to a type of woman, another unfathomable being whose tameness was always threatening to unleash its latent savagery:

> She has two characters ... just so the sea often stands without a
> tremor, harmless, a great delight to sailors, in the summer season;

but often it raves, tossed about by thundering waves. It is the sea
that such a woman most resembles in her temper; like the ocean,
she has a changeful nature.[97]

It was hard to know when the sea's dark side would burst out: hence
the elaborate rituals to invoke divine protection upon a voyage, and
the countless offerings made to saviour divinities like the Dioskouroi
and the great gods of Samothrace, in return for a voyage successfully
accomplished.[98]

The sea's perceived ambiguity is reflected in myths. The positive
side – loveliness, responsiveness to human craft (in both senses) – is
implicit in two lists of names. Amongst Hesiod's fifty Nereids (*Th.*
240ff.) are Saviour, Generous, Calm, Greeneyes, Swiftwave, Honey-
sweet, Island Maid, Shore Maid, Wavecease, Sandy. When the waters
are in this mood, men's skill can cut a troublefree path – none more
adeptly than Homer's clever and nippy Phaiakians: 'Topship and
Quicksea and Paddler, Seaman and Poopman, Beacher and Oarsman,
Deepsea and Lookout, Goahead and Upaboard; there was Seagirt the
son of Manyclipper Shipwrightson.'[99] Of course, it helps if the gods
themselves take a hand. In the poem by the Hellenistic poet Moschos
about Europa's abduction by the tauriform Zeus, the couple's passage
over the calm sea is celebrated by a benign and revelling entourage of
tumbling dolphins, conch-blowing Tritons, and Nereids mounted on
beasts of the deep (115–24) (Plate 8b). But the sea is also a place of
duplicity, being the element where shape-shifting Proteus dwelt.[100]
Threat and danger lurk beneath its surface, as with the Poseidon-
stirred tempests of the *Odyssey*, or the storms which wreck the Greek
fleet returning from Troy. Savage and uncontrollable, the sea is like
Love, which travels 'over the sea and in the wild lands' (Sophokles
Ant. 785–6).

In addition to mirroring the two-faced sea, myths stress certain
specific aspects. The role of imaginary fishermen is to net the

[97] 7.27–42 (trans. H. Lloyd-Jones).
[98] See Wachsmuth 1967, Burkert 1985, pp. 266–7. Höckmann 1985 refers briefly to religion, at
       pp. 157–60.
[99] *Od.* 8.111–14. The sprightly translation of the Phaiakian names, cited by Stanford *ad loc.*, is
       by Rouse; that of the Nereids' names is my own.
[100] Cf. Vermeule 1979, ch. 6 (full of insight, and beautifully written).

unexpected. In so doing they both resemble and subtly differ from the herdsmen who stumble on mountain luck.[101] The herdsman-finder's fortune is by definition extraordinary. It was not his purpose to find, and what he does hit upon was, it had been believed, lost for ever to humanity. The fisherman-finder, like his herding cousin, is venturing into the wild; but his normal livelihood depends on finding. However, because myths refract, what he hands in is hardly ever fish, or hardly ever *just* fish.[102] A frequent motif is the netting of a sacred object. The floating head of Orpheus, still gamely singing in spite of its owner's earlier dismemberment by Thracian maenads, eventually reached land on Lesbos.[103] On the same island, an olive-wood image of Dionysos Phallen was fished up; likewise Hermes in Thrace.[104] The implications of these *Anschwemmungssagen* have been convincingly drawn out by Fritz Graf, who notes the repeated link between an origin or return from the sea and the extraordinary, uncanny and beneficial character of the object retrieved.[105] The positive aspect of the finds should indeed be stressed: the sea yields up unexpected treasure. A statue of Theagenes, the renowned Thasian athlete, was consigned to the deep when the image fell upon and killed some of his enemies, who were whipping the bronze as if it were flesh; miraculously, it was fished out of the sea, to take on curative properties.[106] This sense of the sea's hopefulness is confirmed by the story of the recovery of little Perseus and his mother Danae, cast adrift in a chest. Hauled ashore by Diktys, Net Man, the baby was metaphorically reborn, growing up to a new life of reinstated honour.[107] Baby Oidipous was reborn, too — in the mountains. Sea and mountains are alike in being wild; but, of the two, it is the sea which more often offers renewed hope.

---

[101] Mountains and sea as parallel (both may receive polluted objects): Hp. *Morb. sacr.* , Littré vol. VI, p. 363, with Parker 1983, p. 229, Bremmer 1987, p. 44.

[102] In the Herodotean tale (3.41–2) about Polykrates and the fisherman who brings him a remarkable catch, the fish is significant because it has swallowed a ring that had been cast away: it is not *just* a fish.

[103] Luc. *Adv. ind.* 11–12; Burkert 1983, p. 202.

[104] Paus. 10.19.3, Call. fr. 197; Burkert 1983, pp. 202–3, cf. p. 204 n. 40.

[105] Graf 1985b, p. 302.

[106] Paus. 6.11.6–9. Cf. the netting of Pelops' shoulderblade: Paus. 5.13.4–6.

[107] Burkert 1983, p. 209. Compare the casting adrift of Tennes and his sister: Paus. 10.14.2.

9. The sea and its margin: the peninsula of Koryphasion, near Pylos, Messenia.

The evidence of cult enables us to see more clearly what is at stake in these tales of fishing up. We know of several Greek states in which a statue was carried annually to the sea for a purifying bath. In the case of the Athenian Plynteria, the ritual significantly took place in the last month of the calendar year, marking a break between the old order and the new.[108] In ritual, as in myth, contact with the sea can constitute a fresh beginning, the reinauguration of hope. In this connection it is worth emphasising the exact location of these rituals: the sea-*shore*. In the relatively tideless Mediterranean, the shore is narrow – a line, a boundary, a margin, a place where opposites meet (Plate 9). In cult, it is the site for the transition between polluted and

[108] Burkert 1985, p. 79.

pure. In myth, it is where the human meets the uncanny (Hippolytos and the bull, Andromeda and the sea-monster); where the no-longer-human-but-not-yet-properly-dead belong (like Polydoros, whose body has been cast up on the shore of the Hellespont, and whose ghostly voice speaks the prologue of Euripides' *Hekabe*); and where the marginalised hero withdraws (Achilles in the *Iliad*, Odysseus on Kalypso's isle, Philoktetes).[109] There is even an entire tragedy, Euripides' *Iphigeneia in Tauris*, whose action is located on a series of symbolic and literal margins. From Aulis (on the coast of the mainland opposite Euboea), Iphigeneia has come to the shore-temple of Artemis in the land of the Taurians, where she fulfils a role of multiple marginality, as a Greek virgin priestess in a barbarian land; her no-less-excluded brother Orestes finds himself twice unable to escape from the shore. At length brother and sister do make their getaway, but – perhaps in symbolic enactment of their ultimate failure to belong – their ultimate destinations will be two cults, at Brauron and Halai, on the *coast* of Attica.[110]

One more facet of the mythical sea may be mentioned: the connection with prophecy. Amid the sea's many noises – the seductive song of the Sirens, the roar and crash of furious Poseidon – is the true and authoritative voice of the prophet. Triton, Nereus, Proteus and Glaukos could, if they wished, reveal what was to be; sometimes they had to be forced to wish it.[111] What logic underlies the connection between sea and prophecy? It can perhaps be found in the nature of the knowledge to which the prophet has access. The future is hidden; in Greek metaphor, it lies 'behind'. What is behind is sacred, mysterious: Deukalion and Pyrrha cast behind them the stones from which humanity will magically grow. To know the future, to see that which is behind, is not human, and may therefore be

---

[109] Latin poetry offers several parallels. Palinurus, unburied on the shore, longs in vain for rest: 'nunc me fluctus habet versantque in litore venti' (V. *Aen.* 6.362). In general, to be unburied is to be confined to the margin: 'centum errant annos volitantque haec litora circum', reports the Sibyl (*Aen.* 6.329) of the souls longing to gain passage in Charon's boat. In Catullus 64 Ariadne, inhabiting a no-man's-land between father and husband, dwells alone amid the seaweed ('nec quisquam apparet vacua mortalis in alga', 168).

[110] See Buxton 1992b. For the sea-shore in satyr-plays, see Voelke 1992, pp. 41–2.

[111] Vermeule 1979, pp. 190ff.

10. Real and imaginary caves. Picture (*a*): the cave of Franchthi in the Argolid. As picture (*b*) shows, caves were thought to give access to another, more uncanny world. On this *skyphos*, a beardless Herakles pulls an alien foe from her (?) lair. ('A female death-monster dragged from the cave of hell' – E. Vermeule in *Festschrift Brommer* 1977, p. 297.)

perceived as belonging to the realm of nature as opposed to that of humanity. The word of Zeus is hidden in the rustling of the oak-trees at Dodona, that of Delphic Apollo in the non-human raving of his priestess the Pythia: divine noises remain unintelligible until brought into the human sphere when priests translate them into Greek. Knowledge of the future belongs to the wild, the sacred, the non-human; among other inaccessible spots, it can be found beneath the sea, invisible and unfathomable.

Like mountains and the sea, caves are a characteristic feature of the Greek landscape (Plate 10a). The economic importance of caves was minimal. In the period with which we are concerned, their main

practical function was probably to shelter shepherds or lovers. But in mythology caves figure prominently and repeatedly.

In some respects the mythical cave resembles the mythical mountain. Caves, too, are before. Until Prometheus brought culture, mankind lived 'in sunless recesses of caves'.[112] Being before, caves were associated with birth. Numerous caves were claimed as the birthplace of Zeus, notably on Crete and in Asia Minor; the monster Typhos was bred in the Corycian cave; according to Orphic belief, Phanes and Night produced things 'in the beginning' in a cave.[113] The residents of Lakonian Brasiai showed Pausanias the grotto where Ino nursed the infant Dionysos; babies Jason and Aristaios were reared in Cheiron's cave.[114]

---

[112] A. *PV* 453. The assumption that prehistory is about cavemen still dominates much popular thought on the subject. For an idiosyncratic view, see Vico's *New Science*, 522 and 524. Caves and cavemen: T. E. J. Wiedemann in Moxon, Smart and Woodman 1986, pp. 190–1. Cf. Lucr. *DRN* 5.955, Ovid, *Met.* 1.121.

[113] Zeus: A. B. Cook 1914–40, I, pp. 148–58, also M. L. West's commentary on Hes. *Th.* 477. Typhos: Pi. *Pyth.* 1.16–17. Orphics: West 1983b, pp. 213–14. See also Lane Fox 1986, p. 41.

[114] Dionysos: Paus. 3.24.4. Jason: Pi. *Pyth.* 4.102–3. Cheiron: A. R. 2.509–10.

'Not yet' is an equivalent for 'outside', and caves were for outsiders of all kinds. The monstrous Echidna had her lair in a cave 'deep down under a hollow rock far from the deathless gods and mortal men'; the Harpies withdrew to a cavern below Mount Dikte in Crete; the no less fearsome Lamia/Sybaris dwelt in a cave below Parnassos (Plate 10b).[115] Those isolated individuals Kalypso and Philoktetes lived in their respective remote caves, as did the Cyclopes:

> These people have no institutions, no meetings for counsels;
> rather they make their habitations in caverns hollowed
> among the peaks of the high mountains, and each one is the law
> for his own wives and children, and cares nothing about the others.[116]

(As usual, narrative context inflects the presentation of the theme: in the Theokritean idyll, the cave where the nymph Amaryllis has her home is romantically pastoral rather than savage (3.12–14).) Beyond the narratives about gods and heroes we find other outsider-speleophiles, such as Aristotle's pygmies, that (so they said) non-conformer Euripides, reputed to have composed in a 'grim and gloomy cavern' on Salamis, and Epimenides of Knossos, who withdrew to a cave, slept for forty years, and woke to become a poet and 'purifier'.[117] For mythology was, as we have repeatedly emphasised, a group of narratives which had many of its motifs and patterns in common with other areas of thought.

As the Cyclopes illustrate, caves were associated with activities perceived as outside the norm. An example is sexual love outside, or before, marriage. The secret liaison between the Moon and Endymion was consummated in the Latmian cave near Miletos; the Silenoi and Hermes made love to Nymphs in caves; the same type of location concealed Kreousa's rape by Apollo.[118] (We may compare the

---

[115] Echidna: Hes. *Th.* 301–2. Harpies: A. R. 2.298–9, 433–4. Lamia: Ant. Lib. 8.1.

[116] Philoktetes: Jobst 1970, pp. 38–44. *Odyssey* ref.: 9.112–15.

[117] Pygmies: Aristot. *HA* 597a; see P. Janni in Prontera 1983, pp. 135–71. Euripides: A. Gell. 15.20.5, cf. *Life of Euripides* 62ff. (available in vol. 1 of Budé series of E.). Epimenides: Paus. 1.14.4. To the list of cave-withdrawers one may add Homer, said to have composed in a cave near a spring of sweet water: Paus. 7.5.12. Caves as outside: cf. the symbolic dwelling of the not-yet-philosophical in Plato's *Republic*. The Christian virgin Thekla cured the sick in a mountain cave: Hägg 1983b, p. 159.

[118] Endymion: A. R. 4.57–8. Silenoi: Hom. *H. Ven.* 262–3. Kreousa: E. *Ion* 17. Poseidon and a nymph (Polyphemos' parents) made love in a hollow cave (*Od.* 1.71–3). Compare also the

novelist Achilles Tatios' story about Rhodopis, who broke her oath of virginity in a cave near Ephesos (8.12.7).) Slightly different, but related, is Demeter's withdrawal into a cave in Arkadia after Poseidon had raped her in the form of a stallion, the goddess thus seeking a suitably remote refuge in order to avoid social contact.[119] Finally, unwanted children were left in caves, as when Ion was abandoned by his mother Kreousa, and the twins Amphion and Zethos by their mother Antiope.[120] The analogy with mountains is obvious, but caves are rarer in this role. Presumably the reason is that, if the aim of exposure is to bring about the baby's death, then the shelter afforded by a cave is a hindrance. It is surely no coincidence that in the cases just cited the babies are abandoned *by their mothers*. Here as always, however, we must allow for motivational variation. Even within one narrative, ascribed motive may vary under the pressure of local rhetoric and situational emotion. In Euripides' *Ion* Kreousa's action is described by Hermes as 'putting out [the baby] to die' (18), whereas Kreousa herself at first maintains that she hoped 'that the god would save his own child' (965), but later, in a passionate duet with that newly recognised child whom she thought long dead, recalls how she cast the baby out 'to Hades', to be torn and eaten by birds of prey (1494–6).

In discussing mountains and the sea, we were able to investigate the interplay between tales and life in relation both to everyday, practical activities and to ritual. With caves, the situation is somewhat different. In the temple-based Greek religion of the period which concerns us, the ritual significance of the cave as a cult site was rather restricted.[121] There were, of course, important exceptions. At the cavern into which the violated Demeter withdrew, individuals and, annually, the whole community made offerings of grapes and other cultivated fruit, honeycombs and raw wool, products recalling a 'non-cereal' existence and hence, by implication, reinforcing a sense

sacred bridal bed in a cave in A. R. 4.1131, and of course V. *Aen.* 4.165–6: 'speluncam Dido dux et Troianus eandem | deveniunt.'

[119] Paus. 8.42.2. Ovid's Echo withdraws into a cave after being rejected by Narkissos ('solis ex illo vivit in antris', *Met.* 3.394).

[120] Kreousa: E. *Ion* 18. Antiope: Paus. 1.38.9.

[121] Pre-Classical Crete was another matter. Here the expertise of P. Faure is unrivalled: see e.g. Faure 1960 and 1964; also Burkert 1985, pp. 24–6.

of what humanity owes to Demeter.[122] More often it was Pan or the Nymphs to whom the ritual sacredness of caves was felt to belong.[123] Later, grottoes offered access to the symbolic Beyond whose attainment was the object of the private Dionysiac mysteries which grew up alongside the cults of the *polis*.[124] A world without cereals; the wildness of Pan and the Nymphs; the Dionysiac Beyond: equivalent versions of that extra-civic otherness to which entry to a cave might grant access.

In spite of these instances there is still, I think, a gap between the *relative* lack of prominence of caves in Classical Greek religious and practical life, and the frequency with which we meet them in mythology. If I am right – and I could be the victim of an optical illusion caused by the familiar settlement-oriented perspective of the bulk of our sources – I would explain this frequency by saying that caves were 'good to think with':[125] that is, they recur as often as they do in myths because of their usefulness as symbolic operators. A cave is defined by its anomalous and ambiguous shape: it is both inside and outside. It may also be simultaneously above and below ground, and be located either in the wilds – on a mountain, near the sea, under the sea – or in the heart of a human settlement, as with the cave-sanctuary of the Holy Ones (usually identified with the Furies) below the Athenian Acropolis, even if in this case it is perceived as an element of wildness *within* civilisation.[126] A cave is both like and not like a house: unlike, because natural; like, because sheltering.[127] Caves are also open, yet impenetrable. They give access to the sacred or, ultimately, to the dead (the cave-entrance to the Underworld at Tainaron).[128] These ambiguities are the nourishment on which mythology thrives.

122 Paus. 8.42.11. An excellent analysis of this myth-and-ritual complex is to be found in Bruit 1986.
123 Pan: Lane Fox 1986, p. 131, Osborne 1987, p. 192, Borgeaud 1988, esp. pp. 48ff. Nymphs: see Borgeaud 1988, index *s.v.* 'Nymph(s)'.
124 Burkert 1985, p. 291.
125 G. E. R. Lloyd has domesticated this aspect of Lévi-Strauss's *pensée sauvage* for classical scholars; cf. p. 199 below.   126 Paus. 1.28.6.
127 Cave as house in E. *Cyc.*: see Voelke 1992, p. 36.
128 Cave as entrance to the Other World: Patch 1950, index *s.v.* 'cave', Duerr 1985, pp. 19ff., 63 and 273 n. 26 (cave = womb/mouth).

Without origin, without fail, springs supply the essential of life. They can be tamed for easier access, as with the still-visible fountain-house of Peirene at Corinth, or the previously uncovered Kallirhoe waters which the Athenian tyrants transformed into the Nine Springs.[129] But only a magical horse like Pegasos, or an inspired Bacchant, can *create* a spring, with hoof or wand; ordinary mortals must content themselves with housing or channelling what nature has already proffered.[130] Springs are not, it is true, the only source of drinkable water: in his description of the plague, Thucydides distinguishes between springs (*krēnai*) and wells or storage cisterns (*phreata*) (2.48). But springs, perceived as pure and ultimately mysterious, are a constituent of ideal landscapes. It is not, I think, a common human belief that access to the sacred can be gained through a cistern.[131]

Springs could be in the wilds, like the one called 'Pure' (Hagno) on Mount Lykaion in Arkadia, or at the centre of a city (Peirene).[132] When within or near human settlements they were visited by the community's women, who drew water and did washing; this, together with attendance at religious festivals, seems to have been, at least in some localities, one of the few occasions when Greek women regularly left the home (Plate 11).[133] A place of meeting, for free women as well as slave, the fountain constituted a space comparable with the men's *leschē*.[134]

Great sanctuaries, like the Heraion near Argos and the temple of Apollo at Delphi, were founded near springs, since water was needed for visitors and sacrificial animals as well as for the ceremonial of

---

[129] Thuc. 2.15.

[130] Pegasos: see Nilsson 1967, pp. 450–1, Papathomopoulos 1968, p. 89 n. 15. On the striking hoof, see *RE* XVI.1, col. 700 (H. Kees). Bacchant: E. *Ba.* 704–5.

[131] Springs: Wycherley 1937, Ballabriga 1986, pp. 47–8. For *phreata* and related terms, see Hitzig and Blümner 1896 on Paus. 1.14.1. Spring in *locus amoenus*: Elliger 1975, index *s.v.* 'Quelle', Himmelmann 1980, pp. 81–2, with refs. to X. *Oec.* 5.9, 20.18.

[132] Hagno: Paus. 8.38.3. Contrast between wild water and city water: E. *Hipp.* 225–7.

[133] Cf. also Hom. *H. Dem.* 98–9: grieving Demeter, in the form of an old woman, sits by a well as if waiting for an employer to take her on.

[134] Lissarrague (in Schmitt Pantel 1991, p. 218) compares the women's fountain with the men's 'place publique' rather than with the *leschē*.

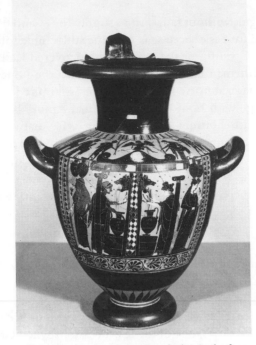

11. Women drawing water at a fountain, which is in the form of two lion's-head spouts – wild, yet (because artificial) domesticated. Any fountain mediates between nature and culture; this one graphically embodies the opposition. (Black-figure *hydria*.)

sacrifice itself.[135] Springs themselves were felt to be religiously powerful, and hence a focus for cult. Pausanias came across many such on his travels. In Messenia there was a source where little children were healed (4.31.4); in Arkadia, a drink from a certain spring of cold water beneath a plane tree would cure rabies (8.19.2–3); in Elis, a bathe in spring waters sacred to the Nymphs would put your rheumatics right (6.22.7). Springs were conducive to truth as well as health. Hot springs would scald the perjurer, leaving the innocent unscathed; a mirror lowered into a spring in Demeter's shrine at Patrai would

[135] See S. G. Cole in Hägg, Marinatos and Nordquist 1988, pp. 161–5.

show an image of the patient as either alive or dead, depending on what the future held.[136] Of course, the power of religious purity might be abused: the woman at Tainaron who washed clothes in a particular spring ended its prophetic virtue for ever.[137] Finally, spring water was used to effect a ritually pure transition into life for the newborn, and into marriage for the betrothed couple.[138]

Aspects of real-life springs are reflected in mythology, but as usual there are refractive emphases. Mythical springs are symbolically central to a community's existence. Kadmos can found Thebes only when he has killed Ares' sacred snake, which was guarding a spring. That sources of fresh water stand for orderly, traditional life is implied in two passages in Homer, relating to societies going about their peaceful, domestic business. On Ithaka there is a fountain near the city, 'sweet-running and made of stone; and there the townspeople went for their water'; not being in the city itself, it appropriately has an altar to the Nymphs built over it.[139] The Iliadic example is poignant. Near Troy there are two springs, one scalding, one ice-cool; and beside them

> are the washing-hollows
> of stone, and magnificent, where the wives of the Trojans and their
>   lovely
> daughters washed the clothes to shining, in the old days
> when there was peace, before the coming of the sons of the Achaeans.

> *(Il.* 22.153–6)

This is the scene of Hektor's race for his life against Achilles. The Trojan springs will still flow, but the Trojan women will be sent to draw water in Greece.

This link with the lives of women is revealingly developed in several myths. On the one hand, women *should* draw water. Thus the Danaids, who showed themselves to be anti-wives by slaying their husbands, underwent appropriate punishment in the Underworld by being obliged endlessly to fill leaking water-jars. But a visit to the

---

[136] Hot springs: Croon 1967. Mirror: Paus. 7.21.12. Cf. Lane Fox 1986, p. 207.
[137] Paus. 3.25.8. Springs and prophecy: Halliday 1913, pp. 116–44.
[138] Garland 1990, pp. 74 and 220.   [139] *Od.* 17.205–6.

fountain might be dangerous, for it was out of doors; and being out of doors brought the risk of erotic encounters. Falassi's account of a modern Italian peasant community suggests an analogous connection between courtship and water-drawing. 'Sooner or later, the girl might agree to meet the young man at the village fountain. Many of my female informants confessed to me that they often emptied their water jugs in the sink, behind their mother's back, so as to have an unquestionably legitimate excuse to go out and fill them up. "So much water in my house has never been consumed as when I was having an affair with Vitaliano."'[140] A comparison from modern Greece goes a step further: when a girl 'goes out on some errand, to gather firewood or carry water, she has a companion to go with her. In the popular mind wells and illicit sexual intercourse are linked together. If a man for any reason wants to see the local girls, he has only to sit by the well and by and by he will see them all.'[141] Ancient Greek myths make explicit a comparable, latent fear of out-of-doors women by, characteristically, carrying it to an extreme. Auge is raped by Herakles at a fountain; Amymone and Poseidon, Oreithyia and Boreas have similar encounters.[142] Themes have variations: springs are associated with several different types of liaison. At Pegai ('Springs') the active lover is female, a Nymph, while the passive is the doomed youth Hylas.[143] Springs mean bathing; mythical springs mean bathing goddesses; bathing goddesses spell trouble for careless hunters like Aktaion and Teiresias. Finally, we cannot omit Narkissos, whose visit to a pool made possible an erotic encounter with himself.

The sacred power of spring water in mythology usually works for human benefit: when Sophokles' Philoktetes is obliged to drink stagnant water (716), he is being deprived of more than just a pleasant taste.[144] One connotation of springs distils their positive qualities into

---

[140] Falassi 1980, pp. 110–11.

[141] Campbell 1964, p. 86 (quoted by Lefkowitz 1986, p. 48).

[142] For Greek, Roman and other examples, see Bremmer and Horsfall 1987, p. 52.

[143] A. R. 1.1221ff., Theoc. 13; A. W. Bulloch in Easterling and Knox 1985, p. 583, compares/ contrasts these versions.

[144] There are occasional non-beneficial springs, though, like the anomalous and mysteriously dangerous one in the Bacchic-mystery underworld (Burkert 1985, p. 293); NB also Apollod. 3.7.3, Ath. 41e (Teiresias dies after drinking from the spring of Tilphoussa, but only because, being old, he cannot tolerate its coldness).

a potent symbol. For the poets who told the myths, spring water offered, through its association with the Muses, everlasting, privileged access to a world beyond human society. On Helikon, where Pegasos' hoof had struck ground and brought forth water at Hippokrene ('Horse Spring'), a poet might meet those who inspired him.[145] Once more there are individual variants on a theme. The refined poetry of Kallimachos claims access to the thin trickle of purest inspiration; not for him a draught from the public fountain.[146]

In reviewing Greek perceptions of sea, caves and springs, we have confirmed our analysis of mountains in some respects and modified it in others. There is no simple formula to express the relationship between the two categories which we have crudely designated as everyday life and mythology: even within our small sample the picture, for example in relation to cult, is variable. But this much is clear: the landscape of mythological narrative is formed from elements which, while they grow out of the practices and perceptions of ordinary life, acquire strongly differentiated and conceptually potent symbolic traits.

[145] Hes. *Th.* 6.   [146] See Bulloch in Easterling and Knox 1985, p. 560.

7
Family

Wives, webs and wiles

Recent academic study of the Greek family has been dominated by the role of women. One paradoxical effect of this huge output of work has been to underline how little we know of Greek women's perceptions of themselves. Given the dearth of information it is not surprising that considerable attention has been devoted to a group of women who, in spite of their mythical status and of the fact that their stories are retold by men, seem to have a solidity seldom found in the countless real but silent women of Greece. Yet the question of how to interpret such figures as Penelope, Antigone, Medea and Klytaimestra is a vexed one: are they reflections of life, or distortions of it? And, first of all, what (again) do we mean by 'life'?

We may take as a point of orientation John Gould's deservedly influential article on women in Classical Athens.[1] Gould stressed the need to differentiate between types of evidence. He showed that the legal provisions relating to Athenian women do not exactly match what can be reconstructed of customary attitudes and behaviour towards them, and in particular that the legally subordinate position of women is by no means always reflected in consistent, and certainly not consistently repressive, behaviour by those to whom the law accorded power over women. He went on to argue that the images of women to be found in mythology coincide neither with law nor with custom, though they do have revealing connections with both. We

[1] Gould 1980.

shall return to Gould's article later, when we have reviewed the material supplied by mythology; for the moment we simply emphasise his demonstration of the heterogeneity of the evidence for 'life'.

Once we look beyond Classical Athens, contexts multiply. The conditions depicted in the Homeric poems are not identical with those of the Classical period, and neither can be assimilated to the Hellenistic world.[2] Geographical distinctions must also be made. For instance, legal provisions affecting women differed at Athens and Sparta, and the argument has been pressed that anecdotes about the dominance of Spartan wives over their husbands are founded on more than simple prejudice.[3] Nevertheless, in spite of this diversity, one generalisation seems to hold throughout: women were felt to be, in a series of fundamental ways, responsible for the *continuity* of the community, a responsibility which they exercised in relation to the past, the present and the future.

First, the past. Women, especially kinswomen, had special duties relating to the dead. From the washing, anointing and dressing of the corpse for the laying-out, to mourning at the funeral itself, to the ritual remembrance of the deceased in offerings and in sung laments, women shouldered the formal burden of coping with the community's losses.[4] Of course, men had roles also: funerary imagery and literary references often represent male mourners, and the Athenian *epitaphios logos* goes so far as to marginalise female lamentation.[5] But the bulk of the evidence tells the other way. When Solon legislated to restrict the demonstrativeness of funerary display, he is credited with having 'subjected the public appearances [lit.: "goings-out"] of the women, their mourning and their festivals, to a law which did away with disorder and licence'.[6] For whatever reason, the *polis* here stepped in to curb what was evidently not seen as purely private

---

[2] Homeric: Lacey 1968, pp. 33–50, Finley 1977, pp. 126ff. Classical: Lacey 1968. Hellenistic: Pomeroy 1984. The literature is vast: the three books cited provide starting-points.

[3] Garland 1990, pp. 231–2.

[4] On all this, see Kurtz and Boardman 1971, pp. 142–61, Alexiou 1974, pp. 4–23, Garland 1985.

[5] See Loraux 1986, p. 45.   [6] Plu. *Sol.* 21.4 (trans. B. Perrin, Loeb edn).

behaviour: preserving and consecrating the past of the *oikos* inevitably brought women into the public arena.

Ensuring continuity in the present meant above all preserving the *oikos*. Spinning and weaving clothes and cooking food – that is, transforming (metaphorically and literally) raw into cooked – were perceived as central to women's existence. Among the grave-goods buried with women were spindle whorls, cooking vessels and model baskets; the law code of the city of Gortyn laid down the proportion of that which she had *woven* to which a divorced or widowed woman was entitled; the hanging of a piece of woollen material on the front door marked the birth of a girl; brides carried a symbolic pot for roasting barley.[7] Corresponding to the nature of women's tasks was the ideal picture of the woman's space as within the *oikos* and the man's outside it – a picture corroborated by women's myth-telling function within the household.[8] Yet this ideal will already have been contradicted by reality in the case of families who could not afford the luxury of a housebound wife, while the prominence of women in public religious cult – another aspect of their role in preserving continuity, and an issue to which we shall return – constitutes a further modification of the ideal.[9]

As mothers, women secured the future in a quite literal way. Even more exclusively than the passage *from* life, the passage *into* life was the province of women.[10] But the securing of the future *of the community* – that is, of the citizen group – was a matter of far more than private significance, since it related to the bearing, formal recognition and rearing of legitimate children within marriage, a state assumed to be the norm for both sexes. Basic to the ideology which underpinned marriage was a stress on the difference between women legitimately

---

[7] Grave goods, Gortyn: see Pomeroy 1975, pp. 43, 39–40. Spinning/weaving: see Jenkins 1985, Moret 1991, L. B. Zaidman in Schmitt Pantel 1991, pp. 379–81. Wool on door: cf. Garland 1990, p. 75. Cooking pot: Pollux 1. 246. (NB also the siege of Plataiai: 480 men, with 110 women 'to prepare the food' (Th. 2.78.3), cf. Pomeroy 1975, p. 72.) On women's work in general, see Herfst 1979. As usual, contextual differences cannot be ignored: Spartan women were said *not* to weave (Pl. *Lg.* 806a, X. *Lac.* 1.3ff., cf. Plu. *Mor.* 241d; see Calame 1977, I, p. 406 n. 102).   [8] Women within: X. *Oec.* 7.21.

[9] The ideal contradicted: Schmitt Pantel 1991, p. 501.

[10] Garland 1990, pp. 61–4, on midwives.

married, and others. On one side of marriage, a stigma usually attached to permanent virginity, a condition which, far from being held to be exemplary, could be regarded as medically pathological.[11] On the other side, wife and prostitute were as a rule strongly distinguished, as in the contrast between the Thesmophoria (a festival for citizen wives only) and the Adonia (celebrated by all women).[12] But in this of all matters it is imperative to notice that Greece does not speak with one voice: as a recent essay on the interpretation of vase-painting has shown, there are some striking visual *equations* between 'good' and 'bad' women, which show that the distinction was neither absolute nor universal, for all that it expressed a basic feature of the dominant self-image of the Greek *polis*.[13]

If we put together these fundamental female roles with the legal disabilities commonly experienced by ancient Greek women, it is hard to miss the contradictoriness, or at least the ambiguity, of a situation in which civic ideology simultaneously registered and denied the importance of one half of the population.[14] As we turn to the evidence of mythology, it will be in part to see what happens to these complexities when they are passed through the filter of fantasy.

The first point to emphasise is that there are major differences between narrative contexts. I take the example of the representations of marriage in praise-poetry and tragedy.

In Pindar, the context of performance concerns the celebration of male prowess. This shapes the way in which relations between the sexes are depicted: women typically appear as beautiful maidens sought after and won by shining gods or illustrious mortals. They are important not for themselves but because they give birth to heroes, who often become the ancestors of the athletic victors for whom Pindar's praise is intended. In *Olympian* 6 the seer Iamos is at once the ancestor of the poem's victor and blessed by a doubly divine lineage, being able to boast descent from both Poseidon and Apollo, who

[11] See H. King in Cameron and Kuhrt 1983, pp. 113ff., also Sissa 1990.
[12] Strong distinction: D. 59.111ff. Thesmophoria: Is. 8.19–20. Adonia: Detienne 1977, pp. 64–6, 78.   [13] M. Beard in Rasmussen and Spivey 1991, pp. 26–30.
[14] This is a central theme of Gould 1980.

bestowed their respective affections on Pitana and her daughter
Euadne. The characteristic flavour of such encounters is given by
Pythian 9, composed for a victor from Kyrene in the race-in-armour.
First the poem bathes in glory the original liaison between Apollo and
the nymph Kyrene. Before Apollo stamped his authority upon her,
the girl was – like all virgins in prevailing Greek metaphor – wild. She
roamed on Mount Pelion, and

> loved not to walk to and fro before the loom
> nor the delight of feasting with her companions
> who kept the house: but with javelins of brass and a sword
> she fought and slew wild beasts . . .
>
> (18–22)

But Apollo found her as she wrestled with a lion. His conversation
with the civilised Centaur Cheiron, a local resident, perfectly conveys
the manner in which the god's taking of the nymph is represented.
Apollo disingenuously asks who the girl is, who her parents are, and
whether it would be wrong 'to lay my mighty hand on her and take
the delicious pasture of her love'. The Centaur replies 'with softened
eyes', and with a laugh. He speaks of the 'secret keys with which
Persuasion knows how to unlock the sanctuaries of love' – for the
imminent act will naturally be fulfilled by consent. 'Why ask me?',
smiles Cheiron: the clear-sighted god knows the truth anyway. This
truth is that Apollo came to Pelion to wed Kyrene, and his purpose
will indeed be accomplished. The nymph will be led to Zeus's garden
over the sea, and will bear her child (Aristaios) in that place – that is,
the city of Kyrene. The whole episode breathes delight, and evokes
the effortless, commanding power of the male divinity:

> When Gods are once in haste,
> their work is swift, their ways short:
> that day, that day determined it.
> In Libya's rich golden room
> they lay together; and there
> she is keeper of a city
> surpassing lovely, and famous in the Games.
>
> (67–70)

The image of marriage implicit in this episode is reinforced elsewhere in the poem. A compatriot of the victor once married off his daughter by organising a race between her suitors. This in turn was modelled on the contest organised by Danaos for his forty-eight daughters, where once again the brides fell to the swiftest. The negative aspect of the Danaids' story – that they slaughtered their grooms on the wedding night and were unendingly punished in Hades – is passed over in silence. The heroines in *Pythian* 9 are pursued as prizes; their role ends either in marriage or in the bringing forth of a glorious hero. The case of the girl the boys ran after at Kyrene is symptomatic: her name is not mentioned, and she moves directly from being Antaios' daughter to becoming Alexidamos' bride. Her reaction is not known, and is irrelevant; what matters is the noble bearing of the victorious suitor, paradigmatic of the athletic champion whom Pindar is praising.

Pindar's poetic world is not unclouded. We need only remember *Pythian* 3 and the fate of Koronis, who lay with a mortal while carrying Apollo's child and was duly killed (along with her unfortunate neighbours) by Apollo's sister Artemis. But the power of the gods remains awesome and instantaneous, for it takes Apollo only one stride to reach Koronis' Thessalian funeral pyre from his seat in Delphi in order to snatch his baby son Asklepios from the flames. What is more, Apollo is in the right: the god's sperm is 'pure', whereas her action was done 'in an error of mind' (12 15).

With tragedy, we leave behind the world of effortless divinity and shining heroism, and confront ambiguities, insoluble dilemmas, and women who take decisions. (Except for choruses and marginals like nurses, the named female characters almost invariably *act*, even if only by choosing how to die.) The union of a woman with a god, far from being the shimmering event which Pindar makes it in *Pythian* 9, may take on a deeply pathetic hue in tragedy, as in Euripides' unflinching drama *Ion* with its tale of the rape of Kreousa by Apollo. In general, tragedy dwells on the pain of women in extreme situations. Sometimes the extremity derives from motherhood (Hekabe), daughterhood (Elektra) or sisterhood (Antigone); more usually it is generated by marriage.

At one end of the spectrum are women whose solid dedication to the family leads them to rank it above their own lives. Alkestis was the only one willing to allow her husband Admetos to accept the gods' gift of a postponement of death, by herself dying in his place. In return she felt able to request him not to take the entirely normal course of remarrying; no less extraordinarily, he agreed (305ff., 328ff.). A woman of like mind was Euadne, who flung herself onto the funeral pyre of her dead husband Kapaneus. In these cases the family is a positive ideal outweighing all other claims upon the woman. In the words of Alkestis' servant,

> How better could any woman show that she loves her husband
> more than herself, than by consenting to die for him?
>
> (E. *Alc.* 154–5)

More frequent are myths where a wife is destroyed as a result of the collapse of her marriage, usually because it has been undermined by Eros or Aphrodite. Sophokles' *Women of Trachis* forms a striking comparison with Pindar. Like the brides awarded as prizes in *Pythian* 9, Deianeira was once a trophy, handed to the victor in the contest between her two suitors, Herakles and the river Acheloos. But, unlike the passive Libyan maid, Deianeira eventually acts. In the crisis represented in the drama she takes the initiative, catastrophically, in a desperate attempt to preserve her marriage, the focus of her existence. Phaidra too, in Euripides' *Hippolytos*, brings about the ruin of her family under the power of love, having been caused by Aphrodite to desire her own stepson. She longs to be in the wilds, her hair flowing free, away from home and city: the collapse of moral order is symbolised by a bridging of the gap between inside and outside. Further along the spectrum still is Medea. In some ways she resembles Deianeira, notably in motivation (being rejected in favour of another woman) and in mode of action (sending a venomous gift), though the two of course differ in that Medea is both aware of what she is doing and successful in escaping. In any case, even for Medea, marriage is the focus and sole context for her existence (E. *Med.* 247).

The preceding account illustrates significant differences of perception between two genres; consideration of other genres would confirm this impression of divergence. But what of common features? I shall focus on marriage and weaving.

Mary Lefkowitz has shown how Greek myths about women's relationship to marriage return again and again to a few stereotypical images or role models.[15] In particular she has shown how, in the lives of mythical heroines, marriage and the bearing of children are presented as both the culmination and the end of normal development, the moment beyond which literally nothing happens; as with Io, whose career of nomadic suffering comes to a full stop when she has given birth to Zeus's child. Despite differences between narrative contexts such as those noted above, the general picture is clear. From Homer's Penelope, to the unnamed Pindaric maiden at the winning post, to Aischylos' Io and Klytaimestra, to Apollonios' Medea, Greek heroines are defined by their relationship to marriage. For a young girl still in the untamed, virginal state presided over by Artemis, to be unmarried is the proper condition for her time of life: she can hunt happily with her mistress in the wilds (Atalanta, Kallisto, etc.). But the moment to which these wild preliminaries should lead is union with a man, followed by childbirth, as in this Homeric vignette:

> The next battalion was led by warlike Eudoros, a maiden's
> child, born to one lovely in the dance, Polymele,
> daughter of Phylas; whom strong Hermes Argeiphontes
> loved, when he watched her with his eyes among the girls dancing
> in the choir for clamorous Artemis of the golden distaff.
> Presently Hermes the healer went up with her into her chamber
> and lay secretly with her, and she bore him a son ...
>
> (*Il.* 16.179–85)

Polymele's baby boy was taken in by his maternal grandfather; Polymele herself found a mortal husband, at which point the Homeric text closes over her. Virginity; birth of a male heir; silence: a proper progress.

To reject marriage can only produce catastrophe. For Kassandra, who spurns Apollo, the result is the complete marginalisation

---

[15] Lefkowitz 1981a, pp. 41–7; 1986 *passim*.

represented by madness and an inability to persuade (= to be believed); for the Amazons, rejection of marriage means a life imagined as physically abnormal and (thus) geographically remote; for the Danaids and the women of Lemnos, it brings the eternal stigma of being husband-slayers (eternity being literal in the case of the Danaids, punished in the Underworld).

As we mentioned earlier, women's role in securing the continuity of the community had its major focus in the household. In mythology this role is explored through the image of weaving. The ideal contrast between husband and wife is that between Hektor and Andromache in the *Iliad*. War is man's work; women have their own to be getting on with. As Hektor urges Andromache:

> Go therefore back to our house, and take up your own work,
> the loom and the distaff, and see to it that your handmaidens
> ply their work also;[16] but the men must see to the fighting.
>
> (*Il.* 6.490–2)

While Hektor was fighting and dying outside the city, his wife

> was weaving a web in the inner room of the high house,
> a red folding robe, and inworking elaborate figures.
>
> (*Il.* 22.440–1)

More complex was the situation of Penelope, whose whole existence centred, in the absence of Odysseus, around her web (Plate 12). But it was a web of intrigue, since she unwove by night what she wove by day: the completion of the work would in effect mark the end of her marriage to Odysseus by signalling her readiness to remarry (*Od.* 19.141ff.). By day she occupied herself like a proper wife; by night she behaved 'improperly' in order, paradoxically, to maintain her fidelity to her husband. The Iliadic Helen is no less paradoxical a weaver: she sits at home like a loyal wife, directing the 'magnificent work' done by handmaidens (6.323–4), yet the subject of the web is the struggles endured by Greek and Trojan because of her adulterous elopement (3.125–8). To complicate still further the portrayal of this most

---

[16] The difference between aristocratic freedom and slavish necessity is that the noblewoman works at her own loom, the slave at that of another (*Il.* 6.323–4, 456).

12. Telemachos before Penelope, with the partially completed web behind her. The grieving, weaving wife. (Attic *skyphos*.)

enigmatic of characters, she is presented not only as loyal wife and as adulteress, but also as a bride-to-be who in traditional fashion will fall to the winner of a contest (3.136–8).[17]

Homer's Helen speaks silently through the imagery of her web, but at least she has an audible voice too. The same cannot be said of Philomela, sister of Prokne and sister-in-law of Tereus. Tereus raped Philomela and tore out her tongue, but, by weaving her own narrative and communicating it to her sister, Philomela made possible a horrific revenge: Prokne murdered and boiled Tereus' child, then

[17] On the ambiguity of Penelope and Helen, see Hunter 1989, p. 29.

served the human meat up to him for dinner, so punishing one form of transgressive closeness between kin with another. This brutal tale points to a common narrative gambit involving women: they characteristically use something from their own sphere of influence in order to exert a power over men through guile which they could not exercise openly by violence.

It may be a robe. Deianeira sends Herakles a poisoned garment; Medea kills her rival for Jason's affection by similar means: Klytaimestra entangles Agamemnon in a fabric; the Danaids threaten to hang themselves with the cords binding their garments unless their supplication for asylum is granted.[18] It may be jewellery. Hekabe and her fellow prisoners used brooch-pins to blind their foe Polymestor, recalling Oidipous' means of self-mutilation. Eriphyle's necklace had a subtler but no less lethal role: it seduced her into causing the death of her husband Amphiaraos when she persuaded him to join a fatal expedition (Plate 13). Food and drink too are agents of domestic harm. Kreousa planned to poison her son; Kirke, another weaver, though hardly a conventional wife, used a potion to drug her victims; Medea had an ostensibly rejuvenative cauldron, which turned ram to lamb but left the aged Pelias as boiled mincemeat. Endowed with the ability to weave, but also adorned with necklaces, Hesiod's Pandora chose another domestic weapon with which to plague mankind, opening a storage-jar that should have remained shut. Myth magnifies the simple act of an imprudent housewife into a deed which shatters human bliss (though not, perhaps, hopes of it).

Another aspect of weaving is the connection with mourning. Penelope was weaving a shroud for Odysseus' father Laertes

> ... lest any
> Achaian woman in this neighbourhood hold it against me
> that a man of many conquests lies with no sheet to wind him.
>
> (*Od.* 19.145–7)

Andromache lamented the possibility that 'clothing laid up that is fine-textured and pleasant, wrought by the hands of women' (*Il.* 22.510–11) would not be used to wrap her husband's corpse. Weaving

---

[18] Danaids: A. *Supp.* 457–65.

13. A golden necklace turns the head of Eriphyle. On this *pelikē*, Polyneikes tries to induce the wife of one of the Argives to get him to agree, against his better judgement, to join the expedition of the Seven against Thebes. As often, myth ascribes *dolos*, 'deception', to a woman.

was thus linked to the tending of the dead, another central function of women in myth as well as life (Plate 14). Burying and mourning might entail problematic choices and over-simplifications in respect of obligation: Sophokles' *Antigone* dramatises such a case. Care for the dead might become exaggerated and almost pathological, as

14. Tekmessa covers the body of the dead Ajax. (Early-fifth-century cup.)

Euripides shows in *Elektra*. But common to the representations of mourning is the prominence of women. The death of Hektor means much to every Trojan, but in *Iliad* 24 it is three women who 'lead out' the song, their voices rising from and blending back into the communal lament.

Finally, an image which brings us back to ambiguity: Odysseus and Kirke on a Boeotian cup (Plate 15). What interests us here is not the deliciously camp treatment, but the emphasis both on Kirke's loom and on her bowl. The latter, as every ancient hearer/reader of the *Odyssey* knew, would be used to administer a magic potion. But what

15. Another wily, weaving woman. Odysseus' knees buckle as Kirke stirs her magic cocktail. (Boeotian *skyphos*.)

of the loom? Is it a symbol of trickery? Or does it offer a *contrast* with the potion, as 'good' (woman) is to 'bad'? Like many questions about the perception of women in Greece, this has to be left open.[19]

We may now revert to the life/myth problem. That myths select symbolically potent features of experience is confirmed by the emphasis on weaving, which combines in one productive image the conflicting implications of staying-at-home and intricacy/trickiness. (Incidentally, in Greek fantasy weaving seems to carry a more powerful ideological charge than spinning.[20] As well as implying cunning – Sappho's Aphrodite is invoked as *doloploke*, 'weaver of tricks' – weaving is a means of communication: a web can bear an image (Philomela), but a thread, even Ariadne's, cannot.) Another aspect of selectivity is stress on the *dangerousness* of golden necklaces and mirrors (Plate 13 again). From Pandora to Prokris (bribed to be unfaithful to her husband in a variant *avant la lettre* of *Così fan tutte*),

[19] Recently an intriguing case has been made out for the presence, in this and similar images, of themes which a later tradition would describe as 'Orphic' (Moret 1991).
[20] This is not of course to deny the frequent portrayal of spinning in art; cf. Lissarrague in Schmitt Pantel 1991, pp. 230–1.

mythical women go out of control whenever they see gold or their own reflections.[21] Yet the possession of golden objects or mirrors by real women evidently carried no automatic whiff of scandal – they were frequently buried with women, displayed on their funeral monuments, or offered as dedications.[22] Myths drew out the latent allure of such things, and brought the threat posed by seductiveness into the open.

The role of myths in making explicit is relevant also to marriage. One form of Greek wedding was staged as an abduction, the groom leading the bride onto a cart or carriage by which he transported her from her father's house to his own.[23] For the bride it was an occasion for mourning lost companions and lost virginity and for regretting the separation from her family, as well as a time for anticipation of the new life after the transition. Mythology reflects such abductions, and transforms into powerful dramas the accompanying feelings of loss and unwilling separation from parents. Persephone, abducted on Hades' chariot, was made to experience in literal truth the equation between marriage and death which is so pervasive in Greek imagery;[24] the brutality of the separation from home is expressed through the inconsolable grief of Persephone's mother Demeter, which expands into a cosmic disaster the ordinary feelings of a mother on the marriage of a daughter. In some ways comparable is the story of the Danaids, obliged to choose between their father and their suitors. When all but one kill their grooms on the wedding night, the girls have opted for father; but the eternal punishment meted out to the murderesses in Hades spells out the dangers involved in rejecting marriage. Those who go through with marriage are, by contrast, placing husband above father: translated into the language of mythology, this means that the groom carries off his prize only after

---

[21] Prokris: Ant. Lib. 41.

[22] Cf. Pomeroy 1975, p. 83, Jost 1992, p. 94. But the epitaph, 'In life she did not marvel at clothes and gold, but was content to love her husband and modesty' (Peek 1955, no. 1810) shows the potential for criticism.

[23] See Jenkins 1983. As described by Plutarch (*Lyc.* 15.3), Spartan weddings began with the *harpagē* (abduction) of the bride.

[24] A girl (a 'maiden honey-bee') who died without marrying was a virgin bride of Hades: *Anth. Pal.* 7.13. For the theme, see Alexiou 1974, pp. 120–2.

causing the death of her father (Plate 16).[25] But, once more, we should not force myths to tell just one story, for they are not *always* extreme. Pausanias (3.20.10–11) records a delicate episode involving the newly-betrothed Odysseus and Penelope. Penelope's father Ikarios wants the couple to stay and live in Lakonia, while the new groom would like to take his bride back with him to Ithaka. Required to make a decision, Penelope covers her face with a veil – a gesture which formed part of the wedding ritual. 'And Ikarios realised she wanted to go with Odysseus.'

The implicit/explicit distinction brings us back to the article by Gould. His contention is that myths about women bring into the open matters which, in the formal regulations and informal attitudes of everyday life, remain partially or completely hidden. In particular, the threat which women pose to men's honour (through their power to diminish that honour by their own conduct, especially sexual conduct) only becomes explicit in mythology, with its gallery of deceitful, destructive, vengeful and above all decisive and powerful women. This is a valuable observation which at the same time needs qualification. Gould draws many of his supporting mythological examples from tragedy. Now tragedy is precisely the arena which concentrates on tensions and disruptions in social relationships. As we have seen, a different picture of women's behaviour emerges from Pindar; the Homeric situation is different again. Nevertheless, it is true, and important, that many mythical women are not only 'visible', but aggressive and even dominant; and Gould's explanation for the functioning of mythology in *these* cases must surely be regarded as persuasive.

Finally: if myths make issues explicit, where do we place ritual? Ritual dramatised many of the same features of women's lives as did myths: weaving (the Panathenaia); dedication to the *oikos* (mourning); women's capacity for sexual continence, for the greater good of the family and hence the state (the Thesmophoria); the susceptibility of women to the 'scorching' power of sexual passion (the Adonia); 'wildness' before marriage (young girls as 'bears of Artemis' in the

---

[25] Like all mythological themes, this was available for comic plunder: cf. the passage from a satyr-play listed as Sophokles fr. 1130 Radt.

16. A wedding/abduction. Pelops drives his bride-to-be Hippodameia away from her pursuing father Oinomaos. (Attic neck-amphora.)

ceremony at Brauron), instead of marriage (the Delphic Pythia), and even within marriage (Dionysiac Agrionia festivals). Ritual, like myth, incorporated women's simultaneous capacity for ideally orderly and catastrophically disruptive behaviour; but, by virtue of its built-in temporal and spatial framing, it confined these extremes within the cultural equivalent of inverted commas. Both myth and ritual brought out aspects of women's lives which remained otherwise latent: to that extent, *both* were making things explicit. The difference is that myth took the metaphors of ritual literally.

Fathers, sons and brothers

If one major influence on recent academic analysis of the family in Greek mythology has been feminism, another has been the rich and

varied tradition which we may label psychological. (Of course the two are not mutually exclusive.) Given the overwhelming emphasis in contemporary psychoanalysis and psychiatry on the importance, for the explanation of adult behaviour, of an individual's childhood relationships with his or her parents, it is understandable that theoretical assumptions about these matters should have affected work on ancient parent/child relationships. However, lack of unanimity about the modern theory has meant that the ancient evidence has turned into a battleground on which adherents of rival schools try to sort out their differences, or at any rate stake their claims.[26]

One prominent reference-point remains Freud's hypothesis of the Oedipus Complex.[27] (The more traditional transliteration seems

[26] Cf. Fages 1991, p. 79: 'le mouvement psychanalytique s'est poursuivi à travers les dissidences'.

[27] Even so traditional a commentator as R. D. Dawe feels compelled to quote at length from the revolutionary Viennese doctor (Dawe 1982, pp. 2–3).

appropriate here.) This Complex was a central feature of Freud's theory of infant sexuality. Freud privileged Oedipus on the grounds that a young boy's desire for his mother, the corresponding wish to eliminate his father, and the eventual overcoming – or failure to overcome – this crisis are universal aspects of the development of the human psyche. This is not the place to add to the millions of words written about the general validity of the hypothesis.[28] There are, however, a few points to make with specific reference to the Greek world.

First, there is no reason to think that the Greeks *themselves* gave special status to the Oidipous story as a model for parent/child relationships. On the contrary, in mythology – to look, for the moment, no further in the Greek evidence – we find a wide range of contrasting paradigms: Niobe and her children, Medea and hers, Agamemnon and Klytaimestra and theirs; Helios and Phaethon; Daidalos and Ikaros; Aigeus and Theseus; Theseus and Hippolytos; Laertes and Odysseus and Telemachos; Oinomaos and Hippodameia; Eriphyle and Alkmaion; Kreon and Haimon; Oidipous and his own children; Demeter and Persephone; Ouranos, Kronos, Zeus; not to mention the complex relationships between the Olympians and their various heroic offspring. Amid all this diversity, the Oidipous story, far from being typical, seems actually to be unique in linking the theme of parricide with that of incest with the mother.[29] Secondly, there is a not entirely negligible difference between a son desiring to eliminate his father, and a father feeling threatened – for example, as a result of a prophecy – by the prospect of being ousted (in the case of a king, overthrown) by his son. Greek mythology is very much richer in the latter motif than in the former.[30] Thirdly, even if we do reduce

[28] Already B. Malinowski argued that the comparative anthropological evidence ruled out the universality of the Oedipus Complex (Malinowski 1927, *passim*). Cf. also Stoetzel 1978, pp. 80–3, on evidence from the Marquesas Islands about a polyandric society in which (it is reported) a child's 'fathers' impose no discipline, and the child experiences no Oedipus Complex. Even within the Freudian tradition there have been persistent doubts, cf. Sacks 1985. For developments in Freud's own thinking on the matter ('Anyone who shoots at the Oedipus Complex is shooting at a moving target', Sacks p. 203) and for possible connections between the theory and Freud's own self-analysis, see B. Simon and R. B. Blass in Neu 1991, pp. 161–74.

[29] Cf. E. Rumpf 1985, p. 57.   [30] As noted by E. Rumpf 1985, p. 71.

these two motifs to the generalised notion of father/son tension, it cannot be simply assumed that what lies at the root of *this* is something deep in a child's – not only a Greek child's – psyche. As we shall see, a perfectly respectable explanation for *some* father/son tensions can be found at a quite different level, namely the legal–economic one. Fourthly – hardly a novel observation, this – there must be some doubt about the viability of regarding the Complex as relevant to the interpretation *even of the Oidipous story itself*, because in Sophokles' classic version, whatever else Oidipous is suffering from, it cannot be a Complex *about Laios*, since as far as he knows his father is Polybos of Corinth.[31] Nor, finally, is it irrelevant that the extant iconography about the Oidipous story virtually ignores both the parricide and the incest. In short, the Oedipus Complex would have achieved less currency in discussions of Greek mythology had it not happened to bear the name of a Greek hero.

Freud's hat is by no means the only one in the ring. C. G. Jung had already added an Elektra Complex. The psychologist Ewald Rumpf canvasses the claims of, amongst others, the Medea Complex, the Phaethon Complex, the Tantalos Complex and the Niobe Complex, this last exemplifying the mother whose affective life is dominated by feelings for her children: '[for such a woman,] losing her children means losing her life . . . Petrifaction is the most telling image of the condition of severe depression.'[32] Philip Slater saw a key to an understanding of Greek culture not in a Complex but in a Syndrome. In his opinion, the protracted absences of Greek fathers created a behavioural configuration according to which mothers sought substitute partners in their sons: 'imprisoned and isolated by her indifferent and largely absented husband, some of the mother's sexual longing was turned upon her son'.[33] Not unrelated is the approach of Jan Bremmer, who attempts to identify a precise historical context for

[31] Cf. J.-P. Vernant in Vernant and Vidal-Naquet 1981, pp. 63–86 ('Oedipus without the Complex'). R. A. Paul (in Neu 1991, pp. 268–9) takes to task those who misguidedly gloat over this absence in Sophokles. The fact remains that Paul's assertion that '*we* . . . *do* have Oedipus Complexes', which govern 'our' reading of *OT*, begs the question (unless P. is here expounding Freud rather than agreeing with him).

[32] E. Rumpf 1985, p. 39 (my translation).

[33] Slater 1968, p. 31.

a specifically *Greek* Oedipus Complex.[34] On his view, when during the Archaic Age (a) fosterage and other types of initiatory education declined, and (b) women in most parts of Greece seem to have enjoyed progressively less social freedom, mothers began to take more direct, personal charge of their children, with consequences of the hothouse kind – a situation for which the Oidipous/Jocasta liaison might have constituted an extreme model.

It has to be admitted that classicists – and, indeed, other modern historians – have seldom shown a sophisticated awareness of contemporary work in psychology.[35] While anthropology has been a regularly plundered treasure-house of data and methods, psychology has often been treated as something about which one's robustly commonsensical intuitions will serve well enough. In this situation, the approaches mentioned in the preceding two paragraphs have the considerable merit of putting their theoretical cards on the table, as opposed to failing to declare what is often a very weak hand. Yet against that must be set a drawback – present in some but not all of our examples – a drawback frequently found both amongst psychologists commenting on ancient Greece and classicists leaning on psychology: namely, a tendency to use mythological material selectively. Freud, for his purposes, dwells on 'Oedipus'; Slater, in the course of an admittedly wide-ranging study, concentrates on heroes whose fathers are absent and whose mothers (notably Hera) constitute a threat to their narcissistic offspring. More worrying than this kind of selectivity is the tendency to underplay or ignore differences of context. Typical is a recent treatment by Garland which, though very helpful as a compilation, tends to use mythology *alongside* other types of evidence in a sometimes haphazard way.[36]

What is needed, surely, is an analysis like Gould's of Athenian women. By *separating out* the messages transmitted by, for example, institutions, customary attitudes and myths – messages which may themselves, even within each of these three areas, be far from

---

[34] Bremmer 1987, pp. 53–5.
[35] Naturally there are honourable exceptions. A recent one is Versnel 1990, the introduction to which exploits the theory of cognitive dissonance in an attempt to throw light on the topic of cultural ambiguity.   [36] Garland 1990, e.g. pp. 147–57.

univocal – we have the best chance of unravelling the relevant contrasts and complexities in the ways in which the Greeks thought about parent/child relationships. Bearing in mind that our aim is not comprehensiveness but the throwing of light on the interaction between mythical narratives and ordinary life, I choose just one relationship to concentrate on: father/son.

We begin with the legal framework. (From the outset we must bear in mind the possibility that, in comparing the predominantly Athenian data about law with the more panhellenic testimony of mythology, we are ourselves reducing the real diversity of a historical situation; but the alternative is to remain completely silent.) From the moment he came into the world, a boy depended on his father for acceptance into the community: at the Athenian ten-day festival, for example, the father would (or would not) acknowledge his son's legitimacy. Until his eighteenth year the child continued to be under the total legal control of his father or guardian. This absoluteness of possession ceased at majority, which thus constituted a point of potential crisis: it then became possible for the young adult to take legal action against his former possessor.[37]

More usually, it was not until a father had grown old that the law stepped in to regulate disputes between himself and his son. The dependent party – now the father – could, as in the case of the wronged minor, expect redress against maltreatment. Athenian sons were obliged to refrain from beating their parents, and to offer them food, shelter and a proper funeral; failure to do so led to a total loss of civic rights.[38] At Delphi, comparable delinquency by a son meant prison.[39] The other side of the coin is represented by inheritance law. What sons could expect from their fathers was a share of the patrimony. But suppose the father lived to such a great age as to become incapable of managing the affairs of the *oikos*, even though he remained its legal head? In that case, a charge of senility could be preferred, though, as with all well-intentioned measures (it was in the interests of the *polis* for its constituent *oikoi* to be well-run) there was

---

[37] Garland 1990, pp. 157–8.
[38] Harrison 1968, pp. 77–8, cites the evidence.   [39] See Lerat 1943.

scope for abuse.[40] The role of the law was, in short, to see that fathers and sons respected what were seen as their mutual obligations; and it was, in particular, at times of the transference of property, or the handing over of authority, from one generation to the next that these obligations were liable to undergo special strain, and hence to require the intervention of the law.

Some of the father/son tensions which gave rise to laws were reflected in customary attitudes. Legal measures about failure to treat parents properly are matched by numerous references to the rightness, or piety, of duly honouring one's father and mother.[41] In Plato's *Laws* we hear the view that 'neglect of one's parents is something which no god or right-minded person would ever recommend to anyone' (930e); indeed, such behaviour might bring one into grave religious danger.[42] Total acquiescence might be a positive quality to claim in court, as in the speech written for a thirty-year-old who had, he asserted, never contradicted his father.[43] Yet the guess that these pieties protest too much is confirmed by extensive evidence of conflict between generations, not just in those Aristophanic caricatures whose apogee is the Strepsiades/Pheidippides relationship in *Clouds*, but in such claims as that recorded in another forensic speech – and, to that extent, presumably designed to sound plausible – that both natural and adoptive sons quarrel with their fathers in their lifetimes, the difference being that natural ones speak well of them when they are dead.[44]

[40] Is. 4.16; cf. Garland 1990, pp. 261–2.
[41] Lyc. *Leocr.* 94–7, Lys. 31.20–3; Aristot. *Ath. pol.* 55.3; M. Reinhold in Bertman 1976, pp. 25ff.
[42] E.g. Pl. *Lg.* 872e, Lyc. (*loc. cit.* in previous note); cf. Parker 1983, pp. 196–7.
[43] Lys. 19.55.
[44] Evidence for conflict: Bertman 1976. (There is a nice example in Thgn. 271–8 (in West 1989–92, I), a father's moan about filial ingratitude.) The speech is Ps.-Dem. 40.47.

   The predominance of *Athenian* evidence for intra-generational conflict may not be coincidental. It has been argued by Reinhold (in Bertman 1976) that the democracy fostered tension by putting fathers and sons on the same political level from the time of the sons' majority. This, combined with the potential for the 'de-authoritization' (R.'s word) of fathers built into a system where slave-tutors as well as fathers might exercise 'paternal' authority, leads R. to the distinctly un-Freudian conclusion that 'in Athens in the fifth century there occurred the first massive challenge to the older generation in the history of mankind' (p. 28). This and other exaggerated claims ('The peoples of the ancient Near East could not even have conceived of the possibility of generational tensions or disequilibrium',

But it will not do, either, to put all the emphasis on conflict, while playing down the respect-and-obedience ideal as wishful thinking. For it is clear from various sources that we have to find room for a broad spectrum of feelings, including love. Numerous evocations of the death of children contribute significantly towards making the Greek epigram one of the most moving of ancient poetical forms. Loss of an adult son might also call forth deep grief, as with the tragic death of Atys, Kroisos' favourite son.[45] As for sons' feelings towards fathers, a 'hard' reading of the inheritance situation should not lead us to forget remarkable passages like this Homeric simile:

> And as welcome as the show of life again in a father
> is to his children, when he has lain sick, suffering strong pains,
> and wasting long away, and the hateful death spirit has brushed him,
> but then, and it is welcome, the gods set him free of his sickness,
> so welcome appeared land and forest now to Odysseus ...
>
> (*Od.* 5.394–8)

In mythology, the absoluteness of the control of real-life infants by their fathers is expressed in extreme form in stories of the abandonment of babies from whom some future threat was perceived, as in the case of Laios and Oidipous, and Priam and Paris. A less drastic arrangement was to make formal provision for the fostering of children. Examples are the boyhoods of Jason and Achilles, brought up by the wise anomaly Cheiron, or Hippolytos, sent away to be raised by his maternal grandfather Pittheus. (This pattern has been seen as a reflection of the practice of archaic aristocratic fosterage; as with abandonment, a period 'in the wilds' or 'apart' precedes adult life.)[46] A reflection of the fact that a child might be felt to be a mere extension of its father is detectable in scenes such as

---

p. 16; '... whatever were the fateful vicissitudes the Hellenistic world experienced ... generational dissension was not one of them', pp. 46–7) detract from the interest of what R. has to say specifically about Athens.

[45] Hdt. 1.36ff. As one of the anonymous referees of this book pointed out, the tragic loss of sons is something of a Herodotean *Leitmotiv*: Harpagos, Prexaspes, Psammenitos, Periandros, Oiobazos and Pythios are among those who endure it.

[46] Bremmer 1983b analyses the special importance of the maternal uncle and the maternal grandfather in relation to fosterage.

that between Hektor and Astyanax in the *Iliad*, or the closely parallel episode between Ajax and Eurysakes in Sophokles' *Ajax*. The child is a smaller version of the father, the repository of his honour, and not yet in a position to contest his wishes or pose any kind of threat to him. In wholly exceptional cases a mythical infant *is* able to assert himself as an individual agent, but for this it takes a god (Hermes, who goes rustling cattle shortly after coming into the world, in his *Homeric Hymn*) or a super-hero (Herakles, who strangles the snakes sent into his cradle by Hera).

A much larger repertory of tales deals with father/son relationships at a stage when the son is adolescent. In the heroic world this means that the son is becoming or has just become a warrior, and is thus able to *act*, to undertake adventures in order to win honour, in the same way as his father does or did. The consequences of this power to act are various. One scenario is a prolongation of the Hektor/Astyanax model: the son defends or avenges or otherwise furthers the father's honour. A classic instance, paradigmatic already in the *Odyssey*, is the avenging of Agamemnon by Orestes; Telemachos' defence of the interests of Odysseus begins in earnest when he has been prompted by Athene no longer to cling to childhood (1.296–7). In the *Iliad*, that world of patronymics, Achilles had been sent out by his father Peleus to learn to be a speaker of words and a doer of deeds (9.443); at the moment of deepest pathos in the poem, the young hero weeps at the memory of his own father, far away (24.511).

But it is noticeable that Orestes and Achilles are both distant from their fathers, and Telemachos is only reunited with Odysseus after long years of separation. Distance between father and son is, in fact, a recurring feature, and it often takes the extreme form of conflict. In the case of Kreon and Haimon in *Antigone*, the son begins by admitting that he remains his father's possession ('Father, I am yours', 635), but goes on to express increasingly open disagreement with Kreon's decision to condemn Haimon's betrothed Antigone for her loyalty to her dead brother Polyneikes. The quarrel reaches its violent resolution when son spits at father, tries to kill him, then stabs himself. Too late (for this is tragedy) Kreon realises what he has done: the broken father walks Learlike onto the stage with his son in his arms.

To the extent that the father at last regrets his action, the conflict may be said to be mitigated; but Haimon dies with hatred on his lips. In Euripides' *Hippolytos* there is a clearer, twofold mitigation: the quarrel derives from a misunderstanding, and is healed before the last gasp. But we should not overlook the fact that the father's hasty authoritarianism is a contributory factor in the disaster. Two other conflicts of authority happen, thanks to Roman sources, to be better known to the modern world than they are well-documented for Greece: Helios and Phaethon, and Daidalos and Ikaros. But it seems clear that in Greek versions too the stories took the form of sons disregarding their father's warnings about using what was, in effect, their inheritance: in both cases the result for the son was quite literally catastrophe. In all these narratives it is the son – Haimon, Hippolytos, Phaethon, Ikaros – that dies. In spite of one or two counter-examples – the accidental murder of Laios by Oidipous, the forgetful causing of Aigeus' death by Theseus (the *mitigation* of the near-unthinkable crime is again noticeable) – the message that lies very close to the surface of several Greek myths is that challenging the authority of the father may be fatal for the son.[47]

A modification of the pattern just discussed occurs in stories where the father is presented as very definitely old. How does the son – not, this time, an adolescent, but a mature adult – react in a situation in which the death and consequent replacement of his father is an immediate possibility? Once more, what is striking is the absence of a simple answer, the *range* of responses possible. Homer incorporates two contrastingly memorable examples of the love between father and son in Hektor and Priam, and Odysseus and Laertes: it is hard to say which is the more moving, the boundless grief of the aged Trojan or the reconciliation, physically overwhelming beyond tears, of the two Ithakans. Cooler, perhaps, but full of explicit piety, is the attitude of Herakles towards Amphitryon in Euripides' *Herakles*: the hero's Labours were, in this version, undertaken out of a wish to see his father restored to the place from which he had been obliged to flee. At

---

[47] In this respect we are not far from Bremmer's conclusion about the Oidipous myth itself, which 'can be read as a warning to the younger generation: "You have grown up but you must continue to respect your fathers."' (Bremmer 1987, p. 53).

the other end of the moral spectrum is the struggle in Sophokles' *Oidipous at Kolonos*. The nub of the conflict is the fact that, according to oracular predictions, the tomb of Oidipous will be a site of power; hence the Thebans, including the sons of the old man, have suddenly taken a new interest in their former king. But so incensed is Oidipous with his sons' disloyalty and self-serving that he curses them. (Once more, it is not the father who suffers the fatal consequences.) It is hardly fanciful to see the conflict over parental authority/sovereignty – does the old man control his own destiny, or do others control it for him? – as a transposition into the realm of myth of the senility cases of real-life courts. Exemplifying the fertile logic so often to be found in Greek anecdotes, the story went that Sophokles was accused of senility by his own son, and dispelled the charge by reading aloud – from *Oidipous at Kolonos*.[48]

Another relevant group of tales involves the gods. One of the basic types of genealogy for Greek heroes was birth from a liaison between a god and a nymph or mortal woman. In these instances the relationship between father and son interacted with that between god and mortal. We shall see in the next chapter that some of the most moving episodes in Greek mythology derive from an exploration of the latter imbalance, as with the tears of blood shed by the Iliadic Zeus over his son Sarpedon. A particular set of problems was highlighted by cases of double parentage, notably Herakles (son of Zeus 'and' Amphitryon) and Theseus (son of Aigeus 'and' Poseidon). With the intellectual and moral daring characteristic of tragedy, it was possible for the suffering hero of Euripides' *Herakles* to express a preference for his mortal over his divine father (1265), while the Herakles of Sophokles' *Women of Trachis* could reflect bitterly about 'Zeus up in the stars' (1106). Of all the heroes, few are at a greater distance from their fathers than those who are the offspring of gods.[49]

What of father/son relationships between divinities? For those Greeks who, like Plato, were disposed to see myths as presenting scandalous paradigms for immoral behaviour, an obvious example was the transfer of sovereignty from Ouranos to Kronos (son castrates

[48] *TrGF* IV *Test*. O Radt.
[49] We may contrast the poignant proximity of Achilles to his divine *mother* Thetis in the *Iliad*.

father) and from Kronos to Zeus (son seizes power through violent revolution). How could this scurrilous stuff be squared with the repeated injunctions to behave piously towards a father, injunctions embedded in myth as well as in law and custom? (In Polygnotos' *Underworld* in the Knidians' *leschē* at Delphi, there were, according to Pausanias, 'very interesting figures below Charon's boat: a man who was wicked to his father is being strangled by him'.)[50] Part of the answer must wait until we consider the gods more directly. But for now we may observe that gods, even more than heroes, presented *extreme* examples of the possibilities of behaviour – not necessarily examples of morally admirable behaviour. The tensions latent in any transfer of sovereignty were incomparably greater in cases where, while the power of the unageing, senior party remained undiminished, that of the junior had grown awesomely formidable, and where the means available to *block* transference were so terrifying. And we may add that the Ouranos/Kronos/Zeus succession is not the only model. Once his authority was established, Zeus's relations with his own sons Apollo and Hermes lacked the brutality of the earlier struggles for power. 'Then clever Zeus was glad, and brought the two together in friendship', observes the author of the *Homeric Hymn to Hermes* (506–7) about the settling of the brothers' quarrel.

It is not easy to arrive at a convincing general description of the relationship of mythical *exempla* to other modes of imagining the father/son relationship. One difficulty concerns genre-differences, with Pindar emphasising inter-generational harmony, tragedy conflict, and so on. But there are other problems. On the life side of the life/myth distinction, it is very hard to get beyond the repeated expressions of what *ought* to happen, to what *did* happen. There are few areas – except perhaps the treatment of beggars and strangers – where there is such unanimity about what one's obligations *ought* to be. Equally, there are plenty of open admissions that what really happened often fell way short of this ideal. We cannot argue away this ambiguity, which seems to be fundamental. But how, in any case, do the mythical narratives fit in to the picture? The Gouldian model for

[50] Paus. 10.28.4. Pausanias goes on to relate how the lava of Etna divided to spare two lads who were trying to escape while carrying their father and mother.

narratives about women – that they bring out a latent sense of threat and danger – will not, I think, quite work here, since father/son relationships – their potential for conflict as well as for harmony – were already in the explicit, public domain in a way that certain aspects of women's lives were not. I would rather say in this case that myths gave *extreme* expression to problems and possibilities which law and custom *already* acknowledged.

We noted earlier that, according to the dominant pattern of Greek family life, while a bride would leave her own household to reside in the house of her husband, her brothers would usually stay behind. Unless disinherited or adopted into another family, the sons would eventually divide the property equally, there being no rule of primogeniture.[51] This legal paradigm had numerous variations in practice (sons leaving to find a livelihood elsewhere, for instance), but seems to have been actualised regularly enough for us to regard it as a norm.[52]

Conflict might obviously arise if more than one brother stood to inherit: how exactly would things be split up?[53] Tensions between father and son over inheritance were to some extent countered (at least ideally) by the debt of respect so often said to be owed by children to parents. But brother/brother relations could rely on no such sense of automatic obligation. However, if we ask how people *did* expect brothers to behave towards one another, the answer is a complex one which covers a wide range of affective territory and is by no means free from paradox and contradiction.

An obvious, though far from unproblematic, place to begin is Hesiod's *Works and Days*. The poem is cast as an exhortation to the poet's own brother who, Hesiod states, has unjustly done him out of his inheritance:

---

[51] Is. 7.5; cf. Lacey 1968, p. 125, Fisher 1976, p. 9.

[52] Son leaving: cf. Dover 1968, p. xxvi n. 2.

[53] This is not to deny that legal systems involving primogeniture generate their own intense sibling rivalries: Jacob and Esau, who quarrelled in the womb; Joseph and his brothers . . .; cf. Slater 1968, pp. 382–3.

For we had already divided our lot, but you seized the greater share
and carried it off, greatly swelling the glory of our bribe-devouring
rulers, who see fit to make such a judgement as this.

(37–9)

Not surprisingly, the theme of brother/brother relationships takes on
a certain piquancy in the poem: 'Even with your brother, smile – and
get a witness' (371); 'There should be an only son to feed his father's
household, for so wealth will increase in their dwelling; but if you
leave a second son you should die old' (376–8) – not to mention the
contrast between Epimetheus and Prometheus.[54] But even in Hesiod
the bonds are there as well as the tensions: 'Do not treat a friend as
[closely as] if he were your brother' (707); get a witness *even* with your
brother. Because of the centrality of *this* theme to *this* poem, we
should think twice before assuming that Hesiod's attitudes are
'typical'. But other sources, from a range of periods and genres,
confirm that brothers were often perceived as staunch friends who
could yet be trusted only up to a point. Alkinoos takes it for granted
that to a sane man a suppliant and guest is 'as good as a brother' (*Od.*
8.546–7); Plutarch records the use of 'brother' as an honorary title;[55]
yet a fable of Aesop starts from a situation in which a farmer's sons are
at loggerheads.[56]

Myths reflect the enormous variety of relationships which could
exist between brothers. One need look no further than the *Iliad*,
which sketches in the background to the lives of numerous minor
warriors, amongst whom are many about whose families we are told
a little. Some have no brothers, some have one, two or more; Nestor
and Dolios each have six sons.[57] But the most notable feature of
mythical brothers – and this looks like a classic case of refraction – is
their tendency to come in mutually contrasting or hostile pairs. To
Prometheus and Epimetheus, the Mr Clever and Mr Silly of Greek
mythology, may be added Atreus and Thyestes, and Danaos and

[54] NB also *Op.* 184: in the declining Iron Age, brother will not be near/dear (*philos*) to brother.
[55] *Mor.* 479d (the treatise is entitled *On Brotherly Love*).
[56] Fable 53 Perry. Cf. Thgn. 299–300 (no one wants to be your friend when you're in trouble –
not even your brother).   [57] *Od.* 3.412–15, 24.497; cf. Garland 1990, p. 99.

Aigyptos, while the pair which makes most extreme and explicit the tension generated by inheritance rivalry is Polyneikes and Eteokles, whose very names (Much Quarrel, True Glory) embody a contrast in fate and temperament (belied in some of the treatments of their story).

Rivalry between pairs of brothers is at its most extreme in the case of twins.[58] This is surely why twins appear with such frequency in mythical narratives. Amphion and Zethos, twin offspring of Zeus and Antiope, were opposed in their temperaments: the musician against the manly cattle-breeder/warrior. More radical still was the opposition of Proitos and Akrisios, twins born to Abas and Aglaia: like Esau and Jacob they quarrelled in the womb, and when full grown they fought over the kingdom, until Akrisios gained the upper hand and drove Proitos out of Argos.[59] Tyro's twin sons Pelias and Neleus at first acted in harmony, putting to death their wicked stepmother Sidero (Iron Woman); but later they fell out, and Neleus had to flee the realm. Nor should we forget Hektor and Polydamas: born on the same day, and contrasted as man of the spear and man of speech (*Il.* 18.249–52). In all this we must as usual allow for differences of context. In tragedy the focus is on disruptions in relationships, in Pindar on family solidarity, including solidarity between brothers. But mythical selectivity – *pairs* of brothers; twins – is evidenced across the genres. Indeed, beyond the genres: once again mythology does not constitute an autonomous area. We need look no further than that absolutely stock theme of New Comedy, the contrasting pair of *adelphoi*.[60]

---

58 The discussion of mythical twins in Slater 1968, pp. 381–6, seems to me to underestimate the extent of the evidence for rivalry.

59 Other mythical brothers whose enmity began with conception are listed by schol. Lyc. *Alex.* 939.

60 A word about mythical sisters. Sibling relationships involving women differ crucially according to whether or not the women are married. After marriage, the relationship of sister is usually overshadowed by that of wife, as with the contrasting fates of Helen and Klytaimestra. Before marriage, sisterhood is of relatively greater importance, as in the cases of Antigone and Ismene, Antigone and Polyneikes, Elektra and Chrysothemis, Elektra and Orestes in tragedy; and compare Medea's drastic abandoning of her tie with her brother Apsyrtos after eloping with Jason. The stories of Prokne, Philomela and Tereus, and of Aedon, Chelidon and Polytechnos (Ant. Lib. 11), are apparent exceptions, but the sisterhood of Prokne and Philomela and of Aedon and Chelidon only becomes decisive when the viciousness of the two husbands has effectively negated the bond of marriage.

8

Religion

Relating the landscape and the family of the Greek *imaginaire* to the world behind and beyond them involves, as we have seen, considerable methodological complexities. When we focus on narratives about gods, matters become more problematic still, since the world which the stories transform may be seen as either (1) the whole fabric of social life, or (2) the practices of ritual, or (3) 'ordinary' beliefs about divinities. Later I shall have a little to say about (2) – a subject which has exercised a perhaps excessive dominance over recent scholarship – and rather more to say about (3), which has, by comparison, been neglected. But I begin by recalling some general features of the Greeks' narratives about gods, in order to raise certain issues relevant to (1).

The nature of divinity

The first general characteristic of the divinities of Greek mythology is that they are neither good nor evil, but powerful.[1] Their powers range over the entire field of experience: whatever a human being is doing – being born, fighting, stealing, sleeping, getting married, committing adultery, dying – his or her activity is related to a

---

[1] This applies even to Zeus. Cf. Nilsson 1951–60, on the inconclusiveness of connections between Zeus and justice: 'Zeus war der einzige Gott, der, abgesehen von blutlosen Personifikationen, sich der Gerechtigkeit annehmen konnte, sie war aber nicht in seinem Wesen begründet, und schwer wog es, dass die Mythen viele ungerechte Taten von ihm erzählten' (p. 315).

structure mapped out at the divine level.[2] Even Ares and the Furies, for whom it is quite possible to express hatred or revulsion, represent activities which are part, perhaps even a necessary part, of human experience: brutal warfare, and vengeance upon kin-murderers.[3] The second characteristic is that divine activities, interrelationships and behaviour towards mortals are to some extent modelled on the institutions and customs of Greek society. But only to some extent: *some* divine activity is, as we shall see, beyond human comprehension, incommensurate with any pattern of real intra-human behaviour.

The presentation varies, of course, according to context. The most detailed picture appears in epic, since it was a convention of the genre that the action unfolded on two levels, to both of which the narrator claimed to have access. As a first illustration we may take the *Iliad*, not because it was typical, but because it was uniquely authoritative.

Relations between the Iliadic Olympians are based on a combination of violence, deception, negotiation and reciprocity. The violence is evident already in Book 1, when Hephaistos ruefully reminds his mother Hera that

> It is too hard to fight against the Olympian.
> There was a time once before now I was minded to help you,
> and he caught me by the foot and threw me from the magic threshold,
> and all day long I dropped helpless, and about sunset
> I landed in Lemnos, and there was not much life left in me.
>
> (1.589–93)

But there are more ways than one of cooking a goose. The use of trickery is famously exemplified in Book 14, when Zeus's wife outwits him 'with deceitful purpose' (300), aided by the irresistible power of Aphrodite. More subtle still is the situation at the beginning of Book 4. Hera wants to enforce the sacking of Troy, a city hateful to her. Acquiescing, Zeus nevertheless retorts that, if ever there is a city

---

[2] The analysis of the structured division of divine power seems to me to be the aspect of the work of J.-P. Vernant and M. Detienne which is most likely – and most justifiably – to endure.

[3] Hatred of Ares: Hom. *Il.* 5.890 (expressed by Zeus himself), S. *OT* 190ff. Revolting Furies: A. *Eum.* 52–4.

which *he* wants to sack, Hera is not to stand in his way. Hera's reply is complex:

> Of all cities there are three that are dearest to my own heart:
> Argos and Sparta and Mycenae of the wide ways. All these,
> whenever they become hateful to your heart, sack utterly.
> I will not stand up for these against you, nor yet begrudge you.
> Yet if even so I bear malice and would not have you destroy them,
> in malice I will accomplish nothing, since you are far stronger . . .
> Come then, in this thing let us both give way to each other,
> I to you, you to me, and so the rest of the immortal
> gods will follow.
>
> (4.51–64)

Within the general framework of the imbalance of power in Zeus's favour, there is room for movement. Even one of the humblest figures in the divine power-hierarchy, Thetis, can rely on the mighty argument of reciprocity to support her case:

> Father Zeus, if ever before in word or action
> I did you favour among the immortals, now grant what I ask for.
>
> (1.503–4)

Again, although Zeus is the most powerful, each divinity has a sphere which the others may not infringe:

> [Hera] went into her chamber, which her beloved son Hephaistos
> had built for her, and closed the leaves in the door-posts snugly
> with a secret door-bar, *and no other of the gods could open it.*
>
> (14.166–8)[4]

In relationships between Iliadic gods and mortals, imbalance of power is always the decisive factor. The mortals sweat, bleed and die, but Athene can protect Menelaos from an arrow 'as lightly as when a mother brushes a fly away from her child who is lying in sweet sleep' (4.130–1). This is not to say that the gap is unbridgeable. The gods can be emotionally involved in the mortals' actions, as when Zeus weeps

---

[4] Cf. *Od.* 8.280–1: Hephaistos' workmanship is so fine that its products are imperceptible even to the other gods.

tears of blood over Sarpedon, whom he is – Hera has convinced him – powerless to save from death (16.459); and Thetis' tenderness for Achilles frames the poem.[5] Yet in other contexts the relationship is more dispassionate, as with the distancing image of Zeus's two urns, from which derives mankind's fate (either a mixture of good and evil, or unrelieved evil) (24.527ff.). This oscillation between divine involvement and divine aloofness constitutes the uncomfortable and unpredictable setting within which Iliadic heroes act. If a god's protégé is insulted, intervention will follow, as with the priest of Apollo in Book 1. If the gods' honours are skimped, there will be consequences: the Greeks' walled ditch, constructed without proper sacrifices, was not to stand for very long (12.8–9). Yet at the crucial moment, mankind may be alone (22.208–13). In the end divine power asserts itself by re-emphasising the boundary with mortality. Although Diomedes is given temporary permission to see the difference between gods and men, and even to wound Aphrodite, his attempt to go too far is rebuked:

> Take care, give back, son of Tydeus, and strive no longer
> to make yourself like the gods in mind, since never the same is
> the breed of gods, who are immortal, and men who walk groundling.
>
> (5.440–2)

When the horses which the gods had given to Peleus, and which had seen the death of Patroklos, weep for their dead master, Zeus remarks conclusively:

> Poor wretches,
> why then did we ever give you to the lord Peleus,
> a mortal man, and you yourselves are immortal and ageless?
>
> (17.442–4)

Features of the Iliadic picture recur throughout Greek mythology in respect both of god/god and god/mortal relations. As to the

---

[5] On the general capacity of Greek myths about immortal beings to be *moving*, one may note the remark of Rudhardt 1958, p. 76: 'La légende toutefois oublie l'immortalité des dieux en traitant un épisode limité de leur histoire; elle les soumet à la durée, à l'intérieur de l'épisode, et, dans cette limite, à la souffrance et au changement; elle achève ainsi de les humaniser.'

former, relationships continue to operate at a variety of points on the scale which leads from violence to negotiation. The use of force in the constitution of the universe is a central theme of Hesiod's *Theogony*; in the same poem, the mode by which wily Prometheus chooses to circumvent Zeus is deception. But negotiation was another option. An amicable arrangement is reached in the *Homeric Hymn to Hermes*, where the honour-dispute between Apollo and Hermes is resolved through Zeus's authoritative arbitration; in Aischylos' *Eumenides* the differences between Apollo and the Furies are settled without violence – though Athene has the keys of Zeus's thunderbolt if her persuasion fails (827–8). A more bitter boundary-dispute forms the plot of Euripides' *Hippolytos*. Artemis maintains (1328–30) that on principle the gods avoid confrontations with each other (which has indeed been true of Artemis and Aphrodite in this play). The balance will simply be restored by the wronged divinity taking it out on a human favourite of the wronger (1420–2). As usual, cookery varies with context. In Pindar, when Helios is accidentally omitted from an apportionment of lots, Zeus helpfully offers to hold the draw again, though Helios gets what he wants anyway (*Ol.* 7). Even violent Ares warms his heart to Apollo's lovely music, and conflict is resolved in the harmony of choral song (*Pyth.* 1.10–12).

The immortal/mortal boundary, so fundamental to the *Iliad*, is explored elsewhere in a variety of ways (though never with greater poignancy than in that work). A typically Pindaric version of the relevant similarity and difference is set out at the beginning of *Nemean* 6:

> There is one
> race of men, one race of gods; both have breath
> of life from a single mother. But sundered power
> holds us divided, so that the one is nothing, while for the other the
>   brazen sky is established
> their sure citadel for ever. Yet we have some likeness in great
> intelligence, or strength, to the immortals,
> though we know not what the day will bring, what course
> after nightfall
> destiny has written that we must run to the end.

Herakles gained Olympos after hard effort; Asklepios raised the dead, and was thunderbolted; Cheiron was agonisingly wounded and wanted to die, but could not unless he found someone (Prometheus) willing to take over his immortality; Tithonos, blessed with immortality but not with immortal youth, shrivelled up beside his eternally young bride: myths about heroes explore the perilous interface between mortality and immortality.

An important area in which this is true is that of reciprocity. Humans nowadays owe the gods certain things; the implications of these debts are examined through myths. One thing humans owe is sacrifice. The reason why Hera supported the expedition of the *Argo* was that Pelias, Jason's foe, forgot her when making offerings to the gods; when Admetos failed to sacrifice to Artemis on the occasion of his marriage, the bridal chamber turned out to be full of coiled snakes.[6] A related debt concerns giving the gods due honour and respect. In Euripides' *Trojan Women*, Athene's wrath towards the Greeks derives from Ajax's crime of dragging Kassandra from her temple in Troy; she urges Poseidon to wreck their fleet 'so that in future the Achaeans will learn to respect my power and to worship the other gods' (85–6). At an earlier stage in the history of Troy, King Laomedon failed to pay the wages of Apollo and Poseidon, who had fortified his city for him; he got a plague and a sea-monster for his reward.[7] Another kind of respect is due acknowledgement of superiority. Here again, heroic myths narrate what happens when proper distances are elided: Thamyras, Arachne, Marsyas and a host of others fail to appreciate the riskiness of competing with those who are, by definition, *hors de concours*.[8]

Many of the themes noted above – power, violence, deception, negotiation, reciprocity, conflicts over interests and honour – have obvious echoes and models in the human sphere. Yet there are striking differences. One has been highlighted by John Gould in a paper which stresses the alien, uncanny and horrific dimension of divinity.[9] This is exemplified in the narrative in Euripides' *Hippolytos* in which the messenger relates the overthrow of Hippolytos on the appearance of

---

[6] Pelias: A. R. 1.13–14. Admetos: Apollod. 1.9.15.
[7] Apollod. 2.5.9.   [8] See Weiler 1974.   [9] Gould 1985.

the monstrous bull from the sea, despatched against him by Poseidon in response to the curse invoked by Theseus. The gods here exceed all human analogy, inhabiting a territory which can best be indicated through the Greek word *deinon*, 'terrible', 'awesome'.

Another quality shared by many mythical narratives is their laying bare of motives and explanations which in the superficial traffic of everyday life remain hidden. What mortal could know as much about the causation operative in his or her existence as the Homeric narrator claims to know about his subject matter? What human being could see with the clear eyes of the gods in Euripidean prologues? Once more, we can see myth as a device for making explicit, for highlighting what is behind life. But, paradoxically, one of the aspects of the world made explicit in myths is the *incompleteness* of human understanding of the world, and the *insufficiency* of human models of behaviour for comprehending divinity. This is above all true of tragedy, in which certain key episodes and scenes are simply inexplicable, certain divine actions baffling, because the drama either provides too few clues to reconstruct a coherent pattern of motivation, or incorporates too much, because conflicting, information. A classic example of the former is the notorious question of why, in the version of the tale given in Aischylos' *Agamemnon*, Artemis grew angry at Aulis before the departure of the Greek expedition to Troy. While explanations of her wrath are easy to find in other versions, this particular account shrouds the matter in mystery. On the other hand, Euripides' *Herakles* positively overflows with explanations for the reason for the downfall of the great hero, to such an extent that, here too, providing a coherent account involves disregarding some information at the expense of the rest.[10] The purposes of the gods are sometimes opaque, their voices silent or beyond interpretation.

Telling and acting

In twentieth-century scholarship, the aspect of Greek social behaviour which has most frequently been juxtaposed with myth is ritual. The history of myth–and–ritual approaches is complicated, not least

[10] Cf. Buxton 1988.

because it is inseparable from the larger question of the shifting relationships between the disciplines of anthropology and classics.[11] But from Jane Harrison to Walter Burkert a golden key to unlock the meanings of 'what is said' has been found in the investigation of 'what is done'. The terms of the enquiry have varied enormously, as have conclusions about, especially, the priority of one of these modes of symbolic expression over the other. There has even been an attempt (by C. Calame) to undermine the polarity altogether by calling into doubt the conceptual identity not just of myth but also of ritual, both being seen as products of western anthropological thought.[12] However, collapsing both into a general category of *énonciations de la pensée symbolique*[13] would seem to leave us with an excessively blunt analytical tool, and in the brief remarks which follow I have, along with virtually all scholars, kept ritual as a potentially useful concept.

That the narration of a Greek myth might actually form part of a ritual is certain. At the mysteries of the Mother Goddess, observes Pausanias *à propos* of a bronze near Corinth representing Hermes with a ram, a story was told: 'I know it, but will not relate it' (2.3.4). Circumstantial details are often lacking, as here; usually we have to make do with suggestive parallels between myths and 'their' festivals, rather than with fully documented accounts which would enable us to describe in proper contextual detail the nature of the integration between the two. Even suggestive parallels have their fascination, however, and they can sometimes generate plausible guesses about a close symbiosis between myth and festival. The inhabitants of Lemnos celebrated a rite of New Fire, when for a nine-day period all fires on the island were extinguished, to be relit afterwards by fire brought from over the sea.[14] Corresponding to this is a myth, according to which the women of the island incur the wrath of Aphrodite: they are afflicted with a bad smell which drives away their husbands and puts a stop to normal conjugal relations.[15] The motif of the disruption of the everyday repeats itself in even more emphatic

---

[11] The best *mise au point* is Versnel in Edmunds 1990, pp. 25–90; see also Bremmer 1992.
[12] See ch. 1 of Calame 1990b.   [13] Calame 1990b, p. 50.
[14] Philostr. *Her.* 207 (Teubner edn).
[15] For the myth and the ritual, see the classic account in Burkert 1970.

form when the husbands, who have consoled themselves with some Thracian slavegirls, are murdered by their wives. But eventually life begins again, as – from across the sea – Jason and the Argonauts sail in to rekindle that which had been extinguished.[16] The structure of the mythical narrative corresponds to the rhythm of the festival, and confirms the observation of one ancient source that the fire was extinguished *epi tōi ergōi*, 'in consequence of the [murderous, Lemnian] deed'.[17] Story and festival go together, even if we are not aware of any role which *narration* of the myth might have played in the ritual.

In cases where correspondences between narrative and ritual make it reasonable to talk of symbiosis, we can frequently observe the now familiar process of clarification and making-explicit, whereby mythology expresses openly or in extreme form that which in ritual remains hidden or disguised. Jan Bremmer has argued convincingly that, in rites enacting the expulsion of a scapegoat, the victim, typically a person of low status who becomes temporarily the focus of attention, is chased alive out of the city; in the corresponding myths the victim is a person of *high* status who is *killed*.[18] Myth translates ritual: to leave one's city is – if you spell it out – to die. Again, the women who worship Dionysos at the *oreibasia* return to their normal lives after the conclusion of the rites. By contrast, the corresponding myths express the disruption of family life in *irreversible* terms, as in the tale of Agaue's murder and dismembering of her son Pentheus. Temporary, ritual disruption of the family is translated mythically into permanence.

If the women who took part in the *oreibasia* had actually killed their kin as opposed to merely abandoning them temporarily, they would have been committing, in addition to murder, an unforgivable category-mistake. It did occasionally happen, or was said to have done; with predictable results.

---

[16] Myrsilos of Lesbos records a custom on Lemnos according to which on one day in the year the women kept their menfolk at a distance 'because of their bad smell': the link between myth and rite is reinforced (*FGrH* 477 1a; cf. Burkert 1970, p. 7).

[17] Philostr., *loc. cit.* in n. 14.

[18] Bremmer 1983a.

> They say that the daughters of Minyas, Leukippe and Arsinoe and Alkathoe, became frenzied and craved for human flesh, and drew lots about their children. The lot fell upon Leukippe and she gave her son Hippasos to be torn in pieces ... And up to the present time the people of Orchomenos give this name to the women of the family descended from them. And once a year at the Agrionia festival there takes place a flight and pursuit of them by the priest of Dionysos holding a sword. And when he catches one of them he may kill her. *And in our own time Zoilos the priest did indeed kill one of them. But this resulted in no good for the people; for Zoilos fell sick of a chance ulcerous wound, and after it had long festered, he died.*[19]

The myth recounts cannibalism and the catastrophic destruction of a family. The corresponding ritual *should* dramatise a symbolic pursuit of women escapers, which should in turn lead to a return to normality after the ritual. By a mischance, the behaviour appropriate to myth has invaded ritual, bringing death upon the agent responsible as well as upon his innocent victim – innocent, because only in the symbolism of the ritual was she guilty. The return to normality has been blocked, the essential temporariness of ritual cancelled.

A further, related difference between mythology and its festival context is worth introducing here. Rituals are designed to fulfil their objectives.[20] They set up dramatic situations, enact them, and at the end return participants and observers to undramatised reality: from *Fest* to *Alltag*. Sacrifice, for example, is a procedure by means of which proper relations with the gods and solidarity between humans are achieved through correct apportioning of cooked meat. The rules of the game are carefully prescribed; if they are followed, the ritual, by definition, works. But myths are, or may be, rather different. They *may* reach an 'end', as with the finale to Aischylos' *Oresteia*, or the eventual arrival of the Argonauts at Lemnos in order to ensure a future. But they may also draw attention to the open-endedness and ambiguity of action, to dilemmas without solution and wounds

---

[19] From no. 38 of Plutarch's *Greek Questions* (= *Mor.* 299e–f, trans. slightly adapted from that by W. R. Halliday; my italics).

[20] Cf. Burkert 1985, p. 264: 'Ritual creates situations of anxiety in order to overcome them ...'

without healing. In tragedy, above all, we regularly find that the shapes into which myths cast experience are baffling and contradictory. Rituals set themselves achievable goals; some myths remind their hearers that any hope of tailoring reality to suit human desires is bound to fail.

We spoke earlier of the symbiosis which can exist between myth and festival. But this is not the only possible relationship between the two. Some deities worshipped in cult are unimportant or even absent from extant mythology.[21] Again, many myths, while drawing on ritual, are not tied to one kind of ceremony, let alone to a particular cult at a particular time and place. Neither epics nor victory songs nor tragic dramas can be reduced to the status of libretti for ritual action, although the festival context undeniably affects the narrative perspectives adopted in those genres. The *Odyssey*, with its complex structure and its remarkable exploration of Greekness as contrasted with the behaviour of the diverse peoples visited by Odysseus, cannot be boiled down to a ritual pattern; yet its recitation at the Panathenaia must have lent it a special resonance, given the narrative's persistent opposing of Athene to Poseidon – the two rivals for the patronage of Athens.[22] No more can Pindar's odes, rich and intricate and full of subtle allusion, be explained away as mere reflections of ritual action; yet the prevalence in the poetry of agonistic imagery and of myths about returning demonstrates a significant link between context and content. Nor, finally, have attempts to shoe-horn tragedy into a ritual pattern won lasting assent. As the Greeks' phrase 'nothing to do with Dionysos' should not mislead us into ignoring the link between this god of changing identities and the masked drama put on to honour him, no more should we mistake the regular *exploitation of ritual themes* in drama (supplication, laments for the dead, sacrifice) for some hypothetically all-pervading ritual structure.

Believing in myths

Paul Veyne's short book *Les Grecs ont-ils cru à leurs mythes?* was published in 1983; several translations soon followed, including one in

---

[21] Cf. Rudhardt 1958, pp. 82–5.   [22] Panathenaia: Pl. *Hipparch.* 228b, Lyc. *Leocr.* 102.

English.[23] Having achieved the status of *savant*, Veyne declaims from beyond the Flannel Barrier; but, if you persevere through the style, you are rewarded. The argument is in two parts. Only one is directly relevant here; I confine discussion of the other to an extended footnote.

The first part of the case can be stated simply: believing in Greek myths, indeed believing *tout court*, is essentially plural. This is already implicit in the Preface, where Veyne cites Dan Sperber's *Rethinking Symbolism*. The Dorzé of Ethiopia believe that leopards, being Christians, observe the fasts of the Coptic church on Wednesdays and Fridays. However, a Dorzé protects his livestock on *all* days of the week, including Wednesdays and Fridays. 'Leopards are dangerous every day; this he knows from experience. They are also Christians; this is guaranteed by tradition.'[24] Beliefs, that is, are plural: persons and communities may hold, without strain, apparently incompatible beliefs. Veyne's Christmas parallel (stockings are filled *both* by Mum and Dad *and* by Santa) is perhaps too close for comfort to the Tylorian equation of the primitive with the childlike; a better example is Veyne's reference to his own views about ghosts: 'For my part, I hold ghosts to be simple fictions but ... I am almost neurotically afraid of them.'[25]

More relevant for us are Veyne's discussions of plurality of belief in relation to Greek stories; or rather, plurality in *expressions* of belief. He is more concerned with the Hellenistic and Roman periods than with the Archaic and Classical, and cites telling examples from Galen and Pausanias. When Galen has a philosophical hat on, he refers at one point (siding with Plato in order to pour scorn on Stoic attempts to make sense of mythology by rationalising it) to 'Hippocentaurs' and the Chimaira; 'and a multitude of such shapes comes flooding in, Gorgons and Pegasuses and an absurd crowd of other impossible and fabulous natures'.[26] But elsewhere, when seeking to persuade, to proselytise, to give an account of medicine within a more generally accepted framework, Galen mentions, with no explicit statement of incredulity, such traditional figures in the early history of medicine as

---

[23] Veyne 1988.   [24] Sperber 1975, p. 95.   [25] Veyne 1988, p. 87.
[26] *De placitis Hippocratis et Platonis* 3.8.33 (Kühn V, p. 357; de Lacy p. 231). Trans. by P. de Lacy.

'the Centaur Cheiron and the heroes of whom he was the teacher', and Asklepios.[27] So belief can figure differently in different works by the same author. But more than that: Pausanias, within one and the same work, refuses to give credence to the myth of Medusa, yet accepts the authenticity of the tale about the werewolf Lykaon: '. . . I believe this legend, which has been told in Arkadia from ancient times and has likelihood on its side'.[28]

Emphasis on the problems involved in deciphering Greek expressions of belief is by no means original to Veyne. In a beautiful article written in 1976, Tom Stinton showed how expressions of *dis*belief can function as 'signifiers' whose 'signifieds' are by no means what they seem.[29] For instance, Herodotos tells a story about men living beyond the Scythians who are bald from birth; beyond them are mountains inhabited, according to the bald men, by a goat-footed race, 'though I do not regard this as credible'; and beyond *them* are men who hibernate for six months: 'but this I *totally* refuse to accept' (4.23–5). The effect is both to convince us of Herodotos' *general* trustworthiness (for he is *so* sensitive to gradations of likelihood) and to encourage the reader to accept the existence of the bald men as going without saying – or with saying.[30] Knowing how to take expressions of belief depends on our assessment of the context and of the strategy of the writer; since Stinton, assumptions about Euripides' famous scepticism have needed very careful handling. Veyne is stylistically a million miles from Stinton, but he too leads us to recognise just how intractable some of the apparently straightforward evidence about belief actually is.[31]

---

[27] *Introductio seu medicus* I (Kühn XIV, pp. 674–5); cf. Veyne 1988, p. 55.

[28] Medusa: 2.21.6–7. Lykaon: 8.2.4 (trans. P. Levi). Cf. Veyne 1988, pp. 96 and 99.

[29] Reprinted in Stinton 1990, pp. 236–64. The Saussurian terms are not Stinton's, but seem appropriate to his argument.

[30] Stinton 1990, p. 237.

[31] At this point I include some comments about the second stage in Veyne's argument. This consists in holding that we must talk, not just of a plurality of beliefs, but of a plurality of truths, or of criteria for truth (p. 113). 'The *Iliad* and *Alice in Wonderland*', declares Veyne, 'are no less true than Fustel de Coulanges' (p. xi). (What shall we say? Finley's *Ancient Economy*? Hammond's *History of Greece*?) Now the nature of this plurality of truths is, intriguingly, itself multiple, or at least dual. At times it seems to be a matter of chronological succession, of one Kuhnian paradigm being replaced by another ('Once one is in one of these

Let us turn to some of this evidence. Scholars sometimes tend to operate, half-unconsciously, with a model which goes like this. Archaic Greeks, with the exception of odd-balls like the Presocratic philosopher Xenophanes, on the whole believed in myths. In the fifth century, more sceptical voices were raised, for example by Euripides. In Hellenistic times a still greater distance opened up between myths and belief. And as for the ultra-knowing Ovid . . . This model cannot, I believe, be dismissed as a straw one. Oswyn Murray was perhaps being over-optimistic when he alluded to 'one of the most dubious and insidious of all *nineteenth-century* postulates, [namely] the idea of social development from the primitive and religious towards the complex and secular'.[32]

What do we do with this model? First, we have to distinguish between belief in myths, that is in *stories*, and belief in gods. It is quite possible to disbelieve in certain *stories* about Artemis while still believing in her existence. This may seem to be merely a trivial debating point, but it is in fact of considerable relevance when we

fishbowls, it takes genius to get out of it and innovate' (p. 118).) But at other times Veyne writes as if at all times a range of strategies – but, as far as one can see, the *same* range of strategies – has existed towards belief (scepticism, total credulity, rationalisation, etc.) – a view in apparent contradiction with the fishbowl approach. These and other inconsistencies have been highlighted in Méheust 1990. (To add another paradox, this time an authorial one, when I telephoned M. Veyne to ask him what *he* recommended that one should read about his work in general and *Les Grecs ont-ils cru* in particular, he immediately cited Méheust's rather critical article.)

If we *are* to assign a consistent view on the truth question to Veyne here, I think it should be done in the terms expressed by C. Brillante (in Edmunds 1990, pp. 116–17), who maintains that for Veyne 'any reflection, whether qualified as mythic or rational, is shown to be the creation of an *imagination constituante*, that is, of a reason that need not account for its own affirmations, except to itself'. If Brillante is right, this is a road down which I have no wish to follow Veyne. However, in the light of recent notorious attempts to deny the genocide practised by the Nazis during the Second World War, it is important to note this observation: 'It is clear that the existence or the nonexistence of Theseus and gas chambers in one point in space and time has a material reality that owes nothing to our imagination . . . [However] the materiality of gas chambers does not automatically lead to the knowledge one can have about them' (Veyne 1988, p. 107). Even the most pachydermatous of epistemological relativists must (fortunately) think twice before espousing views compatible with a denial of that particular historical reality. (Parenthetically, we may observe that those who do follow an extreme 'no closure of historical interpretation' line risk getting into bed with some pretty dubious company.)

[32] In O. Murray and Price 1990, p. 6; my emphasis.

think about what might count as evidence for belief. Whether belief is conceived of as a mental occurrence or a disposition, and whether we are concerned with believing *in* or believing *that*, establishing the nature of a belief held by someone else often entails making inferences from actions as well as utterances.[33] If we want to establish whether X believes in socialism, Y in free love, or Z that charity begins at home, we shall need to canvass their actions as well as what they profess. Of course, there is a potential gap between the two: people may *fail* to act upon their beliefs, or be obliged to act *against* their beliefs; but their actions will still count at least as relevant evidence. Now religion would seem to be one area where actions ought to be taken into account in assessing the extent and strength of beliefs: it is a matter of *ex votos* as well as *credos*. So when Robin Osborne points to the rapid spread of the cult of Pan in Attica after 500 BC as evidence for a changing perception of the countryside, we may well be tempted to describe this process as a development in religious *belief*.[34] Indeed, this is the more so because of the nature of Greek religion. Jean Rudhardt, and more recently Marcel Detienne, have argued that to 'believe' in the Greek gods just *is* to honour them in cult: to sacrifice to them, pray to them, sing and walk in procession for them: these are *ta nomizomena* (things 'thought', things 'customary').[35]

But assessing belief in *stories* is a rather different matter, since in many cases it is not clear what kind of action could count as evidence for or against the presence of a particular belief – say, the belief that the madness of Herakles followed his Labours. In such cases we have characteristically to rely on the evidence of utterances – the fact, for example, that a narrator opts for this version of a tale rather than that. The bulk of our evidence, that is, will consist of explicit statements about, or expressions of, belief, together with mythical narratives from which belief-states have to be inferred. Of course, it would be absurd to deny *all* relevance to what we might inelegantly call the worship-situation: this would, presumably, figure in *some* way in the account we would want to give of a twentieth-century opera which

---

[33] See H. H. Price 1969, for a philosophical analysis of belief.
[34] Osborne 1987, p. 192.
[35] Rudhardt 1958, p. 142; Detienne and Sissa 1989, pp. 191–2.

included, say, Dionysos as a character. But in practice, in an ancient Greek context, we rarely find ourselves well enough informed about the extent or absence of relevant practised religion to limit our uncertainties about belief in myths.

So: utterances: texts in contexts. And the plurals should be emphasised; because the crucial element in the situation is contextual plurality.

Age and gender could be thought of as factors shaping attitudes to the stories. A passage from Plato's *Laws* makes the point in relation to the young:

> '... yet it proved easy to persuade men of the Sidonian story [= the myth of Kadmos], incredible though it was, and of numberless others.'
>
> 'What tales?'
>
> 'The tale of the teeth that were sown, and how armed men sprang out of them. Here, indeed, the lawgiver has a notable example of how one can, if one tries, persuade the souls of the young of anything.'[36]

Old men too are sometimes seen as subject to an intensification of belief. I quote two voices. The first is that of Kephalos, a very old man with whom the Platonic Sokrates likes (he says) to converse. Asked about how life is when one is so near the brink, Kephalos relates how he and other old men often meet together, and talk. They chin-wag about the past, of course, some regretting it, others bidding it good riddance. They speculate too about the future:

> ... when a man begins to realise that he is going to die, he is filled with apprehensions and concern about matters that before did not occur to him. The tales that are told of the world below and how men who have done wrong here must pay the penalty there, though he may have laughed them down hitherto, then begin to torture his soul with the doubt that there may be some truth in them.[37]

[36] 663e–664a (trans. adapted from that by R. G. Bury, Loeb edn).
[37] *R.* 330d–e (trans. P. Shorey, Loeb edn).

The second voice belongs to the lyric poet Anakreon.

> My temples are already grey,
> my head is white,
> delicious youth is here no more;
> my teeth are old, and I no longer
> have much time of sweet life left.
> So I sob, often, in fear of Tartaros.
> For Hades' house is terrible:
> the way down is hard, and once you follow it,
> there is no return.[38]

True reflections of talk in the *leschē*? Perhaps. But we should remember that Plato is the greatest ironist of antiquity, while Anakreon is another Ovid for self-mockery.

Women are presented as another credulous group. According to Polybios, they are characterised by a love of the marvellous (12.24–5). Not only are they *tellers* of old wives' tales: they are also said to be particularly susceptible to them. Referring to the myth of Theseus' abandonment of Ariadne on Naxos, Philostratos observes that '[nurses] are skilled in telling such tales, *and they weep over them whenever they will*'.[39] It goes without saying that these ascriptions of degrees and kinds of credulity need not correspond to anything which an ancient opinion survey amongst children, the elderly or women might have come up with: we have the familiar problem of evaluating utterances – and it is (to say the least) no easier to evaluate a 'they believe' than an 'I believe'.

If age and gender constituted two kinds of relevant plurality, a third concerned a different sort of social division. We may take Martin Nilsson's views as representing a strong form of this approach. For Nilsson, the Greek 'folk' was one thing, the urban sophisticates, especially atypical intellectuals who might go so far as to embrace atheism, quite another.[40] This is an important point to make, in particular in relation to the Hellenistic period – it is easy to forget that the Kallimachean attitude to tradition is contemporary with a huge

---

[38] *PMG* 395 (my translation). [39] *Imag.* 1.15.1. [40] E.g. Nilsson 1940.

proliferation of popular recitation and festival performance, at which myths were also retold. Yet at the same time Nilsson's dichotomy has to be subjected to massive refinement in relation to varying historical contexts. It is evident that analysis of the difference between 'the people' and 'the sophisticates' is going to look very different depending on whether we are dealing with Alkman's Sparta or Lykophron's Alexandria.

But there is another and more interesting kind of plurality which needs to be confronted: plurality of context for a single individual at any one time. Take the case of an Athenian adult male living at the end of the fifth century. His recent experience of mythology includes: looking at temple friezes, vases and coins; being present at a rhapsodic recital which presented excerpts from the *Odyssey*; singing one of Alkaios' hymns at a *symposion*; attending performances of the *Bakchai* and the *Frogs*; and holding those vague, basic, unfocused, lowest-common-denominator views about divine intervention and the afterlife which Jon Mikalson discusses in *Athenian Popular Religion*.[41] Mikalson's essay is like a breath of fresh air in a room usually filled with methodological perfumes that are pungent, contrasting and not always expensive. But it does, quite deliberately, base its conclusions about Athenian belief on a very restricted type of evidence: oratory, inscriptions, Xenophon. And matters are perhaps not quite so clear-cut as Mikalson implies when he maintains that 'in the study of popular religion the need now is for some descriptive work; a theoretical bias would only impede this work'.[42] On the contrary, the really taxing question seems to me to be precisely: how were such lowest-common-denominator attitudes (taking 'little interest in the bleak and uncertain prospect of the afterlife'; having views about *daimones* that were 'quite vague and imprecise')[43] – how were such attitudes integrated with those implicit in the artistic-performance contexts? Or *were* they integrated? For I suggest that we have no idea how, or whether, most people reconciled the perspectives implied by the various ways in which they might confront mythology. Few Greeks will have felt the need to work out for themselves, in the

---

[41] Mikalson 1983.   [42] Mikalson 1983, p. 7.   [43] Mikalson 1983, pp. 82 and 65.

manner of a Plato, an explicit reconciliation between or hierarchisation of the alternative modes of access to the sacred. They will simply have accepted as normal the fact that different ways of imagining the gods were appropriate to different contexts. To ask which constituted their real belief is to miss the point.[44]

All this does not mean that we must rule out entirely the possibility of making generalisations about Greek belief in myths: for example, it would seem that no ancient author denies the *existence* of, say, Theseus, Meleager, or Agamemnon. Nor, needless to say, should we minimise the importance of relating the different kinds of myth-telling that we find in Pindar, Euripides or Kallimachos to the societies for which they composed, or of noting developments in attitudes towards the mythological tradition implicit in their works. The point is, rather, that to describe those changes in terms of strength or weakness in belief, or of the size of the credulity supply in circulation at any one time, needs at the very least to take account of the complicating factors just mentioned.

But there is another way out of the belief maze. For to ask about the extent of *belief* in stories is in fact to ask one of the least rewarding questions about them. Let us return to four images of mythical women which we discussed earlier: Penelope before her web; Polyneikes persuading Eriphyle; Tekmessa tending the dead Ajax; the abduction of Hippodameia by Pelops (Plates 12–14, 16). These are paradigms, types, models of behaviour – sometimes extremely ambiguous models – from which human conduct may diverge or to which it may correspond. The question of the extent of *belief* in such powerful, persistent images seems not just unverifiable, but irrelevant. It might be argued that the belief issue becomes more pressing in relation to verbal narratives in the past tense: 'Zeus hid fire'; 'Oidipous solved the riddle'. But even in such cases the crucial point in relation to functional importance is that the stories are told, retold, and gradually stop being told, to be replaced by other narratives.

A potentially fruitful analogy here is that between myths and

---

[44] Mikalson himself has subsequently attempted to integrate the evidence of tragedy with that of popular religion (Mikalson 1991), but with only mixed success; cf. the review by H. Yunis in *CR* NS 43 (1993), pp. 70–2.

proverbial expressions.[45] The analogy might seem flawed from the outset, since myths are narratives, while proverbs are not. However, in a Greek context at least, proverbs very often *depend* on narratives, which have to be supplied if the force of the proverb is to be understood. Moreover, many of these implied narratives are mythical. A few minutes' browsing in the standard collection of ancient maxims yields references to the nemesis of Adrastos (applied to those formerly happy but later unfortunate), the fiery robe (sent by Deianeira to Herakles; refers to those who inflame quarrels), the cap of Hades (which conferred invisibility on the wearer; said of those who practise concealment), the laughter of Ajax (manic laughter, recalling that of the crazed hero), the glare of Atreus (a baleful look like that on the face of the betrayed husband plotting a ghoulish revenge), the sleep of Endymion (applied to sleepy-heads: Endymion slept for eternity), the sufferings of Io (woe upon woe), not to mention a Kadmeian victory, a Troy of troubles, 'not without Theseus', the madness of Thamyris, Bellerophon's letters, and plenty of others.[46] Such expressions provided a ready-made way of 'locating' certain aspects of behaviour, by implicitly making generalisations about them. But these generalisations do not aspire to the status of *universal* truths: while a given maxim may work in one context, its opposite may be more relevant in another. That too many cooks spoil the broth does not mean that many hands don't make light work: what convinces in one context need not be required to convince in another. So too with myths, whose force, like that of proverbs, is essentially context-bound. (To repeat: myths are not *the same as* proverbs; they are, however, in one important respect *analogous* to them.) Hence the problem of 'reconciling', to which we referred earlier, is really not so intractable, since what are apparently contradictory propositions can happily coexist *provided they are embedded in different contexts*. Nor is the analogy with proverbs irrelevant to belief. If someone asks you how you can *really believe* that too many cooks spoil the broth, while at the same time *really believing* that many hands make light work, you may reasonably retort that they are barking up the wrong tree.

---

[45] *Muthoi* as similar to yet distinct from proverbs: Pl. *Lg.* 913b9–c3; cf. Brisson 1982, p. 124, Detienne 1986, p. 95.   [46] Leutsch and Schneidewin 1839–51.

Greek myths were retold because they were authoritative: partly in virtue of the various authorities conferred on tellers by the context (women in the house, bards at the feast, poets at archon-sanctioned, *polis*-organised dramatic performances); partly because of the authority which tellers created for themselves, thanks to the content of the tale and the manner of its telling; partly because the telling of similar tales in a variety of contexts and at all ages (from nursery stories to adolescent choirs to the old men's *leschē*) can hardly have failed to produce a reinforcing effect. But the authority of myths did not go without saying, in spite of the fact – perhaps even because of the fact – that tellers regularly claimed to be reporting the truth. An audience hears a poet maintain that he is inspired by the Muse; they find his song convincing. But they do so in the knowledge, not only that he is distancing himself from previous tale-tellers (as with Pindar in *Olympian* 1, where stories involving the gods in cannibalism are indignantly rejected), but also that the *next* poet in the tradition will tell his *own* tale, again inspired, again claiming the truth. Greek myths constitute a corpus of plausible, telling tales which aim, within their contexts, at achieving *peithō*, persuasion. But a fuller account of *that* must wait until the final part of this book.

PART THREE

What was the point?

9

The actors' perceptions

We have touched repeatedly on certain functions which Greek myths had in context; we now address this question directly. In Part Three we shall operate with a distinction no less fundamental, and perhaps no less controversial, than that between myth and everyday life. We shall distinguish between the perceptions of the original actors – that is, the narrators and their audiences – on the one hand, and the perceptions of modern observers – scholars and other interpreters – on the other. So presented, the distinction is grossly over-simplified. First, an observer's account of function may overlap with or even coincide with the perceptions of the original actors. Secondly, claims by ancient writers about what they or others were doing in telling tales have to be seen in the light of the persuasive, often polemical strategies of the writers concerned; ascriptions of purpose to earlier by later writers have to be handled with particular care, as for instance with assertions about what were seen in later antiquity as Homeric 'allegories'. Thirdly, the concept of 'the (modern) observer' is itself an artificial construct. In reality, perceptions of function have varied and still vary widely even between competent critics; and there exists, in addition, a nest of theoretical problems relating to the question of how far the interpretation of an ancient text (or any text) can be disentangled from its later 'reception'. Nevertheless, the difference between what ancient myth-tellers and myth-hearers thought (or said they thought) they were doing, and what later observers perceive them to have been doing, can only be regarded as negligible if we are prepared to claim omniscience *for ourselves* in the understanding of our own story-telling – or, for that matter, in our understanding of any other contemporary cultural phenomenon.

Many genres of narrative incorporated the claim that a prime function of myth-telling was to preserve for posterity the great deeds of the past. The delegation which visits Achilles in the *Iliad* finds the hero singing, to his own lyre-accompaniment, about *klea andrōn*, 'the famous deeds of men' (9.189). The bard in Hesiod, in addition to recalling the blessed gods of Olympos, records *kleia proterōn anthrōpōn*, 'famous deeds of former mortals' (*Th.* 99–101). Indeed, the Hesiodic Muse is invoked precisely in order to make events become famous: *kleiete*, 'celebrate' (*Th.* 105) – a power which the Muses exercise also on their own behalf, as they *kleiousin aoidēi*, 'celebrate in song', the earliest generations of gods, then Zeus, then the races of mortal men and Giants (43–52). In Pindar, song immortalises – appropriately enough, in a genre which aspires to transmute evanescent athletic triumphs: 'Even high deeds of bravery have a great darkness if they lack songs'; 'when men pass away, songs and tales bring back their noble achievements for them'.[1] We may add that, though the subject is the poet's beloved rather than a hero of mythology, Theognis gives comparable, contextually precise expression to the imagined poetic future: 'You will be present at every meal and feast, lying upon the lips of many, and young men shall sing of you, well and clearly and in good order, to the shrill-voiced pipe' (239–43).

Tragedy lacks the first-personal stance characteristic of the epic bard or praise-poet, so its claims to immortalise are bound to be indirect. In most cases, tragic references to the power of narrative to confer fame point outwards beyond the frame of the drama, exploiting the audience's sense that they are witnessing events simultaneously past and present. Thus Alkestis 'will' be celebrated at Sparta and Athens after her death (*kleontes*, 447); Hippolytos 'will always be remembered' at Trozen (1428–9); Antigone 'will' be famous (*kleinē*, 817) when she has passed over to Hades; Herakles' persuasion of

---

[1] *Nem.* 7.12–13, 6.29–30. The *topos* is very common in Pindar.

Philoktetes includes the promise of *eventual* glory (*euklea bion*, 1422). In view of the kind of events recorded in tragedy, the fame which reaches posterity may be double-edged: *kleos* in *Philoktetes* is both the report of the hero's disease-ridden misfortune and the prospect of his glory at Troy (251, 1347).[2] Such ambiguity is, for obvious reasons, dysfunctional in and thus foreign to the funeral speech, the tone of which is in this respect closer to Pindar than to tragedy. Lysias here incorporates an appropriate mingling of praise with remembrance:

> So now, in the first place, I shall recount the ancient ordeals of our ancestors, drawing remembrance of those events from their renown. For they also are matters which all men ought to remember, glorifying them in their songs, and describing them in the sayings of noble men; honouring them on such occasions as this, and teaching the living by referring to the achievements of the dead.
>
> (*Fun. Or. 3*)

Lysias' words lead us to a second function of myth-telling often stressed by the actors: teaching. People 'learned' from Homer; the same poet was called (ironically) 'wiser than all the Greeks', while Hesiod was the 'teacher of most'.[3] The assumption underpinning the Aristophanic debate between 'Aischylos' and 'Euripides' in *Frogs* is that poets should teach their fellows to be better by showing them examples of conduct (1019ff.). In Plato, a view is represented according to which poets are aiming at moral instruction; Sokrates in *Lysis* can refer to them as 'like our fathers, so to speak, and leaders in wisdom' (213e).[4] Plato's objection, best known from the *Republic*, is that poets too often depict *bad* conduct for imitation, with deleterious consequences for, in particular, the plastic souls of children.

In the course of his analysis of ancient poetics Malcolm Heath observes that 'when a Greek spoke of the poet as teacher he meant ... that one could find in the poets moral exemplars, cautionary tales and formulations in gnomic utterance of moral, and indeed of technical,

---

[2] Compare E. *Ph.* 576 for negative *kleos*.

[3] Homer: Xenoph. 21B10 DK, Heracl. 22B56 DK; cf. Verdenius 1970. Hesiod: Heracl. 22B57 DK.   [4] Cf. Heath 1987, p. 41.

wisdom'.[5] There is a good deal of truth in this view,[6] yet it needs to be qualified by the observation that our sources' presentation of the didacticist tradition is always coloured by their own context and purpose. For instance, a number of passages in the orators depict poets as educating and advising by providing mythical examples;[7] yet it is conceivable that the poets' intentions are here being assimilated to those of the orators themselves. However, the impressive extent of the evidence for the didacticist approach suggests that this was indeed widely felt to be one of the functions of story-telling.

That the past could be regarded as a source of paradigms is, in fact, a common assumption amongst ancient writers. The Mytilenaians 'use the things that happened before as *paradeigmata*', and hence refuse to trust the Athenians; the orator Lykourgos urges the jury that by voting to condemn they will be leaving a (good) *paradeigma* for future generations.[8] A verb frequently found in conjunction with *paradeigma* is *chrēsthai*, 'to use'. The past is there to be exploited; and this past includes the deeds of the gods and heroes. Sometimes we find the paradigmatic use of mythology spelled out, as when Lykourgos characterises Euripides' *Erechtheus* as a play which offers a *paradeigma* of patriotic behaviour; or when Strabo distinguishes between, on the one hand, accounts of the wanderings of Odysseus, Menelaos and Jason, and, on the other, the useful *paradeigmata* (relating to hardships undergone) which can be drawn from them; or, most famously of all, when the chorus in Sophokles' *Oidipous Tyrannos* takes the fate of the hero as a *paradeigma* to justify the conclusion that 'I call no mortal blessed'.[9] But, more often, we have to tease out the paradigmatic force of myths from the contexts in which they are embedded. In the case of the Meleager story in *Iliad* 9 or the Niobe allusion in *Iliad* 24, it is the observers who describe the rhetoric as paradigmatic.[10] The same goes for many of the cross-references between myths within Greek poetry.[11] Sometimes the point of a cross-reference is clear, and

---

[5] Heath 1987, p. 47.

[6] That is not to say that the whole of Heath's argument is persuasive. See the author's review in *Times Literary Supplement* for 15–21 July 1988, p. 772.

[7] Cf. Heath 1987, p. 44, Rudhardt 1958, p. 73.

[8] Th. 3.10.6, Lyc. *Leocr.* 9.   [9] Lyc. *Leocr.* 100, Str. 1.1.19, S. *OT* 1193–5.

[10] *Il.* 9.527ff., 24.602ff.; cf. Willcock 1964, Braswell 1971.   [11] See Oehler 1925.

the notion of teaching is virtually explicit, as when in Euripides' *Bakchai* Kadmos cites the terrible fate of Aktaion and then warns Pentheus, 'Do not suffer the same fate' (337ff.). But equally, the precise nature of the parallel may be obscure. Attempts continue to decipher the relevance to the main dramatic action of the fourth choral song (944ff.) in Sophokles' *Antigone*, where the stories of Danae (imprisoned by her father), Lykourgos (rash and doomed opponent of Dionysos) and the blinded sons of Phineus stand in an at best enigmatic relationship to the tale of Antigone and Kreon.[12] We shall return to paradigms later, since they constitute a classic case of the overlap between actors' and observers' perceptions.

One way in which the notion of teaching was explored was by setting it up as an opposite, or complement, to 'entertainment'.[13] Here it is worth recalling a longish passage from near the beginning of Strabo's geographical treatise since, although written considerably later than the period which is our main concern, it tackles the distinction head-on. In the course of the standard Greek rhetorical gambit of claiming a distinctive voice for oneself by criticising a well-known predecessor, Strabo presents his rival Eratosthenes as maintaining that poets write for entertainment, not instruction. Strabo, by contrast, holds that poets aim at both. To demonstrate the point, he makes his own contribution to the discussion of the nature of narrative teaching. 'Most of those who live in *poleis*', he observes, 'are incited to emulation by the myths that are pleasing' – examples include 'deeds of manly courage' such as the Labours of Herakles and Theseus, or honours bestowed by the gods, or paintings or images or statues which suggest a happy mythical ending. The contrary type of story – that which dissuades from courses of action – is prompted by 'divine punishments, terrors and threats'. The most *useful* poet is Homer, who 'applies his *muthoi* to the province of education'.[14] Homer adds fantasy to truth; this is how he can simultaneously educate and please.

Strabo's exegesis has the effect of retaining mythological poetry, above all that of Homer, within the bounds of that to which an adult

[12] Cf. for example C. Sourvinou-Inwood in Calame 1988, pp. 167–83.
[13] Cf. *Diss. log.* 90.3.17 DK.   [14] Str. 1.1.10, 1.2.3, 1.2.8–9.

may seriously attend, by the expedient of peeling away that to which he should *not* seriously attend. A related and extremely common form of rationalisation, which had its own implications for the notion of teaching, is the interpretative strategy usually labelled 'allegorical'. On this view, teaching is seen as taking place in (in Saussurian terms) the domain of the signified: 'The real value of a myth lies in the truth which it expresses, not in the image which does the expressing.'[15] The nature of the perceived teaching varies according to the presuppositions and approach of the interpreter, but there is a pervasive assumption that mythological poetry is a source of wisdom whose character it is the task of the interpreter to uncover.[16] This is most obvious when the allegory is moral rather than, say, physical. Thus Athenaios mentions a reading of Homer according to which the poet is seen as desiring to implant moderation, while Plutarch refers to the lessons and instruction to be found in poetry, as when Homer teaches in relation to Aphrodite that 'vulgar music, coarse songs, and stories treating of vile themes, create licentious characters, unmanly lives, and men that love luxury, soft living, intimacy with women and [quoting from the *Odyssey*] "changes of clothes, warm baths, and the genial bed of enjoyment"'.[17] In his interesting and unusually explicit discussion of the *utility* of Greek myths, Dionysios of Halikarnassos cites as a first example their role in 'demonstrating the works of nature *di' allēgorias*, by means of allegory'.[18]

The attractiveness of allegorical interpretation – malleable yet durable – ensured that the conception of myth-teller-as-teacher persisted into late antiquity and far beyond. But already in Archaic Greece expression had been given to a third perception of the purpose of myth-telling, one which at times complemented and at times contrasted with the didactic tradition. This view, or cluster of views,

[15] Buffière 1956, p. 33 (my translation).
[16] Cf. Heraclit. *All.* 70.13, who speaks of *tēn ēllēgorēmenēn sophian*, 'wisdom presented in allegory'.
[17] Ath. 8e, Plu. 'How the young man should study poetry' (*Mor.* 19e–20a, trans. F. C. Babbitt, Loeb edn).
[18] D. H. *Ant. Rom.* 2.20. I am indebted to Prof. Ph. Borgeaud for drawing my attention to the value of this passage.

emphasised the power of myths to arouse feelings: to give sweet pleasure, and to offer consolation for present sorrows by stirring memory of past adventures.

Homeric song regularly conveys a sense of poetry as delightful: *terpō* ('I delight'), *thelgō* ('I enchant') and *himeros* ('yearning') are key words. Achilles in his tent 'delighted (*eterpen*) his heart' as he sang of the glorious deeds of men; Odysseus and the Phaiakians found Demodokos' song about Ares and Aphrodite delightful (*terpet'*); Eumaios likened the disguised Odysseus to a poet who has learned from the gods lovely (*himeroenta*) words to sing: 'so he charmed me (*ethelge*) with his tales as he sat beside me in the halls'.[19] Yet, given a different narrative context, the effect can be far from delightful. After hearing Demodokos sing the story of the Trojan horse, Odysseus 'melted' and cried piteously like a newly bereaved wife (*Od.* 8.521–31). Phemios' song about the grim return of the Achaians from Troy was, similarly, too close to home for Penelope: she bade the singer remember another song, one of the sort with which he could charm mortals' hearts (*thelktēria*) (*Od.* 1.337).

These Homeric themes run, with variations, throughout the poetic tradition. For Hesiod, the song granted by the Muses is *himeroessan*, 'full of desire' (*Th.* 104).

> For though a man have sorrow and grief in his newly-troubled soul and live in dread because his heart is distressed, yet, when a singer, the servant of the Muses, chants the glorious deeds of men of old and the blessed gods who inhabit Olympos, at once *he forgets his heaviness* and remembers not his sorrows at all; but the gifts of the goddesses soon turn him away from these.[20]

The Muses delight even the mind of Zeus; he bore them to be a source of forgetfulness of misfortune, a means of putting an end to care.[21] Yet their mother is Memory. As Apollo both sends and wards off the plague, so the Muses stand Janus-like on the boundary of memory and oblivion, able to exercise power in either direction.

[19] *Il.* 9.189 (cf. ibid. 186, *terpomenon*), *Od.* 8.368–9, 17.518–21. See Latacz 1966, esp. pp. 210–14.
[20] *Th.* 98–103 (trans. H. G. Evelyn-White, Loeb edn); cf. West's commentary on *Th.* 55.
[21] *Th.* 36–7, 51–2, 55.

Like the epic bard, the praise-poet claims to distil sweetness, offering the victor 'the poured nectar of victory, gift of the Muses, the mind's sweet yield', to match the sweetness of the victor's life.[22] Sung praise gives delight through gentle healing:

> The best healer for struggles of pain . . .
> is happiness; and wise songs,
> daughters of the Muses, enchant by their touch.
> Not warm water even laps in such ease
> the body as praise moulded to the lyre's measure.
>
> (*Nem.* 4.1–5)

In tragedy, by contrast, room can be made for the gap between claim and realised effect: the Nurse in Euripides' *Medea* – a play empty of healing – complains that no one has found a way of curing grief through song, in spite of all the jolly music to be heard at banquets (190–202). But it is the contrary point of view which is the more commonly represented, as in the Theokritean assertion that singing is a pleasant drug/remedy (*pharmakon*) for love – the only such remedy which humanity possesses.[23] In the passage from Dionysios of Halikarnassos already noticed, the author punningly observes that one function of *muthoi* is *heneka paramuthias*, 'for consolation' (2.20).

No less than its didactic role, the role of myth-telling in affecting the emotions was noticed by those who attempted to place themselves at a distance from the mythological tradition in order to monitor the social function of poetry. The sophist Gorgias, who had his own philosophical axe to grind in stressing the persuasiveness of language, wrote of the power of *logos* to 'end fear, remove pain, instil joy, increase pity'.[24] Plato's Sokrates, not without irony, described the effect of the purple passages habitually chosen by rhapsodes as 'stunning', 'amazing': the verb is *ekplēttō*, which Aristophanes had selected to convey the effect which his majestic-antique character

---

22 Pi. *Ol.* 7.7–8, cf. *Pyth.* 8.96–7. On poetry (and art) as purveyors of sweet delight, see Webster 1939, p. 172.
23 Theoc. 11.1–4. See Goldhill 1991, pp. 255–61, on the complexities of *pharmakon* in this poem.
24 *Enc.* 8 (= 82B11.8 DK).

'Aischylos' had on his audience.[25] Evaluation of the emotional effect of narrative varies, of course, with moral-philosophical standpoint. Platonic suspiciousness is countered by the Aristotelian recognition that tragic narrative, at least, has a *valuable* function thanks to its arousal of pity-and-fear.

A fourth function discussed in our sources is the role of myths in explaining the present in terms of its origins. In Hesiod's *Theogony* Zeus is offered a choice of portions of a slaughtered ox by the wily Prometheus. The father of the gods opts for the one with the tempting fat concealing the inedible bones within. *Ek tou* – 'out of this', hence 'as a result of this' (556) – mortals have ever afterwards burned bones for the immortals: the sacrificial present is rooted in a past precedent.[26] Comparable patterns of explanation occur at the end of many tragedies. In Euripides' *Hippolytos* it is *in recompense for* (*anti*, 1423) and as a remembrance of the suffering represented in the drama that maidens of Trozen will henceforth sing for Hippolytos; in *Helen*, an island off Attica is named Helene *because* (*epei*) it received the heroine, transported there by Hermes (1674–5). Heroes founded peoples, families, cities, political régimes, arts, professions. The past explains the present by being imagined as having created it. This is aetiology: Kallimachos' long poem known precisely as *Aitia* was devoted to an exploration of just such origins. Narratives of metamorphosis, too, characteristically have an aetiological dimension: the human transformed into bird, beast or flower persists in the present, yet embodies a continuity with the past. Antoninus Liberalis' accounts of mythical transformations habitually conclude with the formulae *achri nun* or *eti nun*: 'still now'.

An aspect of aetiology which is fundamental to an understanding of the role of Greek mythology in its contexts is its tolerance of plurality. Hesiod's *Works and Days* provides a classic instance. Near the beginning of the poem, Hesiod gives an account of why the lot of man is so hard. To counterbalance Prometheus' theft of fire for mortals,

[25] Pl. *Ion* 535b, Ar. *Ra.* 962. For *ekplēxis*, cf. Longinus 15.2, with the note by Russell in his edn *ad loc.*

[26] Rite as aetiology: Calame 1990b, p. 15.

Zeus sent them a bane in the delectable shape of Pandora, the female created by the gods.

> Before, the tribes of humanity lived without troubles and hard work, without the painful diseases which bring death to men. But the woman removed the great lid from the jar and scattered its contents, designing grief and anxiety for humans. Only Hope remained behind within the unbreakable container below the rim of the jar, and did not fly out; before that, she replaced the lid of the jar, through the will of Zeus, the god who wields the aegis and gathers the clouds. But [now] countless misfortunes wander amongst humans: the earth is full of misfortune; so is the sea . . .
>
> (90–101)

What concerns us here is not the complexity and ambiguity of the narrative – this point will be developed later – but the fact that immediately after the Prometheus/Pandora explanation of why things are so rough nowadays comes a story which is explicitly said by Hesiod to be a *different* one: 'or, if you like, I will summarise another *logos*' (106).[27] There follows a narrative no less rich and intricate, this time that about the sequence of races of humanity – gold, silver, bronze, heroes – which has preceded the present age of iron. The point to note is that there is no way in which the two stories can be exactly integrated with one another. To take just one difference: the Pandora story assumes a continuity of population before and after the schismatic act of jar-opening, but the myth of the Races tells us that the break between Gold and Silver was absolute: the earth covered the former (121), and only later did the gods create the latter (127).[28] To accuse Hesiod of inconsistency, of being unable to sustain a logical argument, would be wholly to misunderstand him. He *signals* the fact that the two stories are different. The contrast between past and present is there in each case, but is worked out in different ways, first with an emphasis on guile and concealment, then through a set of

---

27 Doubts about the interpretation of *ekkoruphōsō* (cf. Verdenius 1985 *ad loc.*) do not affect the point I am making.
28 Other incompatibilities have been underlined in Fontenrose 1974, pp. 1–2.

variations on the opposition between fair dealing and aggressive violence. The compatibility of alternatives is basic to Greek mythology. We come back to the question of belief, and of proverbs. 'Look at it this way; or, if you like, look at it *this* way.'

A final, more speculative observation before leaving aetiology. It is entirely plausible, though quite unverifiable, that one of the commonest situations in which adults told myths to children was in answer to the perennial, patience-trying but wonderful question 'Why ... ?' If this were so, we should have another continuity between story-telling to children and story-telling to adults, another way in which listening to stories prepared a child for entry into the mental world of grown-ups.

In dividing up perceived functions into compartments, we have been over-schematic. In fact there was interference and overlap. In particular, a single theme unifies many of the cases which we have classified separately, a theme which is of fundamental relevance to a genuinely contextual reading of Greek mythology.

Some time ago I drew attention to the role of *peithō*, loosely and inadequately translatable as 'persuasion', in a variety of areas of Greek culture.[29] This notion is, I now think, even more significant than my earlier account recognised. *Peithō* is rhetorical, erotic, philosophical, poetical, political. It dwells in the eyes; it rests on the lips. It belongs to kings, to lovers, to those who live in the world of *Realpolitik*. It belongs above all to those who tell stories, and who therefore want to hold an audience by being convincing.

A perfect, idealised example of the power of *peithō* in relation to the telling of a myth can be found in Apollonios' epic about the Argonauts. One of the members of the expedition was Orpheus, peerless singer. To calm a potentially violent quarrel between two of the company, Orpheus takes up his lyre.

> He sang of that past age when earth and sky and sea were knit together in a single mould; how they were sundered after deadly strife; how the stars, the moon, and the travelling sun keep

[29] See Buxton 1982.

faithfully to their stations in the heavens; how mountains rose, and how, together with their Nymphs, the murmuring streams and all four-legged creatures came to be. How, in the beginning, Ophion and Eurynome, daughter of Ocean, governed the world from snow-clad Olympos; how they were forcefully supplanted, Ophion by Kronos, Eurynome by Rhea; of their fall into the waters of Ocean; and how their successors ruled the happy Titan gods when Zeus in his Dictaean cave was still a child, with childish thoughts, before the earthborn Cyclopes had given him the bolt, the thunder and lightning that form his glorious armament today.

The song was finished. His lyre and his celestial voice had ceased together. Yet even so there was no change in the company; the heads of all were still bent forward, their ears intent on the enchanting melody. Such was his charm (*thelktron*) – the music lingered in their hearts . . .[30]

The audience is rapt, charmed, bewitched: the quarrel which prompted the song is not mentioned again.

Such lovingly compelling narrative can in its ultimate form only come from the gods. Hence the old men of Argos who form the all-too-human chorus of Aischylos' *Agamemnon* can only claim to be giving an *authoritative* account of the expedition to Troy in view of the fact that *peithō* has been breathed down upon them from the gods (105). When such backing is absent, *peithō* may fail, as it does in *Iliad* Book 9 when Phoinix unsuccessfully cites the paradigm of Meleager in order to sway Achilles into giving up his steadfast refusal to fight.

The assumption that a central objective of myth-tellers is to achieve *peithō* is confirmed by passages where the framework is what we should describe as philosophical. In several dialogues Plato develops a utilitarian account of the function of myths, based on their perceived role as agents of persuasion.[31] From the *Republic* we learn that the point of the stories to be told in the brave new world is to *peithein* the

---

[30] A. R. 1.496–515; trans. adapted from that by E. V. Rieu.
[31] Cf. Brisson 1982, pp. 144–51.

populace that no citizen has ever been hostile to another.[32] This, doubtless, might be classified as a didactic function for story-telling. But — to echo the point which Strabo made against Eratosthenes — *peithō* can be an agency of teaching precisely because it makes people *want* to listen. As we noted earlier, Gorgias, professionally wedded to persuasion, was keenly aware of the emotional effect of language. Another sophist, Protagoras, in the Platonic dialogue named after him, chose to answer a question about the teachability of excellence by telling a *muthos* rather than by giving a systematic exposition (*logos* — here the 'classic' distinction does hold good); and the reason he gave was that a *muthos* would be *more delightful, chariesteros* (320c). The story he tells is, incidentally, an anthropogony combined with an aetiological account of the distribution of *aidōs* ('restraint', 'inhibition') and *dikē* ('sense of fairness', 'right') in the world, an account couched in terms of the actions of the mythical Titans Prometheus and Epimetheus. Teaching, pleasure and explanation-through-origins meet in a single narrative.

[32] *R.* 378c. In the light of Plato's general philosophical doubts about the exalting of rhetoric, it is no surprise that he ironically underlines the falseness of the means used to achieve the end: *R.* 414b8–c7.

10

Modern perspectives

With hindsight we can see that ancient statements about the functions of myth-telling give at best a partial guide to the complex roles which stories had in Greek society. In discussing the landscape, the family and religion we have already had occasion to go beyond the accounts known to have been given by the original actors, in order to employ perspectives developed by modern anthropology and psychology. In this chapter we shall consider a range of ways in which our explanations of function may justifiably 'go beyond'.

Reflectors and constructors

The first function isolated in the preceding chapter turned on the ancient claim that myths preserve the great deeds of the past. To what extent does this perception remain persuasive for modern observers? At stake are the implications of two metaphors: reflection and construction.

When Schliemann digs at Mycenae and discovers a golden splendour apparently recalling the world of the *Iliad*; when a corner of north-western Turkey yields a site which might be Troy; when the remains of Knossos look decidedly labyrinthine; when Plato's story of the destruction of Atlantis seems to be confirmed by vulcanological evidence about the catastrophic effects of the eruption of Santorini; when, in short, archaeology takes narrative by the hand and leads her out of the shadows; then – and virtually only then – does Greek mythology make the headlines.[1] The passion for reflection is not, of course, confined to the lay public. For the solar mythologists, Greek myths were distorted reflections of an Indo-European past, a time when, it was argued, language referred again and again to natural phenomena. For the historian of religion Martin Nilsson, the same stories reflect the historical reality of Mycenaean times. For the social historian Moses Finley, Homeric epic reflects the social conditions of tenth/ninth-century Greece. These and comparable approaches are variants of the peach theory of story-telling: remove the outer flesh, and the kernel of reality lies revealed.[2] But there is another analogy: with an onion. Strip the layers away, and nothing remains except tears.

The difference between reflection- and construction-oriented criticism can be illustrated from contrasting ways of reading the story of the origins of the Delphic oracle, as narrated by Apollo's priestess at the beginning of Aischylos' *Eumenides*.

> First, in this my prayer, of all the gods I reverence
> Earth, first author of prophecy; then Themis,
> who, legend tells, took possession of this oracle
> next after her mother; thirdly, succeeding
> by consent, not force, there sat
> another Titan, Phoibe, child of Earth;
> and she in turn gave her prerogative
> as a birthday gift to Phoibos [Apollo], her namesake.
>
> (1–8)

[1] The only other sort of case I can think of – and it is so closely related to archaeological–realist explanation as to amount to an extension of it – is when science steps forward to illuminate the truth behind the marvellous. One example is the supposedly real origin of werewolfism in iron-deficiency porphyria (cf. my remarks in Bremmer 1987, p. 77 n. 35). Another is recorded in *Le Figaro* for 5 March 1992: in a five-column feature summarising a paper in the *Bulletin of the American Meteorological Society*, two oceanographers discuss meteorological and geological phenomena which might have caused the Red Sea to part. Back in the Classical world, the Golden Fleece has lured many a scientist: liver damage in sheep is one of the explanations floated (cf. Ryder 1991, Smith and Smith 1992, references which I owe to David Braund).

[2] A variant of the peach theory is the apple theory: 'By "Greek myths", I mean what I take to be the pristine core of the myths, and not necessarily how the myths survive in our day, often more or less adulterated in classical "sources" ...' (Stewart 1977, p. 5).

Many scholars have assumed that the Apolline possession of the Delphic oracle was indeed, in historical actuality, preceded by a period in which the incumbent was Gaia and/or Themis. Recently, however, C. Sourvinou-Inwood has denied the validity of such an assertion.[3] On her reading, even the fact that a lot of Mycenaean female figurines were found at Delphi (though not on the site of the temple of Apollo) cannot be taken to prove that the shrine, supposing there to have been one, was a shrine of *Gaia* – unless, that is, one already assumes the historicity of the myth. For Sourvinou-Inwood, the precedence of Gaia/Themis over Apollo is a 'construction' designed to make a symbolic statement. On this view, the myth 'is structured by, and expresses, the perception that at Delphi the chthonic, dangerous and disorderly aspects of the cosmos have been defeated by, and subordinated to, the celestial guide and law-giver'.[4] Even if tomorrow a spade were to uncover incontrovertible proof of the historical priority of Gaia/Themis over Apollo, this would not damage Sourvinou-Inwood's thesis, for her demonstration, made on the basis of the present state of the evidence, is quite compatible with any *future* discovery of historicity. But in any event, since Sourvinou-Inwood's analysis of the symbolic operation of the Previous Owners myth can stand regardless of the way the historicity question is resolved, it would seem that reflectors and constructors can remain friends: their approaches should be complementary.

So central is the reflection/construction issue to modern treatments of mythology that it is worth exploring with a detailed example. Kadmos' founding of Thebes has the merit of combining an intriguing candidate for reflection with a particularly rich and complex construction.

Kadmos was the brother of Europa. When Zeus fell in love with her and carried her off to Crete, Kadmos and his brothers were sent out by their father to find the girl. Apollodoros provides a no-frills account of what happened next.

> Kadmos came to Delphi to inquire about Europa. The god told
> him not to trouble about Europa, but to be guided by a cow, and

---

[3] In Bremmer 1987, pp. 215–41.   [4] Ibid., pp. 226–7.

to found a city wherever it should fall down from weariness. After receiving such an oracle he journeyed through Phokis; then, falling in with a cow among the herds of Pelagon, he followed it. After crossing Boeotia, it sank down where the city of Thebes now is. Wishing to sacrifice the cow to Athene, he sent some of his companions to draw water from the spring of Ares. But a serpent, which some said was a son of Ares, guarded the spring and destroyed most of those that were sent. In his indignation Kadmos killed the serpent, and on the advice of Athene sowed its teeth. When they were sown there rose from the ground armed men, whom they called Spartoi. These slew each other, some in a chance brawl, some in ignorance. But Pherekydes says that when Kadmos saw armed men growing up out of the ground, he flung stones at them, and they, supposing that they were being pelted by each other, came to blows. However, five of them survived, Echion, Oudaios, Chthonios, Hyperenor and Peloros. [These five become the ancestors of the population of Thebes.][5]

All Greek myths existed in variant versions: that of Kadmos was no exception. Two aspects of the story, in particular, generated a plurality of detail. First, the geographical origin of Kadmos. Several fifth-century sources, including Herodotos and Euripides' *Phoenician Women*, make him a Phoenician; this becomes the commonest version. A variant places his home in Egypt, while a late writer (Nonnos) tries to reconcile the divergences by making Kadmos' *father* the founder of *Egyptian* Thebes.[6] Here is a classic case of equivalents: what the variants agree on is to make Kadmos an outsider, a barbarian. The second principal locus of variants, in both literary and visual representations, is the killing of the serpent and its aftermath. Was the means of slaying stone or sword?[7] Was it Athene who sowed the teeth?[8] Or did Athene and Ares give Kadmos the teeth to sow?[9] Did Kadmos sow *just five* teeth?[10] Nevertheless, in spite of these nuances at the narrative level, it is reasonable to take the bare-bones

[5] Apollod. 3.4.1 (trans. adapted from Frazer 1921).

[6] Kadmos as Egyptian: Hekataios, *FGrH* IIIA, 264 F 6.2. This view was opposed by Pausanias (9.12.2). Nonnos: see Vian 1963, p. 35.   [7] See Vian 1963, p. 112, for refs.

[8] Stesich. *PMG* 195.   [9] Pherekydes, *FGrH* I, 3 F 22a–b.   [10] Hellanikos, *FGrH* I, 4 F 1b.

version given by Apollodoros as something which most myth-tellers of the Classical and Hellenistic periods could have recognised as a persuasive account of the foundation of Thebes.

In antiquity, the part of the story which seemed most intriguing to interpreters – doubtless because it most needed their services – was that involving the Sown Men. A favourite way-in was via etymology. *Spartos*, a 'sown man', could be related to another sense of the root verb *speirō*, namely 'I scatter'. For the fourth-century BC writer of Athenian history Androtion, the *Spartoi* were the companions of Kadmos who came with him from Phoenicia and lived 'scattered' in the world, till Kadmos reassembled them in Thebes.[11] According to Palaiphatos in his *On Incredible Stories* (again fourth century), Thebes once lived under King Drakon ('Serpent'), a son of Ares. When Kadmos had killed Drakon, the latter's sons rose up to avenge him, but, bribed by Kadmos, they *scattered* throughout Greece.[12] Other rationalisations are found. For the mythographer Konon, the Spartoi were warriors who favoured the ambush: to the terrified Boeotians they seemed to be springing fully armed from the soil.[13] Less subtly, Pliny the Elder saw Kadmos as the inventor of stone-quarrying.[14]

Since antiquity until quite recently, the Stone and the Sown have continued to be the focus of attention. The Renaissance mythographer Natale Conti observed in 1567 that the throwing of the stone and the ensuing combat 'signifies the future civil wars between the Thebans'.[15] In his *La Mythologie et les fables expliquées par l'histoire*, written in the second quarter of the eighteenth century, the Abbé Banier regarded the Sown Men as simply 'the people of the country whom Kadmos found a way to bring over to his side'.[16] Far more imaginative was the approach of Banier's contemporary, Giambattista Vico.

> First [Kadmos] slays the great serpent (clears the earth of the great ancient forest). Then he sows the teeth (a fine metaphor for his

---

[11] *FGrH* IIIB, 324 F 60b.   [12] Palaeph. 3 Festa (Teubner edn).
[13] *FGrH* I, 26 F I, ch. XXXVII.   [14] Plin. *NH* 7.195.   [15] *Mythologiae* 9.14.
[16] 6.1.1, ch. 7 (= vol. III, p. 407 of the 1739–40 English trans., reprinted in 1976 by Garland Publishing Inc., New York).

ploughing the first fields of the world with curved pieces of hard wood, which, before the use of iron was discovered, must have served as the teeth of the first ploughs, and teeth they continued to be called). He throws a heavy stone (the hard earth which the clients or *famuli* wished to plough for themselves). From the furrows armed men spring forth (in the heroic contest over the first agrarian law the heroes come forth from their estates to assert their lordship of them, and unite in arms against the plebs, and they fight not among themselves but with the clients that have revolted against them; the furrows signifying the orders in which they unite and thereby give form and stability to the first cities on the basis of arms . . .).[17]

The details of the hypothetical class-struggle are bizarre, Roman-sounding and wholly implausible, but Vico's pyrotechnic mind as usual comes up with something which few of his contemporaries would have dared to think.

We mentioned that two aspects of the tale were particularly productive of variants: the non-Greek origin of Kadmos, and the Stone-and-the-Sown. In modern times the former has generated far the greater scholarly interest, thanks to the availability of a new means of getting purchase on the 'real' origins of Kadmos. With the strides made by classical archaeology in the late nineteenth and twentieth centuries, it seemed to have become possible for the first time to quantify the amount of historical fact preserved in Greek mythology. At the forefront of the process of coming to terms with the implications of the new data was Martin Nilsson. As the title of his book *The Mycenaean Origin of Greek Mythology* (1932) reveals, Nilsson was an extreme reflector, arguing for an overwhelming degree of congruence between sites of archaeologically proven Mycenaean importance and locations prominent in later Greek mythology. But Thebes presented a problem. Keramopoullos' excavations had uncovered the remains of an impressive Mycenaean palace; what was conspicuously absent was evidence of the oriental connection so emphatically present in the myth. Nilsson's answer was

[17] *The New Science* 679 (trans. Bergin and Fisch, revised trans. of 3rd edn, Cornell Univ. Press, 1968).

to remain faithful to his hypothesis, but to refine it. 'Boeotia was an outpost of Mycenaean civilisation', and it was in reminiscence of the assumed fact that 'a Mycenaean tribe really founded a new town here' (p. 125) that Thebes was said to have been founded by an outsider. But why a Phoenician? In Nilsson's view, since the precise origin of the founder had been forgotten, mythology simply stepped in to fill the gap; and it did so at a time when the foreigners with whom the Greeks most often came into contact were Phoenicians (p. 126).

The trouble with this thesis was that it was not just speculative but dependent on special pleading. How, though, on a reflection-oriented view, *could* one deal with Kadmos' oriental connections? In the course of a detailed re-examination of the whole matter, Ruth Edwards assessed the importance of a new, potentially exciting piece of evidence: a collection of oriental seal-stones brought to light in the 1960s as a result of continuing excavations at Thebes.[18] Much has been thought to hinge on the interpretation of this collection. N. G. L. Hammond, a confirmed reflector, wrote with typical confidence of its being 'clearly a royal heirloom brought by Kadmos and lost in the sack by the Epigoni'.[19] Knowing Professor Hammond's luck, one may expect to read at any moment of the discovery in a Bronze Age Theban midden of an inscription in Phoenician characters reading 'Kadmos was here.' But until then it is more prudent to follow the lead of those Mycenaean experts who, like J. T. Hooker, view the seal-find as indeed a collection, but 'perhaps the acquisition of a single traveller *and, therefore, not representative of the imports current at the time*'.[20] There is, in other words, still no external corroboration of an oriental foundation of Thebes.

However, the reflectors' ardour has not been quenched. Martin Bernal's remarkable *Black Athena I*, which combines the revolutionary with the old-fashioned in equal proportions, has a good deal to say

[18] Edwards 1979; see the generally favourable review by Brillante 1984. B. himself gives a balanced account, but is over-sanguine in his view (p. 174) that 'once the mythical and fantastic elements of the narrative have been excluded, we may consider that what is left includes elements which are in part historically genuine' (my translation).

[19] Hammond 1986, p. 654.

[20] Hooker 1976, p. 111. Edwards is more bullish: '[The seals] do at least provide indisputable proof of contact between Thebes and the Semitic orient ...' (p. 134).

about the myths which ascribe an oriental or otherwise barbarian origin to various Greek states. Unfortunately for us, this is exactly the area on which Bernal is at his least convincing, since he takes a naively fundamentalist, no-smoke-without-fire line which rests ultimately on faith: ' ... I am certain that all the legends contain interesting kernels of historical truth ...'[21] Although this aspect of Bernal's case amounts to mere assertion, he has performed the valuable service of linking the story of Kadmos with that of the 'Argive' Danaos, said to have come from Egypt. These tales – along with that of Pelops, who originated in Phrygia or Lydia before migrating to the Peloponnese – do surely pose a common problem.[22] How is it that the Greeks – some Greeks – could retell myths which linked them originally with The Barbarian?

If there is no evidence to confirm the reflection hypothesis, what of an alternative but not necessarily conflicting approach, one which concentrates on the way in which myths *invent* a past, deploying themes and patterns which echo or contrast with the emphases of other narratives told in Greece?

The site of Thebes is favoured, since (1) it has a spring; (2) it was established thanks to the gods (Apollo at Delphi; Athene); (3) the help of the natural world – in the form of a cow – was instrumental in the foundation. But the imposition of order was not achieved without difficulty: (4) the serpent had first to be defeated. In all these respects the narrative is typical of Greek stories *about the founding of colonies at the periphery of the Greek world.*[23] (1) Kyrene was founded near Apollo's spring; the founder of Syracuse, Archias, had been told to choose a site near the spring of Arethusa; the future inhabitants of Aigai were instructed to found their city near the springs of the river Haliakmon; Thourioi was named after the spring of Thouria.[24] (2) It is sufficient to recall the pivotal role of the Delphic oracle in relation to

[21] Bernal 1987, p. 84. Fruit again (cf. n. 2 above).

[22] Hall 1992, p. 184 n. 3: 'B. singularly overlooks Pelops, since the idea that Greece was colonised from the north-west corner of the Asiatic seaboard does not fit the argument of his book.' The comment is brutal but not unjust.

[23] See Vian 1963, pp. 76–82, an exceptionally interesting analysis to which I am much indebted.

[24] Hdt. 4.158, Paus. 5.7.3, schol. Clem. Alex. *Protr.* 11.8, D.S. 12.10.

the colonising movement of Archaic Greece. (3) Among the animals which lead humans towards the sites of colonies are the crow, eagle, dove, lark, wolf, dog, fox, boar, sow, stag, goat, hare, rat and seal.[25] (4) Many foundation-stories incorporate the motif of the overcoming of a powerful animal adversary. Before settling in Rhodes, Phorbas got rid of a plague of poisonous snakes.[26] In order to found Byzantium, Byzas had first to overpower a bull.[27] Seleukos Nikator killed a boar, and with its dripping blood marked the perimeter of the future city of Laodikeia.[28] A serpent was killed at the moment of the foundation of Alexandria, and a canal was named after it.[29]

The crucial difference between the Kadmos story and the colony-narratives which it so closely resembles is, of course, that tales about Kyrene, Syracuse, Thourioi and the rest dealt with *second-order* foundations, established by Greeks from already-existing Greek communities, and populated by Greeks from those states. Kadmos' Thebes was imagined at one stage further back: a *first-order* foundation, a city established *ab ovo* in the heart of Greece, with no ready-made population of immigrants to people it. Hence, generating a population for the city becomes itself a central feature of the story. In this respect the narrative finds its cousins in a quite different group of tales, namely those relating the origins of *non*-colonial states in the Greek homeland, and, more specifically, those states believed to have originated through autochthony. The Attic king Kekrops emerged from the earth, as did his successor Erechtheus; when Aiakos grew up on Aigina, he asked Zeus for settlers, 'and they say Zeus raised humans out of the ground'; the first men to dwell in Phliasia and in Patrai were aboriginal sons of the soil.[30] So too the population of Thebes has an all-important pedigree to add to and complicate its foundation from outside: it comes from the earth.[31]

---

[25] See Vian 1963, p. 78, for full details.   [26] D.S. 5.58.5.

[27] Hesychios of Miletos, *FGrH* IIIB, 390 F 1.11.

[28] Pausanias of Damascus, *FGrH* IIIC, 854 F 10.1, 9 and 10.

[29] Ps.-Callisth. 1.32. Note also that in Pi. *Pyth.* 1, which celebrates Hieron's founding of the city of Aitna, Pindar recalls the defeat by Zeus of the monster Typhon – the prototype of all victories of order over chaos; cf. Trumpf 1958.

[30] Kekrops/Erechtheus: see Parker in Bremmer 1987, p. 193. Aigina: Paus. 2.29.2. Phliasia, Patrai: Paus. 2.12.4, 7.18.2.

[31] On autochthony, see Loraux 1981, index *s.v.* 'autochtonie, autochtone', Rosivach 1987.

Or partly from the earth. For one of the many complexities in the
Kadmos story concerns the interplay between non-sexual and sexual
reproduction. The men who spring from the soil apparently owe
nothing to Kadmos as a literal parent; yet Kadmos is represented as a
sower in a furrow – a standard Greek metaphor for male sexual
activity. To this already ambiguous situation must be added a
biologically *un*remarkable feature of the prehistory of Thebes:
Thebes' population was imagined as descending partly from the
union of Kadmos with his wife Harmonia. The Thebans are
simultaneously the descendants of a human couple and of a monstrous
army. (Pentheus' father was Echion, one of the Sown; but his mother
was Kadmos' all-too-human daughter Agaue.) The symbolic prehistory of the Thebans, inheritors both of the pure warfare of Ares and of
the concord of Harmonia, is riddled with ambiguities.

Not the least of these is the fact that the Thebans are both Greeks
and barbarians. That Thebans themselves should have retold a
narrative incorporating a claim to aboriginality hardly needs exegesis,
for an autochthonous past is regularly presented as something of
which one can be proud.[32] But why retell a story claiming
simultaneously an origin in the East? In 1913 A. W. Gomme argued
that the hero's eastern origins were a fifth-century fiction fuelled by
anti-Theban prejudice; Emily Vermeule subsequently adopted a
similar approach, suggesting that stories of Kadmos as an oriental only
became popular after the notorious Medising of Thebes in the Persian
Wars.[33] Lack of evidence makes it impossible to draw up a balance-
sheet of Theban as against non-Theban versions of the myth. But
there is no reason to ascribe the oriental dimension exclusively to
sources hostile to Thebes. That this feature *could* be exploited in an

[32] Cf. X. *HG* 7.1.23: the Arkadian Lykomedes 'filled the Arkadians with a sense of their own
importance. According to him, only the Arkadians could call the Peloponnese their
fatherland, since they were the only *indigenous* people who lived there . . .' – a version of the
past which is used to back up a real-world refusal to follow the leadership of others. The
Athenians went further: 'We Athenians are the only people never to have left the land we
spring from' (Hdt. 7.161). Thucydides agrees that 'the same people' have always lived in
Attica, but, typically, accounts for this in terms of a sharp-eyed observation about a general
pattern of behaviour: Athens' land is *poor*, and so was not beset by disunity or changes of
population (1.2).

[33] Gomme 1913, discussed at length in Edwards 1979, ch. 4; Vermeule 1971.

anti-Theban way is no guarantee that it necessarily or always had such a thrust. There is, then, room for another approach.

A clue is available in a myth dealing with another aboriginal population, the Leleges, whom tradition associated with a wide range of regions in western, central and southern Greece. Just as the Pelasgians, themselves aboriginals, are linked with the eponymous figure of Pelasgos, so the Leleges find their identity focused in Lelex. But there is a significant discrepancy of view about his origins. For the Spartans and the Leukadians, he was autochthonous. But elsewhere, as at Megara, he was thought of as an outsider – in fact, as a *barbarian* outsider who came from Egypt.[34] This version retains the crucial before/after difference which any tale about origins had to accommodate, while avoiding the politically unwelcome consequences which might follow from a tale which placed the origin of Lelex elsewhere *in Greece*. The equivalence between autochthonous and barbarian origins is persuasively described by C. Calame as follows: 'Oscillating between autochthony and its opposite, territorial exteriority, the Lelegian ruler embodies in any case the otherness that will allow the assertion of identity.'[35]

The case of Kadmos is analogous. Implicit in the notion of the hero's 'barbarian' origins is an idea of otherness which is the equivalent of autochthony. To speak of Thebes as originating both from the earth and from an external source looks like a reduplication, at the level of narrative, of one and the same emphasis on the crucial before/after distinction. Or perhaps we should be more exact and say that Thebes originates *first* from outside and *afterwards* from the earth: there is a *passage* in this 'act' of foundation, which is indeed not complete until the building of the city walls by Amphion and Zethos. There are thus *several* before/after transitions, several 'others' to serve as foils for the assertion of civic identity which the myth narrates.[36]

All this is not to deny that, in changing political circumstances, ascription of barbarian origins might sometimes take on a new and

---

[34] Spartan tradition: Paus. 3.1.1. Leukadian: Str. 7.7.2 (citing Aristotle). Megarian: Paus. 1.39.6, 1.44.3. I am indebted here to Calame's analysis in Bremmer 1987, pp. 156–9.

[35] Calame, *loc. cit.*, p. 158. More on Lelex in Dowden 1992, pp. 81–2.

[36] This point was brought home to me by my students in a Strasbourg research seminar.

potentially negative meaning. But no explanation of the myth which refers *exclusively* to such circumstances can hope to deal with the richly ambiguous structure at the heart of the story. It should not, finally, be forgotten that Kadmos' own ancestry, like that of Danaos, leads eventually back to Greece: to the Argive Inachos.[37] No other foundation myth before the advent of Rome can compare for complexity with this one.

Paradigms (and shoes)

That the narrating of myths was in some sense an exercise in teaching – the second of the actor-functions which we discussed above – is a view which a modern observer may wish to modify and refine, but surely not to reject outright.[38] A number of aspects of ancient myth-telling do indeed look as if they can reasonably be described as educative. We have already considered the socialising function of domestic story-telling. The widespread participation of adolescents in choral singing can legitimately be regarded as representing the continuation of an analogous function. As for myth-telling to adults, there can be no doubt that such a work as Hesiod's *Theogony* had the effect, among other effects, of conveying *information* to hearers/ readers about how to imagine the world as having begun and developed. Tragedy, too, has often been credited with a didactic dimension, even if the exact sense in which a tragic drama may be said to teach is very hard to define.[39] One way in which tragic didacticism has been understood is as a function of the incorporation of moral *exempla*. This is surely an over-simplification, but it at least reminds us of the notion of paradigm, with which no modern account of the functions of myth-telling can dispense. The value of this concept of myth-as-paradigm is that it highlights the question of how far mythology was functionally significant in relation to Greek *behaviour*.

[37] Rightly stressed by Hall 1992, p. 188.

[38] Cf. the more general point made in Halbwachs 1952, p. 296: 'Tout personnage et tout fait historique, dès qu'il pénètre dans cette mémoire [sociale], s'y transpose en un enseignement, en une notion, en un symbole.'

[39] Croally (forthcoming), ch. 1, has some perceptive comments on this.

We begin with the area in which such behavioural integration may be seen at its starkest. Throughout and beyond the period with which we are dealing, stories about the gods and heroes lent shape, authority and legitimation to political rhetoric and political action. Arguments from mythological precedent were often used to bolster a political case. *Because* an Athenian (Triptolemos) had first bestowed the gift of corn on the Peloponnese and initiated Herakles and the Dioskouroi into the Eleusinian mysteries, *therefore* Athens and Sparta should not be enemies.[40] When Pyrrhos of Epiros, claiming descent from Achilles, helped the people of Taras against Rome, he did so on the grounds that the Romans, *qua* Trojans, were natural enemies of the Greeks.[41] There was, to be sure, nothing conclusive about the citing of a precedent from mythology, precisely because the authority of myths was limited. When the Tegeans and the Athenians both adduced mythological arguments to back their right to have precedence at the battle of Plataiai, the claims cancelled each other out: 'Anyway, enough of these exploits of olden days . . .'[42] But in political debate mythology was always potentially available: to be regarded with common sense, and thus, if necessary, with scepticism, yet at the same time able to confer its own peculiar authority.

The frequency with which myths were invoked in life-and-death political situations must enforce the conclusion that they were, or at any rate could be, taken seriously in such contexts. But the involvement of myths-as-paradigms in politics goes further. The re-enactment of myth sometimes became political action. Before crossing to Asia Minor, the Spartan king Agesilaos wanted to sacrifice at Aulis, as Agamemnon had done; the Spartans sought the bones of Orestes; the Athenians brought those of Theseus home from Skyros.[43] In celebration of his victory over the Persians at Eion, the fifth-century Athenian commander Kimon was permitted by his city to dedicate three stone images of Hermes, one of which bore the following inscription:

[40] X. *HG* 6.3.6.

[41] Paus. 1.12.1, with Momigliano 1987, pp. 275–6. On consanguinity in Hellenistic diplomacy, see Musti 1963, Habicht 1985, p. 127.   [42] Hdt. 9.27.

[43] Agesilaos: X. *HG* 3.4.3. Orestes: Hdt. 1.67; cf. Dowden 1992, p. 91. Theseus: Plu. *Thes.* 36, Paus. 3.3.7.

With the Atreidai of old, from this our city, Menestheus led his
men to the holy plain of Troy. Once, said Homer, among well-
armoured Achaeans, he was leader of the fight, best of all who
came. Thus there is nothing unseemly in calling the Athenians
leaders both for their warfare and their courage.

(Plu. *Cim.* 7.5)

The continuity of experience here assumed between Kimon's
campaign and the Trojan War has numerous parallels. Such authority
was especially useful in situations where a person or group felt in need
of legitimation, as, for instance, when political change had to be
justified before a sceptical or hostile public. Already the tyrant
Peisistratos tried to bring himself in from (literally and metaphorically) the periphery to the centre by enacting a drama in which he was
restored to Athens by the goddess Athene in person.[44] Another well-
known example is the use by the Macedonian 'outsiders' of the
precedents offered by Greek mythology, notably through the
identification of Alexander with Achilles;[45] the same ruler 'imitated'
Herakles, 'envied' Perseus and 'followed in the footsteps' of
Dionysos.[46] Later crises too called forth political behaviour couched
in the language of mythology. 'After his triumph over Jugurtha and
the Cimbri and the Teutones, [Marius] would always drink from a
kantharos, because Dionysos was supposed to have used such a vessel
on his triumphal procession through Asia to India. He wanted in this
way, with each draught of wine, to compare his own victories with
those of the god.'[47] This in turn pales into insignificance beside the
conduct of Mark Antony, whose role-playing as Bacchus eventually
seemed to amount to near self-identification – a posture deliberately
countered by Octavian/Augustus' own cultivation of Apollo.[48]
Here, on the face of it, is one respect in which Calame's warning about
the dangers of putting 'Greek mythology' on all fours with 'Roman
mythology' looks unduly sceptical: the political use of mythical

[44] Hdt. 1.60.
[45] On Alexander/Achilles, see Mossman 1988. Cf. Nilsson 1951, pp. 101–5, on Philip.
[46] Plu. *Mor.* 332a–b.   [47] Val. Max. 3.6.6, quoted by Zanker 1988, p. 8.
[48] See Zanker 1988, pp. 46–53.

paradigms seems to be shared by both cultures. Yet even in this case it must be remembered that the Romans were quite consciously redeploying *Greek* myths, with all the varying connotations which Greekness had for different groups of Romans at different periods.[49]

The habit of mind revealed by the cases of Peisistratos and Kimon informed other areas of Greek experience. Ritual is a notable example. In Tegea, at the feast of Apollo the Lord of Streets, a priestess of Artemis ceremonially chased someone as if she were Artemis chasing Leimon (a mythical murderer shot by the goddess).[50] At Thespiai, the virgin priestess who served at Herakles' sanctuary until she died was re-enacting the precedent of the fiftieth daughter of Thestios, who refused the hero what her forty-nine sisters had granted him.[51] In Thebes, pederastic lovers traditionally took mutual vows at the tomb of Iolaos, who fought shoulder to shoulder with Herakles and so provided a role-model for their own behaviour.[52] Again, there is evidence to suggest that real-life Greek weddings might make paradigmatic allusion to the weddings of mythology.[53]

In all these instances, myths function like shoes: you step into them if they fit. Old shoes, like traditions that are (or seem) ancient, are usually the ones you feel most comfortable with. But, just now and again, a new occasion may require the use of something more appropriate. Furthermore, at one and the same time an individual may possess several pairs of shoes, to be worn in different circumstances. So it is with myths. At one moment you might have seen yourself or those close to you as Klytaimestra or Jason, at another as Penelope or Hektor. Myths provided powerful, authoritative schemata in terms of which the Greeks could see. But their authority was limited, like that of proverbs. Too many cooks . . .

In spite of the confidence with which mythical precedents were often invoked, seeing one thing or person 'as' another was far from being a

---

49 An expert on Roman painting speaks of 'intellectual snobbery' and of 'a desire on the part of Roman patrons to surround themselves with an aura of great Greek art' (Ling 1991, p. 5). This was certainly one Roman response, though not the only one.

50 Paus. 8.53.3.   51 Paus. 9.27.6.   52 Plu. *Pel.* 18.

53 Seaford 1987, p. 109, with n. 38.

straightforward matter; especially when that other belonged to the world of mythology. When a link is asserted with the world of gods and heroes, authority, albeit limited and potentially questionable authority, is conferred. But the nature of this paradigmatic authority is complex.

Sometimes, as in certain poems by Pindar, the reader is confronted with an unambiguous distinction between mythical conduct to be emulated and that to be shunned: even the enormously intricate *Pythian* 1 develops a series of sharp *oppositions* between the orderly, harmonious and liquid (Zeus, Apollo, Muses, Hieron, Greeks) and the chaotic, furious and fiery (Typhon, barbarians). But far more frequently we encounter mythical characters and situations whose exemplariness in any *moral* sense is extremely dubious. To look no further than Homer: any attempt to place Achilles in moral terms is a highly complex matter; the same goes for an evaluation of Penelope's intention to remarry or of Odysseus' vengeance on the suitors, both of which are rendered problematic by the wholly exceptional status of a woman whose husband is at once known (by some) to be alive, and yet 'bound' to be dead. The point could be extended to cover the behaviour of any number of heroes, starting with Herakles. And of course in tragedy expression is given to the rich moral ambiguities latent in the bare narratives about some of the heroes. If myths can be said to constitute or contain paradigms, then this must, in most cases, be for some other reason than that they offer straightforwardly protreptic or dissuasive patterns for conduct.

Imagery gives us a useful way into the problem. Many Athenian vases represent wedding scenes. A common type involves the wedding procession of Peleus and Thetis, mortal hero and divinity, their union blessed by the presence of gods and goddesses. In the words of a recent interpreter, this mythical procession 'would long serve as a paradigm' for real weddings.[54] Such images form part of a much wider series of representations, many of them on the *lebēs gamikos* or the *loutrophoros*, vessels deployed in real-life wedding ceremonies. These images constituted a model for the unions of

---

[54] Lissarrague in Schmitt Pantel 1991, p. 165.

ordinary life. Typically, aspects of a given image would create a distance from the world of the real–life Greek observer, for instance through the (from the ancient observer's point of view) anachronistic use of a chariot to transport the bridal couple to the groom's house, or through the visible presence of divinities such as Erotes and Nikai, graphically confirming the attendance of Desire and Successful Accomplishment upon the happy pair.[55] Such representations bring out the fundamental ideology of marriage – for example, its being in a quite literal sense a passage – and in so doing express what a human wedding should ideally be like.

But this is by no means the only sort of relationship to obtain between image and ordinary life. Many of the scenes painted on vessels designed for use at a *symposion* seem far from ideal in the sense just discussed. The Greek drinker was frequently confronted with images of conduct in downright opposition to that usually considered proper in the sympotic context. Satyrs who ignore the custom of mixing their wine with water, drunken Centaurs who violently disrupt a respectable feast: the limits of allowable behaviour are, apparently, being explored through the depiction of its antithesis. But are matters in fact so simple and so prim? Is the rampant sexuality of the satyr really something which the male reveller would wish to avoid? Could it not (also?) be a condition to which he might aspire? (Has no male Member of Parliament ever made a speech condemning pornography, only to buy it the same evening on his way back to his London flat?) The reading of such images of excess has to be provisional, being peculiarly susceptible to the qualification that, for different viewers/users on different occasions, and even in different moods, the same image might be perceived in very different ways.

Mapping

Our third observer-function is related to the notion of paradigm, but deserves to be looked at separately. That it can be seen to stand out in relief is principally due to the work of anthropologists, who have for

[55] Lissarrague (as in n. 54) figs. 6, 7, 8 and 9 on pp. 170–7.

some time concerned themselves with the way in which, in the societies which they visit and study, the world is classified – mapped – in terms of empirical objects and categories (gold, fox, pool; rotten, upstream), objects and categories which are characteristically deployed in myths and rituals. The most influential, or at least the most often invoked, writer here is Claude Lévi-Strauss, whose *Le Totémisme aujourd'hui*, *La Pensée sauvage* and *Mythologiques* offered a series of virtuoso demonstrations of the operation of the 'science of the concrete'. Times change, and many would now be happier to talk of natures and cultures rather than Nature and Culture. Nevertheless, the general point – that contrasts within a series of empirical objects/categories can constitute a sophisticated means of dividing up and describing the world – this point unquestionably stands; and it is highly pertinent to the world of ancient Greece.[56]

Food provides numerous symbolic operators in Greek stories.[57] Nowhere is this clearer than in the *Odyssey*.[58] Entertaining the guest with culturally appropriate nourishment is the mark of good hosts like Alkinoos and Menelaos. By contrast, the monstrous Laistrygonians eat people, as do Skylla and the Cyclops Polyphemos. The lotus-eaters are non-violent, but still abnormal: eating lotus makes a sailor forget his *nostos*, 'return', and this is unnatural. In other Greek tales, food again marks distinctions between centre and periphery, Greek and non-Greek, wild and civilised. The Arkadians, who existed before the moon, eat acorns, as befits a people perceived (at least by others) as marginal.[59] But if acorns are on the periphery, what is in the middle? The answer is: sacrificial meat, and bread.[60] In Hesiod's *Theogony*, man is the sacrificer: to follow the procedures inaugurated by Prometheus' founding act is to distinguish oneself simultaneously from the gods and from the beasts. The same poet's *Works and Days* portrays man as a creature whose life is dominated by working to

[56] Needless to say, this is neither to accept that Greek thought should to this extent be regarded as primitive, nor to accept that a division between primitive and (say) 'hot' or 'civilised' or 'Western', is an analytically useful one.

[57] A valuable collection of the *Realien* of 'die Kultur des Essens und Trinkens' in the Hellenistic period can be found in Schneider 1967–9, II, pp. 42–69.

[58] Vidal-Naquet's paper, available in Gordon 1981, pp. 80–94, is fundamental.

[59] See Borgeaud 1988, pp. 7, 14–15.   [60] Cf. Hom. *Od.* 9.89.

grow corn: the word *bios* is used to mean 'one's daily bread' as well as 'life' (42). By contrast, animals, who are said to have no sense of what is right, eat each other (276ff.).

However, cannibalism between humans was certainly not unthinkable: in myth, it was often thought.[61] Two well-known tales link it with a particular sort of sexual transgression. Thyestes committed adultery with his brother's wife, thus getting 'too close'; his punishment consisted of his being unwittingly led to get too close to his own son, by eating him. Tereus also approached, in kinship terms, too close, by raping his wife's sister: once more, what followed was involuntary cannibalism of his son. Excess of another kind figures in the myth of Tydeus. His uncontrollable lust for war led him to eat the brains of a slain foe, an act at once milder than those of Thyestes and Tereus (it is an enemy, not a son, who is consumed) and graver (because intentional). Athene's punishment was to withhold the immortality she had planned for him.[62] Nor, of course, do such themes respect the territorial integrity of myth. Pausanias observes that the invading Gauls ate the flesh of their enemies' babies, and drank their blood (10.22.2). Thucydides records a less ghoulish but equally interesting case. The Eurytanians, the largest tribe in Aitolia, were not (unlike the Gauls) beyond the fringe, so the symbolism applied to them is more moderate: 'they speak a language which is the least intelligible [sc. of all the Aitolians] and eat their meat raw' (3.94).

Drink is another classic marker of difference, both in mythical texts and in authors conventionally classified as historians. Homer's Polyphemos drinks neat milk (9.297) as well as neat wine: doubly uncivilised. Herodotos' Scythians drink mares' milk (4.2), while Plato notes that Scythians and Thracians take no water with their wine (*Lg.* 637e). One explanation for the out-of-mindedness of Kleomenes was that he acquired the habit of drinking his wine Scythian fashion (6.84).[63] Herodotos gives this as an alternative to another explanation of the Spartan king's madness, namely that it was punishment for sacrilege – two equivalent excesses.

[61] In the tales told by the Kabyle of Algeria, ogres and ogresses normally eat human flesh. But once they consume couscous – symbol of culture – they can no longer remain anthropophagous. See Lacoste-Dujardin 1970, p. 248.   [62] Apollod. 3.6.8.
[63] On wine, see also Graf 1980. A good Greek mixes wine and water: Ath. 431d–e.

Animals are another powerful tool for mapping. The complex reality of species is pared down to a few salient characteristics, which are used, in turn, to point to features of the world of human culture. Snakes are favourite participants in narratives where the boundaries between above and below, life and death, are explored or called into question. When a serpent lays a special herb upon the corpse of its fellow and immediately restores it to life, the act provides a model for the seer Polyidos to follow in order to revive Glaukos, son of Minos.[64] Wolves, savage outsiders, figure in tales of banishment and transgression: when Lykaon goes beyond the boundary of acceptable human conduct by sacrificing a child on Zeus's altar, he is turned into a wolf.[65] Dogs are both like and unlike wolves, being both wild and domesticated. Their potential as vicious predators is clear from the story of Aktaion, ripped to death by his own hounds, and from the fact that the ultimate dishonour with which a heroic corpse can be threatened is consumption by dogs (and birds).[66]

Horses too are ambiguous, though differently so. Silent and compliant in countless journeys and battles involving chariots, they occasionally strike back. The downfall of Hippolytos ('he who is torn apart by horses') implicates them only instrumentally, since the prime mover of the hero's death is the monstrous bull from the sea, sent by Poseidon in response to the curse invoked by Hippolytos' father Theseus. But the objects of one of Herakles' Labours, the man-eating mares of Diomedes, represent a more extreme expression of the potential of horses for wildness, as do the animals who killed Lykourgos for denying Dionysos: 'On hearing this, the Edonians led him to Mount Pangaion and bound him, and there by the will of Dionysos he died, destroyed by horses.'[67] The motif is equivalent to that found in accounts of the deaths of Pentheus and Orpheus: on mountains horses, like women, are outsiders.

From the bee that builds a honeycomb in the mouth of the sleeping poet Pindar, to the joyous dolphins into whose form Dionysos changes the pirates who would bind him, Greek myths make use of the animal series, a vocabulary of terms for dividing up and thinking

---

[64] Apollod. 3.3. See Bodson 1978, pp. 68ff.
[65] See Burkert 1983, pp. 84–93, and the author's chapter in Bremmer 1987, pp. 60–79.
[66] See Redfield 1975, index *s.v.* 'dogs'.   [67] Apollod. 3.5.1 (trans. Frazer 1921).

about the world.[68] Here, once more, no barrier can be erected
between mythical and other narratives. Herodotos reports a tale
about horses devouring snakes in the outer part of the city of Sardis, an
unnatural event not unnaturally interpreted as a portent (1.78). The
diviners announce that snakes signify dwellers-in-the-land, while the
horse 'is' an invader. Is this history or myth? Instead of replying to the
question, we may more profitably note that the autochthonous
quality of snakes figures also in stories of gods and heroes. Kekrops,
the first king of Athens, emerged from the earth but remained a snake
below the waist;[69] a similar association continued in connection with
the later king(s) Erechtheus/Erichthonios, in whose precinct dwelt a
protecting, sacred snake. The animal series pervades the whole fabric
of Greek story-telling. Homeric similes and Homeric insults ('You
drunkard, with a dog's eyes and a deer's heart', *Il.* 1.225); Semonides'
poetic categorisation of women (the bee, the cat, the monkey[70]);
behaviour towards animals varying according to whether they are to
be sacrificed and eaten, or hunted: all this is a complex and interrelated
network of attitude and action.

It is not difficult to multiply instances of the phenomenon we are
examining. Plants constituted another series between whose terms the
significant contrasts served to make symbolic statements about the
social world. The menacing luxuriousness of Dionysiac ivy runs
through Euripides' *Bakchai*.[71] Several myths, from the downfall of
Pentheus, to Theseus' combat with Sinis the Pine-bender, to the
ferocity of Centaurs, link the pine with wildness and aggressive
violence (Plate 17). The cultural centrality of the olive matches the
marginality of the acorn.[72] Metals, too: the Hesiodic tale of
mankind's prehistory depends on a set of contrasts between gold,
silver, bronze and iron. Rather than extending the list, however, it
will be more useful to ask just what is entailed in the process which I
have called 'mapping'.

[68] Bee: *Life* of Pindar, 2 (in Lefkowitz 1981b, p. 156), cf. Waszink 1974. Dolphins: see the *Homeric Hymn* to Dionysos.

[69] Cf. Parker in Bremmer 1987, p. 193: 'Having emerged from the earth, he still in part resembled the creature that slips to and fro between the upper and lower worlds.'

[70] On monkeys, see Vegetti 1983a, pp. 59–70.   [71] Cf. Gould 1987.

[72] On the olive, see Detienne 1973.

17. Trees, too, can be good to think with. The mountain pine is frequently associated with aggressive violence. Here a branch is wielded by a Centaur (who also has a rock at the ready). (Late-sixth-century red-figure cup.)

In none of our examples is the explicit *point* of the story to map. Hesiod's myth of the Races is not an exercise in formal metallurgical classification; rather, metals are used to make statements about the moral world. Again, the Hesiodic fable of the Hawk and the Nightingale is not a piece of zoological taxonomy, but a use of animals to think about power politics. Here, perhaps, is the beginning of a workable distinction between two categories sometimes referred to as 'traditional' and 'scientific'. In the former, animals (plants, metals ...) are good to think *with*; in the latter, they are thought *about*. We shall return to this issue in due course.

Every religion implies a system of classification. The classificatory function of Greek myth must be understood within the wider framework of Greek belief and practice relating to the sacred. Sacrifice, the fundamental ritual act, involved the drawing of a number of crucial distinctions, including, as we have said, that between domesticated animals (from which group sacrificial beasts were normally taken) and wild animals (for hunting).[73] The pervasive concept of *miasma* ('pollution') depended on a network of differentiations marking off situations of religious danger from situations of religious safety, and governing the rules for passing from one of these states to the other.[74] The very existence of a sanctuary – *temenos*, a strictly delimited portion of land consecrated to the god or gods worshipped there – implies the separation of that which was *hieron* ('sacred') from that which was profane. The vast range of cults in honour of individual deities rests on a set of demarcations within the sphere of divine power: the worshipper has somehow to keep all the plates spinning.

Within such a framework, myths often fulfil the role of pathfinders, testing out boundaries, imagining the consequences of interferences between categories. The three areas just mentioned – sacrifice, pollution, the power of divinities – exemplify the point. The nature and classificatory implications of sacrifice are tried out in several stories. In *Agamemnon* one of the central themes is that of perverted sacrifice: the sacrifice of the wrong sort of creature in the wrong way.[75] Quite a different tone is set by the *Homeric Hymn to Hermes*, in which the recently born god in whose honour the work is composed undertakes a sacrifice which is a remarkable distortion of

---

[73] Just occasionally, wild animals might be sacrificed; see Paus. 7.18.12, on the festival of Artemis Laphria at Patrai.   [74] Discussion must start from Parker 1983.

[75] See Zeitlin 1965.

normal sacrifice by humans – as it must be, since it is a sacrifice by a god to the gods. Here again it is the sense of anomaly which predominates, an anomaly through which the norm is explored.

The best-known boundary-dispute in the matter of pollution must be that dramatised in Aischylos' *Eumenides*, which examines the extreme case of one who has committed a crime, who has been declared free of the consequent pollution by Apollo, and who yet, because of the heinousness of the deed, continues to be persecuted by the divinities charged with upholding ties between kin. At issue here are not only the location of the boundary of religious danger, but also the limits of the rights and duties of the divinities in question: Apollo, the Furies, even Athene herself.

Other demarcations between divinities frequently come into prominence in mythology. The Sarpedon episode in the *Iliad* highlights both the mutually defining powers of Zeus and Hera, and the apparent, ultimate restriction even on the power of Zeus, limited by Moira (Fate, Portion, i.e. what one is allotted).[76] In Euripides' *Hippolytos*, Aphrodite and Artemis are the two plates, one of which the imprudent hero catastrophically fails to keep spinning. No less unwise are the Minyads, too fond of work to have time for Dionysos; while the children of Eumelos of Kos honour only Earth, provoking the retributive intervention of Artemis, Hermes and Athene.[77]

As a final example of the interest which myths take in classification, and specifically in the boundaries between classes, we may mention the notion of monstrosity.[78]

A monster is chaotic, conforming to no existing class. As the case of the benevolent Centaur Cheiron shows (Plate 18), monsters are not necessarily characterised by the savage violence of a Minotaur or a Medusa. But a monster is always by definition an outsider. The theme of combat with monsters is common enough: Perseus and Medusa, Bellerophon and Chimaira, Herakles and ... We have already seen how battles between the heroic Lapiths and the monstrous Centaurs

---

[76] And yet . . . Zeus claims that he *could* save Sarpedon – and Hera does not deny it (16.443). Few passages better illustrate the complexity of the Iliadic notion(s) of fate.

[77] Ant. Lib. 10 and 15.   [78] NB Farkas, Harper and Harrison 1987.

18. The friendly Centaur: Cheiron receives Achilles from his father Peleus. (Early-fifth-century *stamnos*.)

were capable of symbolising a much broader contrast between the civilised and the savage. But the two categories are not always clearly distinguishable: in *Women of Trachis* Sophokles depicts a Herakles who shares the same wild violence exhibited by his foe, the Centaur Nessos. As often, myths focus on the interference between categories.

A revealing aspect of monstrosity, and one which introduces another facet of mythological mapping, is the connection with genealogy. Monsters are nearly always the product of a liaison which is itself abnormal. Centaurs are the offspring of a union between the rash Ixion, would-be lover of Hera, and a cloud fabricated by Zeus. When the father of the gods shed his seed on the ground while asleep, the result was a monstrous creature called Agdistis, endowed with both male and female genitals.[79] Not surprisingly, unions *between* monsters generate that which is abnormal: Echidna and Typhon had a

[79] Paus. 7.17.5.

most remarkable brood, including the Hydra and Kerberos.[80] Such logic is a function of the fact that a major feature of the symbolism of mythological genealogies is the expression of relationship. When Zeus unites with Themis (Due Order) in orthodox fashion, the result is the birth of Eunomia, Dike and Eirene (Good Order, Right, Peace).[81]

Before leaving the topic of symbolic cartography, it is important to emphasise that the degree to which Greek mythology provided a *systematic* map must not be exaggerated. A crucial aspect of the classification to be found in myths is incompleteness. Because Greek mythology is an open, context-driven set of utterances, the maps which it draws do not always match one another. It is only – or so it has been argued – with the arrival of those whom we call scientists and philosophers that explicit reflection begins to occur on the implicit classifications of mythology. With this most difficult of issues we reach the next stage in our discussion.

Explanation

One of the functions ascribed to myths by the actors was, as we saw, that of aetiology. Most modern observers agree that explanation should be regarded as an important aspect of the function of myths. But in what sense do myths explain? *What* do they explain? What, if anything, is characteristic about the kinds of explanation to be found in myths? Is it possible that an understanding of these kinds of explanation could contribute towards an eventual, satisfactory demarcation of the category 'myth'?

In a series of studies, beginning with *Polarity and Analogy* and culminating in *The Revolutions of Wisdom*, G. E. R. Lloyd has explored the interface in ancient Greece between, on the one hand, philosophy and science, and, on the other hand, the pre-scientific, 'traditional' forerunners of the theories and practices of those disciplines.[82] It is impossible to do justice here to this sequence of

---

[80] Hes. *Th.* 306ff.   [81] Hes. *Th.* 902.   [82] Lloyd 1966, 1979, 1983, 1987, cf. also 1990.

works, which combines a daring breadth of reference to anthropology and the history of scientific method with scrupulous attention to
argumentation and the definition of issues.[83] Lloyd is not directly
concerned with the analysis of mythological narratives, but rather
with various differentiations in which the concept of myth may be
involved. The question to which he repeatedly addresses himself,
with reference to areas as diverse as logic, pharmacology and
astronomy, is: in exactly what terms was the theory and practice of
scientific method differentiated from non- or pre-scientific modes of
apprehending and explaining the world? Confronting this problem
entails the repeated juxtaposition of notions such as 'reason' and
'rational' with 'myth', 'magic' and 'religion'. It should be stressed that
Lloyd does not argue – indeed, he emphatically (and of course rightly)
denies – that Greek culture witnessed the *replacement* of myth by
science, by philosophy, or by reason; the evidence already assembled
by Dodds, for example in relation to magical papyri, is sufficient to
demonstrate the continued presence of 'irrational' elements in Greek
life long after the advent of philosophy.[84] Rather, Lloyd is interested
in exploring what is at stake within what *we* call the natural and life
sciences, at certain crucial periods, e.g. the sixth–fourth centuries BC,
in relation to the undeniable growth of innovative theories and new
practical techniques.

   The key contrast which permeates Lloyd's analysis is that between
the explicit and the implicit. Introducing a reprinted version of his
own article on 'Right and left in Greek philosophy', he states that an
aspect of his earlier argument which should have been presented with
even greater emphasis was the view that for the Greeks the
assumption of a basic right/left polarity became 'the object of analysis
and criticism'; he refers to 'this self-consciousness, the *explicit analysis
of their own conceptual schemata and of the logic they presuppose*'.[85]
That, in a nutshell, is already the programme of *Polarity and Analogy*: a
demonstration of the development of explicit reflection upon two
basic modes of thought. The same point recurs in *Magic, Reason and*

---

[83] The scholarship deployed is formidable, even at times oppressive: *The Revolutions of Wisdom*
    contains an 82-page bibliography.
[84] Dodds 1951, ch. 6 and Appendix II, cf. Lloyd 1979, p. 5.   [85] Lloyd 1991, p. 30.

Experience, where Lloyd sets explicit and generalised ideas about nature and causation against earlier implicit assumptions.[86] Clearer still, and, incidentally, indicative of Lloyd's alertness to the importance of discriminating between disciplines, is this, from *Science, Folklore and Ideology*: 'Many of the problems correspond to what are already implicit concerns in popular or traditional thought (though this is less true of physiology or of embryology than of zoological taxonomy). But they had to be brought out into the open, made explicit and become the subject matter of deliberate enquiry.'[87]

The relevance of the implicit/explicit distinction for the concept of myth is spelled out in a passage at the beginning of *The Revolutions of Wisdom*:

> myth is not, and does not aim to be, explicitly systematic and coherent. I am not denying, of course, the findings of structuralism, which has decoded remarkably coherent messages in groups of myths, even whole mythologies. But those messages, as structuralism itself insists, remain implicit, below the surface. On the surface, the intelligibility provided by myth is metaphorical, both in the sense that it is of the nature of metaphor and in the sense that it is a qualified intelligibility ... To be effective, myth must work below the surface, while on the surface the appearance is often of inconsistencies, of a lack of coherent unity.[88]

Basic to Lloyd's position is the view that the meaning of myths is to be found below their relatively disorganised surface. As we have seen, the — itself metaphorical — distinction between surface and deep structure has characterised many approaches to myth; as we have also seen, this distinction is indeed a convenient way of representing some of the regularities-within-variety that the narratives exhibit. More individual, perhaps — at least, more in need of analysis — is Lloyd's claim that myths provide only a 'qualified intelligibility', like metaphors, on the grounds that the messages of mythology remain implicit. How far is this true?

We must first ask: implicit in relation to what? Suppose we begin

[86] Lloyd 1979, p. 265.   [87] Lloyd 1983, p. 217.
[88] Lloyd 1987, pp. 4–5, cf. Lloyd 1990, e.g. p. 8.

with the area discussed by Lloyd. He is surely right that myths show little concern with the kind of explicit and self-conscious generalisation which he identifies as characteristic of science. In the matter of zoological taxonomy, for instance, while myths repeatedly use monstrosity as a theme of their narratives, such stories do not occupy themselves with the *definition* of what it is to be monstrous, at least in the sense of 'definition' which would be recognised by a modern philosopher of science. The same is true of, for example, the motif of madness. While the state of being out of one's proper mind may be an important dimension of the plots of Sophokles' *Ajax* and Euripides' *Herakles* and *Bakchai*, it could not be said that these works explicitly tackle the moral-philosophical *definition* of what it is to be mad.

However, the essential implicitness of myth is not borne out in some other respects. For example, earlier we found it appropriate to speak of one possible relationship between myths and rites as deriving from the way that myths *spell out* the implications of their ritual counterparts, by taking literally that which ritual presents as metaphor, e.g. the killing as opposed to the expulsion of the scapegoat. Again, we saw that one operation which *some* myths may be seen as performing is a paring down, a clarification of the data of experience in such a way as to render ambiguity, for instance, more visible. In that way, too, myths can be seen as agents of *explicitness*. Thirdly, as was argued in our discussion of the mythical representation of women, there are good reasons for believing that myths are bringing to the surface aspects of social life which are otherwise concealed, masked or repressed. Here, once more, it looks as if myths make for *explicitness*.

Again, particularly in regard to moral and political issues, myths do indeed seem to be able to tackle certain questions as direct objects of their 'thought' at the surface ('explicit') level. The ethical dilemmas dramatised in the choices of Antigone or Orestes are spelled out in detail, sometimes in general as well as specific terms (witness the debate between Kreon and Antigone in Sophokles' play). While mythical animals and plants are mostly to be interpreted as good to think *with*, relationships within the *oikos* and the *polis*, and the conflicts and tensions generated by competing claims upon the individual, do seem to be good to think *about*, even if the thinking is not done in the systematic terms with which at least *some* later moral philosophers would acknowledge an affinity.

At this point it will be relevant to develop another aspect of Lloyd's view of mythology, though not quite in the direction which he envisages. This concerns his phrase 'qualified intelligibility'. How far, in fact, do myths give explanations which are 'satisfactory' – at least in the terms posed by the myths themselves – and how far do they contain gaps and contradictions?

In many cases, Greek myths lay out the causality and motivation of the events they narrate in a way which seems transparent and problem-free. An example would be the common sequence of transgression leading to retribution, such as that found in Dionysos' prologue at the beginning of Euripides' *Bakchai*. Semele's sisters have denied the divinity of Dionysos: *'therefore (toigar)'*, says the god, 'I have driven them from their homes in madness . . .' (32). Pentheus is 'fighting against that which is divine': *'because of which (hōn hounek')*, I shall reveal my divinity to him and to all the Thebans' (47–8). Similarly clear is Apollodoros' account of the events surrounding the building of Troy. Apollo and Poseidon fortified it for the king, Laomedon. But he refused to pay their wages: *'therefore (dia touto)* Apollo sent a plague and Poseidon a sea monster' (2.5.9). Such a sequence poses few interpretative problems. It is governed by the pervasive Greek assumption of the central role played by reciprocity in human affairs, a notion underpinning numerous customs and beliefs, such as the practice of hospitality and the moral imperative sometimes abbreviated to 'help friends and harm enemies'.[89]

However, such examples of clear causation far from exhaust the evidence. Maurice Bloch, after an analysis of two Malagasy myths, speaks of 'the wealth of mythology which . . . is not a matter of giving us lessons about simple and resolved matters but is a continuing speculation on problems which are irresolvable'.[90] This is true of Greece also. One of the functions of Greek myths is to probe the

[89] On this imperative, see Blundell 1989.   [90] Bloch 1989, p. 186.

interstices of Greek culture, its ambiguities and paradoxes, its conflicts and contradictions. At the end of Euripides' *Elektra* (1244), Kastor announces *ex machina* that, while what Klytaimestra has suffered – being murdered – is just, what Orestes has done in murdering her is *not* just. Myths focus on extreme dilemmas, which expose in the starkest terms the competing claims which may present themselves to an individual. Shall I be a deserter, or a killer of my daughter? Kill my mother, or fail to avenge my father? Myths explore: the nature of Greekness (the *Odyssey*) and of heroic worth (the *Iliad*), the paradoxes of social marginality (*Iphigeneia in Tauris*), the pressures on a wronged but hardly innocent wife and mother (*Medea*).

Nor is it just that mythical explorations are often extreme and problem-filled. The presentation of issues is often actually *baffling*, especially when characters in the narratives are confronted with the uncanny. I argued above that this phenomenon is typical of tragedy, as in the case of the ineradicable obscurity surrounding the anger of Artemis and the omen of the eagles' feast in Aischylos' *Agamemnon*.[91] But it is found outside tragedy also, for example in the episode in Hesiod's *Works and Days* dealing with the confining of Hope within Pandora's jar.

Scholars continue to debate the logic behind this narrative, especially the significance of the fact that Hope (or Expectation, an alternative and possibly preferable translation) is originally kept in the jar along with (other?) evils. Is Hope/Expectation, then, a good or a bad thing? Does its remaining in the jar mean that human beings have it (in that it is stored for their use) or that they do not (in that it is imprisoned)? The permutations of these and other options, together with countless refinements on them, have elicited endless debate.[92] If only Hesiod had had the grace to be like the late fabulist Babrios, whose version of the tale (58) is simplicity itself: Hope is a good thing, and was originally kept within the jar *along with a lot of other good things*. Opening the jar means that the good things fly away, except for Hope, the one good which remains at humanity's disposal. The Hesiodic version has none of this limpidity.[93] But this does not make

[91] See above, p. 151.   [92] See Verdenius 1985, pp. 66–71.
[93] See e.g. Rudhardt 1986, who also discusses the contrast with Babrios.

it automatically confused, nothing but a botched amalgam of earlier, simpler and more comprehensible accounts. On the contrary, it could be argued that it is precisely the puzzling, provocative ambiguity of some myths – including this one – which is at the heart of their power and their persistence. Because myths can symbolically confront experience in a way which cannot be simply superseded by explicit logical or scientific reasoning, their power to convince *even while remaining baffling* remained and remains one of the most enduring facts about them. Furthermore, if this view is tenable – the view, that is, that part of the *point* of some myths is to be 'unsatisfactory' – then it represents, I think, a distinctively modern perception of the working of mythology, part of the massive emphasis currently placed on the ambiguity of cultural phenomena.[94]

Psychology, emotion and (again) pluralism

The one actor-function which we have not so far picked up in relation to modern perceptions is that dealing with the arousal of feelings. The power of Greek myths to move modern readers/audiences is unquestionable: the stories still retain the capacity to shock, even after three millennia of de- and re-contextualisation. True, this is not directly relevant to the question of function in *ancient* contexts. However, if we bear in mind the evidence that myth-telling not only did but was expected to affect feelings – by, for example, stirring up pity and fear (to look no further than Aristotle's famous formulation) – then it becomes impossible to resist the conclusion that emotional as well as cognitive functions have to be taken into account. Or better – since the opposition between intellect and emotion is as good as vacuous in relation to stories – we should recognise that myths were able to shape perceptions *precisely in virtue of their power to move.*

But how is this power to be characterised? I would make one general point, so obvious that it is sometimes overlooked. Especially in the case of the greatest works of ancient literature and art, a critical analysis which described their effects as *simple* would – or at any rate

---

[94] Cf. the superlative Introduction to Versnel 1990.

should – be found unconvincing. This is as true of the *Iliad* and the *Oresteia* as it is of the *Divine Comedy* and *The Brothers Karamazov*. (As for Shakespeare, Dover Wilson regarded the meaning of *King Lear* as coincident with the meaning of the universe. He was over-stating his case, but I can see what he meant.[95]) *A fortiori*, the range of effects produced by a *combination* of works – say, the *Homeric Hymn to Hermes*, Euripides' *Medea* and Apollonios' *Argonautika* – such a range is, to say the very least, difficult to resume in a single formula. This means, in turn, that it becomes wholly implausible to ascribe a single psychological *function* to such works or combinations of works.

The truth of the proposition just set out should be self-evident to classicists working on texts, vases or sculptures. But when these same literary and artistic products are used (sometimes by these same classicists, although more often by others) as evidence for that magical category, 'myth', there seems to be a temptation to fly in the face of the facts and to look in the opposite direction, towards a unitary theory of function. This approach often goes together with what we may call a panpsychic perspective.

The commonest generalisation about the psychological functioning of Greek myths sees them as having satisfied an emotional need: typically, the relief of anxiety.[96] Within this broad area of interpretation, the closest thing to a fully-fledged theory is that (or those) developed under the umbrella of psychoanalysis. A serious, recent statement of this position is available in R. Caldwell's *The Origin of the Gods*.

As early as the third sentence of the Preface, Caldwell rightly concedes that myths are multifunctional, so that psychological functions are to be seen not as rivals to other types of function but as partners with them. (That concession is one important reason why Caldwell's book can be called serious.) However, for Caldwell they are emphatically *senior* partners: 'the most important function of myth in general and of most individual myths is to answer an emotional need through the representation in some way of uncons-

---

[95] Dover Wilson 1932, p. 127.

[96] Cf. Kluckhohn 1942, Caldwell 1989, p. 17 ('to maintain the emotional integrity and collective health of the group').

cious ideas'.[97] The sting is in the tail, and leads directly into orthodox Freudian territory (oral, anal, phallic phases) before the Greek myths are tackled head-on. Caldwell's interpretation of the myth of the blinding of Teiresias will illustrate his method.

The young hero's punishment was, according to ancient testimony, variously motivated. He revealed the secrets of the gods. Or, he saw Athene bathing. Or, he was asked by Zeus and Hera to adjudicate the question of which group, men or women, derive more pleasure from intercourse (he was in a uniquely favoured position to answer, since he had been himself at one time female, having changed sex on witnessing two snakes copulating); he revealed the answer (women), and Hera vengefully took his sight.[98] For Caldwell, the three stories have a common structure, but a structure which it takes a psychoanalytically trained eye to detect. The variants show the hero punished for an act of sexual curiosity; more specifically, for having witnessed and revealed what happens at the 'primal scene'. This is the Freudian term for the traumatic situation when a child observes the copulation of his parents; becoming suddenly anxious owing to fears of paternal revenge, the child gives up his Oedipal desires in the course of an adaptation to reality. The myth, therefore, in evoking this painful, subsequently repressed, and developmentally crucial transition, can be seen, on this reading, as enabling the individual who hears it to adapt to 'reality'.

In its own terms, Caldwell's account is consistent, and accords with the importance given by Freud's followers to the primal scene. In addition, there is nothing forced about privileging the importance of sexual matters in this particular myth since there is clear evidence, already at the surface level of the narrative, that sexuality is one of its central themes. The problem is not with a sexual reading, but with an *Oedipal* reading. That Zeus and Hera – not to mention the poor old snakes – are to be seen as standing for Teiresias' *parents* certainly does not go without saying.[99] Caldwell's psychological–functional account will convince you in this particular case only if you are already convinced that his general approach is correct. To maintain that the

[97] Caldwell 1989, p. 17.   [98] Apollod. 3.6.7.   [99] Caldwell 1989, pp. 37–8.

Teiresias myth is (a) about sexual curiosity and (b) more generally, about the limitations on all human knowledge (thus neatly bridging the artificial intellect/emotion divide) seems to me in the case of (a) obvious, and in the case of (b) true and interesting.[100] But to link this punishment of sexual curiosity with the end of a child's Oedipal phase will be accepted only by those who have *already* accepted both the correctness of a Freudian interpretation of infant development and the consequent ubiquity of the related symbolism.

Caldwell's line of interpretation exemplifies the kind of thing which I have deliberately eschewed. Throughout this book I have steered clear of panpsychic approaches, preferring the anthropological–historical avenue of contextual analysis. Naturally, I do not deny that general theories of human psychology will, to the extent that they are valid, be relevant to the understanding of particular societies. Indeed all anthropologists and historians have, in the course of their explanations, constantly to balance factors common to all humanity against purely local considerations. The problems arise when contextual differences are elided *unjustifiably* in favour of the quest for universality.

What is or is not 'justifiable' will naturally have to be argued in any given case. If we revert now to our present inquiry, the chief and in my view insurmountable difficulty for unitarians, especially those panpsychists who deal in universal symbols, lies in the extraordinary plurality of tones on offer in Greek mythology. These stories are irredeemably diverse. The gods range from the horrific figure of Madness portrayed by Euripides, and the foul, rheum-eyed Furies of Aischylos' *Eumenides*, to the mischievous baby trickster-god Hermes, who farts and sneezes when his brother Apollo picks him up. Heroes: from the absurd Herakles of *Frogs* to the glorious, shining Odysseus wreaking vengeance on the suitors who have dared to feast in his home. What is a monster? The awesome bull from the sea in *Hippolytos*, or the love-lorn, cheese-obsessed Polyphemos of Theokritos' idyll? No explanation in terms of a single emotional effect or a

100   Caldwell 1989, p. 47.

19. Ajax prepares for suicide. (Attic black-figure amphora by Exekias.)

single psychological function can hope to cover the fantastic aesthetic variety of these tales.[101]

I conclude with two images, which make the same point about plurality. The first (Plate 19), from a famous amphora by Exekias, depicts the final preparations of Ajax before his suicide. Other artists chose a more obviously dramatic moment, showing for instance the warrior already impaled on his blade. Exekias prefers to *imply* the tragedy: the quiet care with which Ajax places his sword enacts his resolution, and contrasts poignantly with the violence which is to come. The second (Plate 20) is of a satyr, *alias* Herakles, confronting the serpent on guard over the 'apples' of the Hesperides – which in this case look uncommonly like wine-jugs. Whenever I feel the urge for a Grand Theory of Function, I first look over my shoulder. There is always a satyr there, waiting to have the last laugh.

[101] On this I cannot disagree with the position taken by G. S. Kirk (Kirk 1970, 1974), though the tone of disparagement which he so often adopts in writing about proponents of single-function explanations is regrettable.

20. One of Herakles' Labours was to pick the golden apples of the Hesperides, guarded by a snake. Here a satyr, brandishing a club, eyeballs the reptile, which is protecting a wine-jug tree. (The vessel bearing the image is itself an *oinochoē*, wine-jug.)

Epilogue

We ended the last chapter with pluralism, one of the key themes running through this book. In symbolically refashioning the landscape, the family, and the perceptions and practices of religion; in paring down, clarifying, exaggerating; in imitating the limited authority of proverbs; in explaining and mapping; in exposing and exploring ambiguities; in working through an indissoluble combination of thought and feeling; in doing all this, Greek myths showed themselves capable of signifying many things. But not an infinite number of things. It is the task of the cultural historian to recover contexts and horizons of expectation which simultaneously make possible *and limit* meanings. One of my objectives has been to demonstrate how the seemingly endless variations of Greek mythology are a product of *this* kind of community, situated in *this* landscape, with *these* institutions.

I would draw attention to two other aspects of my argument. First: compared with the majority of recent critics, I have underplayed myth's symbiosis with ritual. This is not because I follow Calame all the way in his scepticism about the very concept of ritual, but rather because, for all its undoubted pay-offs, modern myth–ritual theory has sometimes tended to exaggerate the importance of something which was, after all, only one part of social life. Myth transmutes *Alltag* as well as *Fest*.

Secondly: in stressing (for example in relation to mapping and explanation) the cognitive as well as the emotional dimension of function, I am implicitly disagreeing with the view that myths were merely a kind of soil or compost from which 'real thought' grew. While we rightly celebrate the exhilarating extraordinariness of the Greeks' achievement in developing the tools of logical and scientific analysis, we should register also that the discriminations and perceptions built into their 'traditional' thought constitute a deeply serious vehicle for coping with the dilemmas, crises and contradictions of living. There are indeed more things in heaven and earth than are dreamt of in your *philosophy*. Greek mythology is one of the languages in which those 'more things' are eloquently and unflinchingly faced.

BIBLIOGRAPHY

Alexiou, M., 1974: *The Ritual Lament in Greek Tradition*. Cambridge University Press.

Ashmole, B., 1972: *Architect and Sculptor in Classical Greece*. London: Phaidon.

Baladié, R., 1980: *Le Péloponnèse de Strabon*. Paris: Les Belles Lettres.

Ballabriga, A., 1986: *Le Soleil et le Tartare*. Paris: Editions de l'Ecole des Hautes Etudes en Sciences Sociales.

Barnes, J., 1987: *Early Greek Philosophy*. London: Penguin.

Bažant, J., 1981: *Studies on the Use and Decoration of Athenian Vases*. Prague: Academia.

Beazley, J. D., 1948: 'Hymn to Hermes', *AJA* 52: 336–40.

Bérard, C., 1983: 'Héros de tout poil: d'Héraklès imberbe à Tarzan barbu', in F. Lissarrague and F. Thélamon, eds., *Image et céramique grecque* (Actes du Colloque de Rouen). Publications de l'Université de Rouen, no. 96, 111–19.

Bérard, C., Bron, C., and Pomari, A., 1987: *Images et société en Grèce ancienne*. Lausanne: Institut d'Archéologie et d'Histoire Ancienne, Université de Lausanne.

Bérard, C., et al., 1989: *A City of Images* (trans. of *La Cité des images*, 1984). Princeton University Press.

Bernal, M., 1987: *Black Athena. The Afroasiatic Roots of Classical Civilisation*. Vol. I: *The Fabrication of Ancient Greece 1785–1985*. London: Free Association Books.

Bertman, S., ed., 1976: *The Conflict of Generations in Ancient Greece and Rome*. Amsterdam: Grüner.

Bettelheim, B., 1976: *The Uses of Enchantment*. London: Thames and Hudson.

Bieber, M., 1955: *The Sculpture of the Hellenistic Age*. New York: Columbia University Press.

1977: *Ancient Copies*. New York University Press.

Bielohlawek, K., 1940: 'Gastmahls- und Symposionslehren bei griechischen Dichtern', *WSt* 58: 11–30.

Binder, G., 1964: *Die Aussetzung des Königskindes*. Meisenheim am Glan: Hain.

Bloch, M., 1989: *Ritual, History and Power*. London: Athlone Press.

Blok, J., and Mason, P., eds., 1987: *Sexual Asymmetry*. Amsterdam: Gieben.

Blundell, M. W., 1989: *Helping Friends and Harming Enemies*. Cambridge University Press.

Boardman, J., 1970: *Greek Gems and Finger Rings*. London: Thames and Hudson.

1972: 'Herakles, Peisistratos and sons', *RA* 57–72.

1975a: *Athenian Red Figure Vases: The Archaic Period*. London: Thames and Hudson.

1975b: 'Herakles, Peisistratos and Eleusis', *JHS* 95: 1–12.

1978: 'Herakles, Delphi and Kleisthenes of Sikyon', *RA* 227–34.

Bodson, L., 1978: '*IEPA ZΩIA*. Académie royale de Belgique: mémoires de la classe des lettres, 2ᵉ série, vol. 63, fasc. 2.

Bond, G. W., ed., 1981: *Euripides: Heracles*. Oxford: Clarendon Press.

Borgeaud, Ph., 1988: *The Cult of Pan in Ancient Greece* (trans. of *Recherches sur le dieu Pan*, 1979). Chicago University Press.

Boswell, J., 1988: *The Kindness of Strangers*. London: Allen Lane.

Bouvier, D., 1986: 'La tempête de la guerre', *Métis* 1: 237–57.

Bowie, E. L., 1986: 'Early Greek elegy, symposium and public festival', *JHS* 106: 13–35.

Bowra, C. M., 1953: *Problems in Greek Poetry*. Oxford: Clarendon Press.

Braswell, B. K., 1971: 'Mythological innovation in the *Iliad*', *CQ* NS 21: 16–26.

Brelich, A., 1958: *Gli eroi greci*. Rome: Ateneo.

1969: *Paides e parthenoi*. Rome: Ateneo.

Bremmer, J. N., 1978: 'Heroes, rituals and the Trojan War', *SSR* 2: 5–38.

1983a: 'Scapegoat rituals in ancient Greece', *HSCP* 87: 299–320.

1983b: 'The importance of the maternal uncle and grandfather in Archaic and Classical Greece and Early Byzantium', *ZPE* 50: 173–86.

1984a: 'Greek maenadism reconsidered', *ZPE* 55: 267–86.

1984b: 'Analyse van de mythe: theorie en praktijk', *Lampas* 17: 126–41.

ed., 1987: *Interpretations of Greek Mythology*. London: Croom Helm.

1992: 'Mythe en rite in het oude Griekenland: Een overzicht van recente ontwikkelingen', *Nederlands Theologisch Tijdschrift* 46: 265–76.

Bremmer, J. N., and Horsfall, N. M., 1987: *Roman Myth and Mythography*. BICS Supplement 52.

Bremond, C., 1980: 'Comment concevoir un index des motifs', *Actes sémiotiques, Bulletin* 16: 15–29.

Brillante, C., 1984: 'Cadmo fenicio e la Grecia micenea', *QUCC* 17: 167–74.

Brilliant, R., 1984: *Visual Narratives*. Ithaca: Cornell University Press.

Brisson, L., 1982: *Platon, les mots et les mythes*. Paris: Maspero.

Bruit, L., 1986: 'Pausanias à Phigalie', *Métis* 1: 71–96.

Brunvand, J. H., 1981: *The Vanishing Hitchhiker*. New York: Norton.

Buck, C. D., 1949: *A Dictionary of Selected Synonyms in the Principal Indo-European Languages*. Chicago University Press.

Buffière, F., 1956: *Les Mythes d'Homère et la pensée grecque*. Paris: Les Belles Lettres.

Bulloch, A. W., ed., 1985: *Callimachus: The Fifth Hymn*. Cambridge University Press.

Burford, A., 1972: *Craftsmen in Greek and Roman Society*. London: Thames and Hudson.

Burke, P., 1978: *Popular Culture in Early Modern Europe*. London: Temple Smith.

Burkert, W., 1970: 'Jason, Hypsipyle, and New Fire at Lemnos', *CQ* NS 20, 1–16.

   1979: *Structure and History in Greek Mythology and Ritual*. Berkeley: University of California Press.

   1983: *Homo Necans* (trans. of original with same title, 1972). Berkeley: University of California Press.

   1985: *Greek Religion: Archaic and Classical* (trans. of *Griechische Religion der archaischen und klassischen Epoche*, 1977). Oxford: Blackwell.

   1993: 'Lescha-Liškah. Sakrale Gastlichkeit zwischen Palästina und Griechenland', in *Religionsgeschichtliche Beziehungen zwischen Kleinasien, Nordsyrien und dem Alten Testament*, ed. B. Janowski, K. Koch and G. Wilhelm (Freiburg, Switzerland: Universitätsverlag), 19–38.

Burn, A. R., 1949: 'Helikon in history: a study in Greek mountain topography', *ABSA* 44: 313–23.

   1951: 'Thermopylae and Callidromos', in *Studies Presented to David Moore Robinson*, ed. G. E. Mylonas (Saint Louis: Washington University Press) vol. I, 480–9.

Burnett, A. P., 1985: *The Art of Bacchylides*. Cambridge, Mass.: Harvard University Press.

Buxton, R. G. A., 1980: 'Blindness and limits: Sophokles and the logic of myth', *JHS* 100: 22–37.

   1982: *Persuasion in Greek Tragedy*. Cambridge University Press.

   1988: 'Bafflement in Greek tragedy', *Métis* 3: 41–51.

   1992a: 'Imaginary Greek mountains', *JHS* 112: 1–15.

   1992b: 'Iphigénie au bord de la mer', *Pallas* 38: 209–15.

Cairns, F., 1979: *Tibullus: A Hellenistic Poet at Rome*. Cambridge University Press.

Calame, C., 1977: *Les Chœurs de jeunes filles en Grèce archaïque*. Rome: Ateneo e Bizarri.

   ed., 1988: *Métamorphoses du mythe en Grèce antique*. Geneva: Labor et Fides.

   1990a: 'Illusions de la mythologie', *Nouveaux actes sémiotiques* (Université de Limoges) 12: 5–35.

   1990b: *Thésée et l'imaginaire athénien*. Lausanne: Payot.

   1992: 'Espaces liminaux et voix discursives dans l'*Idylle* I de Théocrite: une civilisation de poète', *Etudes de Lettres* (Revue de la Faculté des Lettres de l'Université de Lausanne), April–June, 59–85.

Caldwell, R., 1989: *The Origin of the Gods*. New York and Oxford: Oxford University Press.

Cambitoglou, A., and Trendall, A. D., 1961: *Apulian Red-figured Vase-painters of the Plain Style*. Archaeological Institute of America.

Cameron, A., ed., 1989: *History as Text*. London: Duckworth.

Cameron, A., and Kuhrt, A., 1983: *Images of Women in Antiquity*. London: Croom Helm.

Campbell, J. K., 1964: *Honour, Family and Patronage*. Oxford: Clarendon Press.

Carpenter, T. H., 1991: *Art and Myth in Ancient Greece*. London: Thames and Hudson.

Càssola, F., ed., 1975: *Inni omerici*. Milan: Mondadori.

Colin, G., 1938: 'L'Oraison funèbre d'Hypéride', *REG* 51: 209–66; 305–94.

Collard, C., ed., 1975: *Euripides: Supplices*. Groningen: Bouma.

Cook, A. B., 1914–40: *Zeus. A Study in Ancient Religion*. Cambridge University Press.

Cook, R. M., 1987: 'Pots and Pisistratan propaganda', *JHS* 107: 167–9.

Croally, N., forthcoming: *Euripidean Polemic*. Cambridge University Press.

Croon, J. H., 1967: 'Hot springs and healing gods', *Mnemosyne*, 4th series, 20: 225–46.

Davison, J. A., 1955: 'Peisistratus and Homer', *TAPA* 86: 1–21.

Dawe, R. D., ed., 1982: *Sophocles: Oedipus Rex*. Cambridge University Press.

Demand, N. H., 1982: *Thebes in the Fifth Century: Heracles Resurgent*. London: Routledge.

Detienne, M., 1973: 'L'Olivier: un mythe politico-religieux', in M. I. Finley, ed., *Problèmes de la terre en Grèce ancienne* (Paris: Mouton) 293–306 (reprint of article first publ. in 1970).

    1977: *The Gardens of Adonis* (trans. of *Les Jardins d'Adonis*, 1972). Hassocks: Harvester Press.

    1986: *The Creation of Mythology* (trans. of *L'Invention de la mythologie*, 1981). Chicago University Press.

    ed., 1988: *Les Savoirs de l'écriture. En Grèce ancienne* (vol. xiv of *Cahiers de Philologie*). Lille: Presses Universitaires.

Detienne, M., and Sissa, G., 1989: *La Vie quotidienne des dieux grecs*. Paris: Hachette.

Dillon, J. E. M., 1989: 'The Greek Hero Perseus: myths of maturation'. Unpubl. Oxford D. Phil. thesis.

Dodds, E. R., 1951: *The Greeks and the Irrational*. Berkeley: University of California Press.

Dorson, R. M., 1977: *American Folklore²*. Chicago University Press.

Douglas, M., 1954: 'The Lele of Kasai', in *African Worlds*, ed. D. Forde (Oxford University Press) 1–26.

Dover, K. J., ed., 1968: *Aristophanes: Clouds*. Oxford: Clarendon Press.

    1972: *Aristophanic Comedy*. London: Batsford.

    1974: *Greek Popular Morality in the Time of Plato and Aristotle*. Oxford: Blackwell.

    ed., 1980: *Plato: Symposium*. Cambridge University Press.

    1987: *Greek and the Greeks*. Oxford: Blackwell.

    1988: 'Anecdotes, gossip and scandal', in Dover, *The Greeks and their Legacy* (Oxford: Blackwell) 45–52.

Dover Wilson, J., 1932: *The Essential Shakespeare*. Cambridge University Press.

Dowden, K., 1992: *The Uses of Greek Mythology*. London: Routledge.

Dozeman, T. B., 1989: *God on the Mountain*. Atlanta: Scholars Press.

DuBois, P., 1982: *Centaurs and Amazons*. Ann Arbor: University of Michigan Press.

Ducrey, P., 1985: *Guerre et guerriers dans la Grèce antique*. Paris: Payot.

Duerr, H. P., 1985: *Dreamtime* (trans. of *Traumzeit*, 1978). Oxford: Blackwell.

Dundes, A., ed., 1984: *Sacred Narrative*. Berkeley: University of California Press.

Durand, G., 1992: *Les Structures anthropologiques de l'imaginaire*[11]. Paris: Dunod.

Easterling, P. E., and Knox, B. M. W., 1985: *The Cambridge History of Classical Literature*. Vol. I: *Greek Literature*. Cambridge University Press.

Edmunds, L., ed., 1990: *Approaches to Greek Myth*. Baltimore: Johns Hopkins University Press.

Edwards, R. B., 1979: *Kadmos the Phoenician*. Amsterdam: Hakkert.

Eliade, M., 1977: *Forgerons et Alchimistes*. Revised edn. Paris: Flammarion.

Elliger, W., 1975: *Die Darstellung der Landschaft in der griechischen Dichtung*. Berlin: de Gruyter.

Engels, D., 1980: 'The problem of female infanticide in the Greco-Roman world', *CPh* 75: 112–20.

Euben, J. P., ed., 1986: *Greek Tragedy and Political Theory*. Berkeley: University of California Press.

Fages, J.-B., 1991: *Histoire de la psychanalyse après Freud*. Toulouse: Privat.

Falassi, A., 1980: *Folklore by the Fireside: Text and Context of the Tuscan Veglia*. Austin: University of Texas Press.

Falivene, M. R., 1990: 'La mimesi in Callimacho: *Inni* II, IV, V e VI', *QUCC* 65: 103–28.

Falkner, T. M., and de Luce, J., 1989: *Old Age in Greek and Latin Literature*. Albany: State University of New York Press.

Farkas, A. E., Harper, P. O., and Harrison, E. B., eds., 1987: *Monsters and Demons in the Ancient and Medieval Worlds: Papers Presented in Honour of Edith Porada*. Mainz am Rhein: von Zabern.

Faure, P., 1960: 'Nouvelles recherches de spéléologie et de topographie crétoises', *BCH* 84. 189–220.

— 1964: *Fonctions des cavernes crétoises*. Paris: de Boccard.

Fehling, D., 1972: 'Erysichthon oder das Märchen von der mündlichen Überlieferung', *RhM* 115: 173–96.

— 1974: *Ethologische Überlegungen auf dem Gebiet der Altertumskunde*. Munich: Beck.

— 1989: *Herodotus and his 'Sources'* (trans. of *Die Quellenangaben bei Herodot*, 1971). Leeds: Francis Cairns (Publications) Ltd.

Festschrift Brommer 1977: *Festschrift für Frank Brommer*, ed. U. Höckmann and A. Krug. Mainz: von Zabern.

Festschrift Schefold 1967: *Gestalt und Geschichte. Festschrift Karl Schefold*. Bern: Francke.

Finley, M. I., 1977: *The World of Odysseus*[2]. London: Chatto and Windus.

Finnegan, R., 1977: *Oral Poetry*. Cambridge University Press.

Fisher, N. R. E., 1976: *Social Values in Classical Athens*. London: Dent.

Fontenrose, J., 1974: 'Work, Justice and Hesiod's five ages', *CPh* 69: 1–16.

Fraenkel, E., ed., 1950: *Aeschylus: Agamemnon*. Oxford: Clarendon Press.

Frazer, J. G., ed., 1921: *Apollodorus: The Library*. London: Heinemann.

Garland, R., 1985: *The Greek Way of Death*. London: Duckworth.

　　1990: *The Greek Way of Life*. London: Duckworth.

Gathorne-Hardy, J., 1985: *The Rise and Fall of the British Nanny*[3]. London: Weidenfeld and Nicolson.

Gentili, B., 1988: *Poetry and its Public in Ancient Greece* (trans. of *Poesia e pubblico nella Grecia antica*, 1984). Baltimore: Johns Hopkins University Press.

Georgoudi, S., 1974: 'Quelques problèmes de la transhumance dans la Grèce ancienne', *REG* 87: 155–85.

Ginouvès, R., 1962: *Balaneutikè. Recherches sur le bain dans l'antiquité grecque*. Paris: de Boccard.

Golden, M., 1981: 'Demography and the exposure of girls at Athens', *Phoenix* 35: 316–31.

Goldhill, S. D., 1986: *Reading Greek Tragedy*. Cambridge University Press.

　　1991: *The Poet's Voice*. Cambridge University Press.

Gombrich, E. H., 1977: *Art and Illusion*[5]. Oxford: Phaidon.

Gomme, A. W., 1913: 'The legend of Cadmus and the logographi', *JHS* 33: 53–72; 223–45.

　　1945: *A Historical Commentary on Thucydides,* vol. 1. Oxford: Clarendon Press.

Goody, J., 1977: *The Domestication of the Savage Mind*. Cambridge University Press.

Goody, J., and Watt, I., 1963: 'The consequences of literacy', *Comparative Studies in Society and History* 5: 304–45.

Gordon, R. L., ed., 1981: *Myth, Religion and Society*. Cambridge University Press.

Gould, J., 1980: 'Law, custom and myth: aspects of the social position of women in classical Athens', *JHS* 100: 38–59.

　　1985: 'On making sense of Greek religion', in P. E. Easterling and J. V. Muir, eds., *Greek Religion and Society* (Cambridge University Press) 1–33.

　　1987: 'Mothers' Day. A note on Euripides' *Bacchae*', in *Papers given at a Colloquium on Greek Drama in honour of R. P. Winnington-Ingram*, ed. L. Rodley, Soc. Prom. Hellen. Stud. Suppl. Paper 15, 32–9.

Graf, F., 1980: 'Milch, Honig und Wein', in *Perennitas. Studi in onore di Angelo Brelich* (Rome: Ateneo) 209–21.

　　1985a: *Griechische Mythologie*. Munich: Artemis.

　　1985b: *Nordionische Kulte*. Schweizerisches Institut in Rom.

Graves, R., 1960: *The Greek Myths*. Revised edn. London: Penguin.

Guarducci, M., 1927–9: 'Poeti vaganti e conferenzieri dell' età ellenistica. Ricerche di epigrafia greca nel campo della letteratura e del costume', *MAL* 6.2: 629–65.

Guthrie, W. K. C., 1962–81: *A History of Greek Philosophy*. Cambridge University Press.

Habicht, C., 1985: *Pausanias' Guide to Ancient Greece*. Berkeley: University of California Press.

Hägg, R., ed., 1983a: *The Greek Renaissance of the Eighth Century B.C.* Stockholm: Swedish Institute at Athens.

   1983b: *The Novel in Antiquity* (trans. of *Den Antika Romanen*, 1980). Oxford: Blackwell.

Hägg, R., Marinatos, N., and Nordquist, G. C., eds., 1988: *Early Greek Cult Practice*. Stockholm: Swedish Institute at Athens.

Halbwachs, M., 1952: *Les Cadres sociaux de la mémoire*. New edn of work publ. in 1925. Paris: P. U. F.

Hall, E., 1989: *Inventing the Barbarian*. Oxford: Clarendon Press.

   1992: 'When is a myth not a myth? Bernal's "Ancient Model"', *Arethusa* 25: 181–201.

Halliday, W. R., 1913: *Greek Divination*. London: Macmillan.

Halperin, D. M., Winkler, J. J., and Zeitlin, F. I., eds., 1990: *Before Sexuality*. Princeton University Press.

Halstead, P., 1987: 'Traditional and ancient rural economy in Mediterranean Europe: plus ça change?', *JHS* 107: 77–87.

Hammond, N. G. L., 1986: *A History of Greece³*. Oxford: Clarendon Press.

Hanfmann, G. M. A., 1957: 'Narration in Greek art', *AJA* 61: 71–8.

Harris, W. V., 1989: *Ancient Literacy*. Cambridge, Mass.: Harvard University Press.

Harrison, A. R. W., 1968: *The Law of Athens*, vol. I. Oxford: Clarendon Press.

Hartog, F., 1988: *The Mirror of Herodotus* (trans. of *Le Miroir d'Hérodote*, 1980). Berkeley: University of California Press.

Haug, W., and Warning, R., eds., 1989: *Das Fest*. Munich: Fink.

Havelock, E., 1980: 'The oral composition of Greek drama', *QUCC* NS 6: 61–113.

   1982: *The Literate Revolution in Greece and its Cultural Consequences*. Princeton University Press.

Heath, M., 1987: *The Poetics of Greek Tragedy*. London: Duckworth.

Henderson, W. J., 1989: 'Criteria in the Greek lyric contests', *Mnemosyne*, 4th series, 42: 24–40.

Henrichs, A., 1978: 'Greek maenadism from Olympias to Messalina', *HSCP* 82: 121–60.

   1982: 'Changing Dionysiac identities', in *Jewish and Christian Self-definition*, ed. Ben F. Meyer and E. P. Sanders (London: SCM press) vol. III, 137–60.

Herfst, P., 1979: *Le Travail de la femme dans la Grèce ancienne*. New York: Arno Press. (Reprint of 1922 edn, Utrecht.)

Herington, J., 1985: *Poetry into Drama*. Berkeley: University of California Press.

Herter, H., 1936: 'Theseus der Jonier', *RhM* 85: 177–91; 193–239.

   1939: 'Theseus der Athener', *RhM* 88: 244–86; 289–326.

Heubeck, A., West, S., and Hainsworth, J. B., 1988: *A Commentary on Homer's Odyssey*, vol. I. Oxford: Clarendon Press.

Himmelmann, N., 1980: *Über Hirten-Genre in der antiken Kunst*. Opladen: Westdeutscher Verlag.

Hinks, R., 1939: *Myth and Allegory in Ancient Art*. London: The Warburg Institute.

Hitzig, H., and Blümner, H., 1896: *Des Pausanias Beschreibung von Griechenland*, 1. Leipzig: Reisland.

Höckmann, O., 1985: *Antike Seefahrt*. Munich: Beck.

Hölscher, T., 1973: *Griechische Historienbilder des 5. und 4. Jahrhunderts v. Chr.* Würzburg: Triltsch.

Holtsmark, E. B., 1981: *Tarzan and Tradition*. Westport, Conn.: Greenwood Press.

Hooker, J. T., 1976: *Mycenaean Greece*. London: Routledge.

Hopkinson, N., 1988: *A Hellenistic Anthology*. Cambridge University Press.

Hornblower, S., 1987: *Thucydides*. London: Duckworth.

Humphreys, S. C., 1978: *Anthropology and the Greeks*. London: Routledge.

Hunter, R. L., ed., 1989: *Apollonius of Rhodes: Argonautica Book III*. Cambridge University Press.

Hurst, A., 1991: Introduction to edn of *Licofrone: Alessandra*, by Massimo Fusillo, André Hurst and Guido Paduano. Milan: Guerini e Associati.

Hyatt, S. L., ed., 1981: *The Greek Vase*. Latham, New York: Hudson-Mohawk Association of Colleges and Universities.

Jacoby, F., 1944: '*Patrios nomos*: state burial in Athens and the public cemetery in the Kerameikos', *JHS* 64: 37–66.

Janko, R., 1992: *The Iliad: A Commentary*. Vol. IV: *Books 13–16*. Cambridge University Press.

Jeanmaire, H., 1939: *Couroi et Courètes*. Lille: Bibliothèque Universitaire.

Jedrkiewicz, S., 1987: 'La favola esopica nel processo di argomentazione orale fino al IV sec. a. c.', *QUCC* 56: 35–63.

Jenkins, I. D., 1983: 'Is there life after marriage? A study of the abduction motif in vase paintings of the Athenian wedding ceremony', *BICS* 30: 137–45.

    1985: 'The ambiguity of Greek textiles', *Arethusa* 18.2: 109–32.

Jobst, W., 1970: *Die Höhle im griechischen Theater des 5. und 4. Jahrhunderts v. Chr.*, *SAWW* 268, no. 2.

Jost, M., 1992: *Aspects de la vie religieuse en Grèce*. Paris: Sedes.

Kaibel, G., 1878: *Epigrammata graeca ex lapidibus conlecta*. Berlin: Reimer.

Karpodini-Dimitriadi, E., 1981: *The Peloponnese*. Athens: Ekdotike Athenon.

Kebric, R. B., 1983: *The Paintings in the Cnidian Lesche at Delphi and their Historical Context*. Leiden: Brill.

Keuls, E., 1974: *The Water-carriers in Hades*. Amsterdam: Hakkert.

Kirk, G. S., 1970: *Myth: Its Meaning and Functions in Ancient and Other Cultures*. Cambridge University Press.

    1974: *The Nature of Greek Myths*. London: Penguin.

Kluckhohn, C., 1942: 'Myths and rituals: a general theory', *HThR* 35: 45–79.

Koch, H., 1914: 'Zu den Metopen von Thermos', *MDAI(A)* 39: 237–55.

    1915: 'Studien zu den Campanischen Dachterrakotten', *MDAI(R)* 30: 1–115, at 51–74.

Kraay, C. M., 1966: *Greek Coins*. London: Thames and Hudson.

Kraiker, W., 1958: *Die Malerei der Griechen*. Stuttgart: Kohlhammer.

Kullmann, W., and Reichel, M., 1990: *Der Übergang von der Mündlichkeit zur Literatur bei den Griechen*. Tübingen: Narr.

Kunze, E., 1950: *Archaische Schildbänder*. *(Deutsches Archäologisches Institut, Olympische Forschungen, II.)* Berlin: de Gruyter.

Kurtz, D. C., 1975: *Athenian White Lekythoi*. Oxford: Clarendon Press.

Kurtz, D. C., and Boardman, J., 1971: *Greek Burial Customs*. London: Thames and Hudson.

Lacey, W. K., 1968: *The Family in Classical Greece*. London: Thames and Hudson.

Lacoste-Dujardin, C., 1970: *Le Conte kabyle*. Paris: La Découverte.

Lanata, G., 1963: *Poetica pre-platonica: testimonianze e frammenti*. Florence: La Nuova Italia.

Lane Fox, R., 1986: *Pagans and Christians*. London: Viking.

Langdon, M. K., 1976: 'A sanctuary of Zeus on Mount Hymettos', *Hesperia Supplement* 16.

Latacz, J., 1966: *Zum Wortfeld 'Freude' in der Sprache Homers*. Heidelberg: Winter.

Lauter, H., 1985: *Der Kultplatz auf dem Turkovuni*, *MDAI(A) Beiheft* 12.

Lefkowitz, M. R., 1981a: *Heroines and Hysterics*. London: Duckworth.

1981b: *The Lives of the Greek Poets*. London: Duckworth.

1986: *Women in Greek Myth*. London: Duckworth.

1988: 'Who sang Pindar's victory odes?', *AJPh* 109: 1–11.

Lerat, L., 1943: 'Une loi de Delphes sur les devoirs des enfants envers leurs parents', *RPh* 17: 62–86.

Leutsch, E. L., and Schneidewin, F. G., eds., 1839–51: *Paroemiographi graeci*. Göttingen: Vandenhoeck and Ruprecht.

Lévi-Strauss, C., 1963: *Totemism* (revised trans. of *Le Totémisme aujourd'hui*, 1962). Boston: Beacon Press.

1964–71: *Mythologiques*, vols. I–IV. Paris: Plon.

1966: *The Savage Mind* (trans. of *La Pensée sauvage*, 1962). London: Weidenfeld and Nicolson.

Lienhardt, G., 1961: *Divinity and Experience: The Religion of the Dinka*. Oxford: Clarendon Press.

Ling, R., 1991: *Roman Painting*. Cambridge University Press.

Lissarrague, F., 1990: *The Aesthetics of the Greek Banquet* (trans. of *Un Flot d'images*, 1987). Princeton University Press.

Lloyd, G. E. R., 1966: *Polarity and Analogy*. Cambridge University Press.

1979: *Magic, Reason and Experience*. Cambridge University Press.

1983: *Science, Folklore and Ideology*. Cambridge University Press.

1987: *The Revolutions of Wisdom*. Berkeley: University of California Press.

1990: *Demystifying Mentalities*. Cambridge University Press.

1991: *Methods and Problems in Greek Science*. Cambridge University Press.

Long, T., 1986: *Barbarians in Greek Comedy*. Carbondale and Edwardsville: Southern Illinois University Press.

Loraux, N., 1981: *Les Enfants d'Athéna*. Paris: Maspero.

   1986: *The Invention of Athens* (trans. of *L'Invention d'Athènes*, 1981). Cambridge, Mass.: Harvard University Press.

   1987: *Tragic Ways of Killing a Woman* (trans. of *Façons tragiques de tuer une femme*, 1985). Cambridge, Mass.: Harvard University Press.

   1989: *Les Expériences de Tirésias*. Paris: Gallimard.

Mackenzie, M. M., and Roueché, C., eds., 1989: *Images of Authority*. Cambridge Philol. Soc. Suppl. vol. 16.

Macleod, C., 1983: *Collected Essays*. Oxford: Clarendon Press.

McLeod, M. D., 1981: *The Asante*. London: British Museum Publications.

Macqueen, J. G., 1982: 'Death and immortality: a study of the Heraclitus epigram of Callimachus', *Ramus* 11: 48–56.

Malinowski, B., 1927: *Sex and Repression in Savage Society*. London: Routledge.

Malkin, I., 1987: *Religion and Colonization in Ancient Greece*. Leiden: Brill.

Martin, R., 1974: *L'Urbanisme dans la Grèce antique*². Paris: Picard.

Massaro, M., 1977: 'Aniles fabellae', *SIFC* 49: 104–35.

Mayo, M. E., ed., 1982: *The Art of South Italy*. Richmond: Virginia Museum.

Méheust, B., 1990: 'Les Occidentaux du XXᵉ siècle ont-ils cru à leurs mythes?', *Communications* 52: 337–56.

Merkelbach, R., 1952: 'Die pisistratische Redaktion der homerischen Gedichte', *RhM* 95: 23–47.

Metzger, H., 1951: *Les Représentations dans la céramique attique du IVᵉ siècle*. Paris: de Boccard.

Mikalson, J. D., 1983: *Athenian Popular Religion*. Chapel Hill: University of North Carolina Press.

   1991: *Honor thy gods*. Chapel Hill: University of North Carolina Press.

Momigliano, A., 1975: *Alien Wisdom: The Limits of Hellenization*. Cambridge University Press.

   1987: *On Pagans, Jews, and Christians*. Middletown, Conn.: Wesleyan University Press.

Moret, J.-M., 1984: *Oedipe, la Sphinx et les Thébains*. Institut suisse de Rome.

   1991: 'Circé tisseuse sur les vases du Cabirion', *RA*, fasc. 2, 227–66.

Mossman, J. M., 1988: 'Tragedy and epic in Plutarch's *Alexander*', *JHS* 108: 83–93.

Moxon, I. S., Smart, J. D., and Woodman, A. J., eds., 1986: *Past Perspectives*. Cambridge University Press.

Murray, O., ed., 1990: *Sympotica: A Symposium on the Symposion*. Oxford: Clarendon Press.

Murray, O., and Price, S., eds., 1990: *The Greek City from Homer to Alexander*. Oxford: Clarendon Press.

Murray, P., 1981: 'Poetic inspiration in early Greece', *JHS* 101: 87–100.

Musti, D., 1963: 'Sull'idea di συγγένεια in iscrizioni greche', *ASNP* 32: 225–39.

Muth, R., 1954: '"Hymenaios" und "Epithalamion"', *WSt* 67: 5–45.

Nagy, G., 1979: *The Best of the Achaeans*. Baltimore: Johns Hopkins University Press.

Neu, J., ed., 1991: *The Cambridge Companion to Freud*. Cambridge University Press.

Nicolson, F. W., 1891: 'Greek and Roman barbers', *HSCP* 2: 41–56.

Nilsson, M. P., 1932: *The Mycenaean Origin of Greek Mythology*. Cambridge University Press.

    1940: *Greek Folk Religion*. New York: Columbia University Press.

    1951: *Cults, Myths, Oracles and Politics in Ancient Greece*. Lund: Gleerup.

    1951–60: 'Die Griechengötter und die Gerechtigkeit', *Opuscula selecta* (Lund: Gleerup) vol. III, 303–21.

    1967: *Geschichte der griechischen Religion*[3], vol. I. Munich: Beck.

Oehler, R., 1925: *Mythologische Exempla in der älteren griechischen Dichtung*. Diss. Basel.

Osborne, R., 1987: *Classical Landscape with Figures*. London: Philip.

Page, D. L., 1934: *Actors' Interpolations in Greek Tragedy*. Oxford: Clarendon Press.

    ed., 1951: *Alcman: The Partheneion*. Oxford: Clarendon Press.

Papathomopoulos, M., ed., 1968: *Antoninus Liberalis: Les Métamorphoses*. Paris: Les Belles Lettres.

Parke, H. W., 1967: *The Oracles of Zeus*. Oxford: Blackwell.

Parker, R. C. T., 1983: *Miasma*. Oxford: Clarendon Press.

Patch, H. R., 1950: *The Other World*. Cambridge, Mass.: Harvard University Press.

Patterson, C., 1985: '"Not worth the rearing": the causes of infant exposure in ancient Greece', *TAPA* 115: 103–23.

Patzer, H., 1952: "Ραψωδός", *Hermes* 80: 314–25.

Pavese, C. O., 1972: *Tradizioni e generi poetici della Grecia arcaica*. Rome: Ateneo.

Pearson, A. C., ed., 1917: *The Fragments of Sophocles*. Cambridge University Press.

Pease, A. S., 1961: 'Notes on mountain climbing in antiquity', *Appalachia* 132: 289–98.

Peek, W., ed., 1955: *Griechische Vers-Inschriften*, vol. I. Berlin: Akademie-Verlag.

Pfister, F., 1951: *Die Reisebilder des Herakleides*, *SAWW* 227, no. 2.

Philippson, A., 1950–9: *Die griechischen Landschaften*. Frankfurt am Main: Klostermann.

Pickard-Cambridge, A., 1988: *The Dramatic Festivals of Athens*[2], revised by J. Gould and D. M. Lewis. Oxford: Clarendon Press.

Podlecki, A. J., 1966: *The Political Background of Aeschylean Tragedy*. Ann Arbor: University of Michigan Press.

Pöhlmann, E., 1988: 'Mündlichkeit und Schriftlichkeit gestern und heute', *WüJbb* NF 14: 7–20.

Pohlenz, M., 1948: 'Zu den attischen Reden auf die Gefallenen', *SO* 26: 46–74.

Pollitt, J. J., 1986: *Art in the Hellenistic Age*. Cambridge University Press.

    1990: *The Art of Ancient Greece: Sources and Documents*. Cambridge University Press. (First publ. by Prentice-Hall, 1965, as *The Art of Greece, 1400–31 B.C.*)

Pomeroy, S. B., 1975: *Goddesses, Whores, Wives, and Slaves*. New York: Schocken Books.

1984: *Women in Hellenistic Egypt.* New York: Schocken Books.

Powell, A., ed., 1989: *Classical Sparta.* London: Routledge.

Prag, A. J. N. W., 1985: *The Oresteia: Iconographic and Narrative Tradition.* Warminster: Aris and Phillips.

Price, H. H., 1969: *Belief.* London: Allen and Unwin.

Pritchett, W. K., 1965: *Studies in Ancient Greek Topography*, vol. I. Berkeley: University of California Press.

1974: *The Greek State at War*, vol. II. Berkeley: University of California Press.

1982: *Studies in Ancient Greek Topography*, vol. IV. Berkeley: University of California Press.

Prontera, F., ed., 1983: *Geografia e geografi nel mondo antico.* Bari: Laterza.

Propp, V. J., 1969: *Morfologija skazki*². Leningrad: Nauka. Translations are available in several languages, though some are based on the inferior 1928 edition.

Raeck, W., 1984: 'Zur Erzählweise archaischer und klassischer Mythenbilder', *JDAI* 99: 1–25.

Rasmussen, T., and Spivey, N., eds., 1991: *Looking at Greek Vases.* Cambridge University Press.

Redfield, J. M., 1975: *Nature and Culture in the Iliad.* Chicago University Press.

Reitzenstein, R., 1893: *Epigramm und Skolion.* Giessen: J. Ricker'sche Buchhandlung.

Richardson, B. E., 1933: *Old Age among the Ancient Greeks.* Baltimore: Johns Hopkins University Press.

Richardson, N. J., 1974: *The Homeric Hymn to Demeter.* Oxford: Clarendon Press.

Richter, G. M. A., and Milne, M. J., 1935: *Shapes and Names of Athenian Vases.* New York: Metropolitan Museum of Art.

Ridgway, B. S., 1990: *Hellenistic Sculpture*, vol. I. Bristol: Classical Press.

Ritoók, Zs., 1962: 'Rhapsodos', *AAntHung* 10 (1–3): 225–31.

Robert, L., 1949: 'Epitaphe d'un berger à Thasos', *Hellenica* 7: 152–60.

1955: 'Dédicace d'un berger', *Hellenica* 10: 28–33.

1966: 'Inscriptions d'Aphrodisias', *AC* 35, at pp. 383–4.

Robinson, D. M., 1936: 'A new *lebes gamikos* with a possible representation of Apollo and Daphne', *AJA* 40: 507–19.

Rogerson, J., and Davies, P., 1989: *The Old Testament World.* Cambridge University Press.

Rohde, E., 1914: *Der griechische Roman und seine Vorläufer*³. Leipzig: Breitkopf und Härtel.

1966: *Psyche.* New York: Harper and Row. (First edn of German original was publ. in 1894.)

Rose, H. J., 1958: *A Handbook of Greek Mythology*⁶. London: Methuen.

Rosivach, V. J., 1987: 'Autochthony and the Athenians', *CQ* NS 37: 294–305.

Rowe, C. J., 1978: *Essential Hesiod.* Bristol: Classical Press.

Rudhardt, J., 1958: *Notions fondamentales de la pensée religieuse et actes constitutifs du culte dans la Grèce classique.* Geneva: Droz.

1986: 'Pandora: Hésiode et les femmes', *MH* 43: 231–46.

Rumpf, A., 1953: *Malerei und Zeichnung der klassischen Antike*. Munich: Beck.

Rumpf, E., 1985: *Eltern-Kind-Beziehungen in der griechischen Mythologie*. Frankfurt am Main: Lang.

Russell, D., 1981: *Criticism in Antiquity*. London: Duckworth.

Rutherford, R. B., ed., 1992: *Homer Odyssey: Books XIX and XX*. Cambridge University Press.

Ryder, M. L., 1991: 'The last word on the Golden Fleece legend?', *OJA* 10: 57–60.

Sacks, M. H., 1985: 'The Oedipus complex: a reevaluation', *JAPA* 33: 201–16.

Sartre, M., 1979: 'Aspects économiques et aspects religieux de la frontière dans les cités grecques', *Ktèma* 4: 213–24.

Schefold, K., 1966: *Myth and Legend in Early Greek Art* (trans. of *Frühgriechische Sagenbilder*, 1964). London: Thames and Hudson.

   1985: 'Homer und der Erzählungsstil der archaischen Kunst', in *ΕΙΔΩΛΟΠΟΙΙΑ. Actes du Colloque sur les problèmes de l'image dans le monde méditerranéen classique* (Rome: Bretschneider) 3–25.

Schlingloff, D., 1981: 'Erzählung und Bild', *Beiträge zur allgemeinen und vergleichenden Archäologie* 3: 87–213.

Schmitt Pantel, P., ed., 1991: *Histoire des femmes en Occident*, vol. 1: *L'Antiquité*. Paris: Plon. (Originally *Storia delle donne*, 1990.)

Schnapp, A., 1973: 'Représentation du territoire de guerre et du territoire de chasse dans l'œuvre de Xénophon', in *Problèmes de la terre en Grèce ancienne*, ed. M. I. Finley (Paris: Mouton) 307–21.

Schneider, C., 1967–9: *Kulturgeschichte des Hellenismus*. Munich: Beck.

Scobie, A., 1979: 'Story-tellers, storytelling and the novel in Graeco-Roman antiquity', *RhM* 122: 229–59.

Seaford, R., 1981: 'Dionysiac drama and the Dionysiac mysteries', *CQ* NS 31: 252–75.

   ed., 1984: *Euripides: Cyclops*. Oxford: Clarendon Press.

   1987: 'The tragic wedding', *JHS* 107: 106–30.

Sealey, R., 1957: 'From Phemios to Ion', *REG* 70: 312–55.

Seznec, J., 1953: *The Survival of the Pagan Gods* (trans. of *La Survivance des dieux antiques*, 1940). New York: Pantheon Books.

Sifakis, G. M., 1967: *Studies in the History of Hellenistic Drama*. London: Athlone Press.

Simon, E., 1983: *Festivals of Attica*. Madison, Wisconsin: University Press.

Sissa, G., 1990: *Greek Virginity* (trans. of *Le Corps virginal*, 1987). Cambridge, Mass.: Harvard University Press.

Slater, P. E., 1968: *The Glory of Hera*. Boston: Beacon Press.

Smith, G. J., and Smith, A. J., 1992: 'Jason's Golden Fleece', *OJA* 11: 119–20.

Snell, B., 1960: *The Discovery of the Mind* (trans. based on *Die Entdeckung des Geistes*[2], 1948). New York: Harper and Row.

Snodgrass, A., 1980: *Archaic Greece*. London: Dent.

   1982: *Narration and Allusion in Archaic Greek Art*. London: Leopard's Head Press.

Sokolowski, F., 1969: *Lois sacrées des cités grecques*. Paris: de Boccard.

Sourvinou-Inwood, C., 1985: 'Altars with palm-trees, palm-trees and *parthenoi*', *BICS* 32: 125–46.

    1991: *'Reading' Greek Culture*. Oxford: Clarendon Press.

Sperber, D., 1975: *Rethinking Symbolism*. Cambridge University Press. (A near-equivalent French version came out in 1974.)

Stewart, D. J., 1977: 'Falstaff the Centaur', *Shakespeare Quarterly* 28: 5–21.

Stinton, T. C. W., 1990: *Collected Papers on Greek Tragedy*. Oxford: Clarendon Press.

Stoetzel, J., 1978: *La Psychologie sociale*. Paris: Flammarion.

Swindler, M. H., 1929: *Ancient Painting*. New Haven: Yale University Press.

Taplin, O., 1993: *Comic Angels and Other Approaches to Greek Drama through Vase-Paintings*. Oxford: Clarendon Press.

Thomas, R., 1989: *Oral Tradition and Written Record in Classical Athens*. Cambridge University Press.

Trendall, A. D., 1967: *Phlyax Vases*². *BICS Supplement* 19.

Trenkner, S., 1958: *The Greek Novella in the Classical Period*. Cambridge University Press.

Trilling, L., 1951: *The Liberal Imagination*. London: Secker and Warburg.

Trumpf, J., 1958: 'Stadtgründung und Drachenkampf', *Hermes* 86: 129–57.

Vegetti, M., 1983a: *Tra Edipo e Euclide*. Milan: Il Saggiatore.

    ed., 1983b: *Oralità, scrittura, spettacolo*. Turin: Boringhieri.

Verdenius, W. J., 1970: 'Homer the educator of the Greeks', *Meded. Nederl. Akad. van Wet., Afd. Letterk.* 33, no. 5.

    1985: *A Commentary on Hesiod 'Works and Days' vv. 1–382*. Leiden: Brill.

Vermeule, E., 1971: 'Kadmos and the Dragon', in *Studies presented to George M. A. Hanfmann*, ed. D. G. Mitten et al. (Mainz: von Zabern) 177–88.

    1979: *Aspects of Death in Early Greek Art and Poetry*. Berkeley: University of California Press.

Vernant, J.-P., 1980: *Myth and Society in Ancient Greece* (trans. of *Mythe et société en Grèce ancienne*, 1974). Brighton: Harvester.

    1983: *Myth and Thought among the Greeks* (trans. of *Mythe et pensée chez les Grecs*, 1965). London: Routledge.

    1985: *La Mort dans les yeux*. Paris: Hachette.

    1986: 'Le Dionysos masqué des *Bacchantes* d'Euripide', in Vernant and P. Vidal-Naquet, *Mythe et tragédie II* (Paris: La Découverte) 237–70.

Vernant, J.-P., and Vidal-Naquet, P., 1981: *Tragedy and Myth in Ancient Greece* (trans. of *Mythe et tragédie en Grèce ancienne*, 1972). Brighton: Harvester.

Versnel, H. S., 1990: *Inconsistencies in Greek and Roman Religion*. Vol. 1: *Ter Unus*. Leiden: Brill.

Veyne, P., 1988: *Did the Greeks believe in their Myths?* (trans. of *Les Grecs ont-ils cru à leurs mythes?*, 1983). Chicago University Press.

Vian, F., 1963: *Les Origines de Thèbes*. Paris: Klincksieck.

Vickers, B., 1973: *Towards Greek Tragedy*. London: Longman.

Vickers, M., 1985: 'Artful crafts: the influence of metalwork on Athenian painted pottery', *JHS* 105: 108–28.

Vidal-Naquet, P., 1986: *The Black Hunter* (trans. of *Le Chasseur noir*, 1981). Baltimore: Johns Hopkins University Press.

Voelke, P., 1992: 'Ambivalence, médiation, intégration: à propos de l'espace dans le drame satyrique', *Etudes de Lettres* (Revue de la Faculté des Lettres de l'Université de Lausanne) April–June, 33–58.

Vollgraff, W., 1952: *L'Oraison funèbre de Gorgias*. Leiden: Brill.

Wachsmuth, D., 1967: *ΠΟΜΠΙΜΟΣ Ο ΔΑΙΜΩΝ. Untersuchung zu den antiken Sakralhandlungen bei Seereisen*. Diss. Berlin.

Ward, A. G., ed., 1970: *The Quest for Theseus*. London: Pall Mall Press.

Waszink, J. H., 1974: *Biene und Honig als Symbol des Dichters und der Dichtung in der griechisch-römischen Antike* (Rhein.-Westfäl. Akad. Wiss. Vorträge G. 196).

Webster, T. B. L., 1939: 'Greek theories of art and literature down to 400 B.C.', *CQ* 33: 166–79.

1964: *Hellenistic Poetry and Art*. London: Methuen.

1967: *Hellenistic Art*. London: Methuen.

Weiler, I., 1974: *Der Agon im Mythos*. Darmstadt: Wissenschaftliche Buchgesellschaft.

Weiss, P., 1984: 'Lebendiger Mythos. Gründerheroen und städtische Gründungstraditionen im griechisch-römischen Osten', *WüJbb* NF 10: 179–208.

West, M. L., 1971: 'Stesichorus', *CQ* NS 21: 302–14.

1981: 'The singing of Homer and the modes of early Greek music', *JHS* 101: 113–29.

1983a: 'Tragica VI', *BICS* 30: 63–82.

1983b: *The Orphic Poems*. Oxford: Clarendon Press.

1985: *The Hesiodic Catalogue of Women*. Oxford: Clarendon Press.

1989–92: *Iambi et elegi graeci*[2]. Oxford: Clarendon Press.

Whittaker, C. R., ed., 1988: *Pastoral Economies in Classical Antiquity*. Cambridge Philol. Soc. Suppl. vol. 14.

Wiedemann, T. E. J., 1989: *Adults and Children in the Roman Empire*. London: Routledge.

Willcock, M. M., 1964: 'Mythological paradeigma in the *Iliad*', *CQ* NS 14: 141–54.

Williams, D., 1985: *Greek Vases*. Cambridge, Mass.: Harvard University Press.

Winter, F., 1908: *Altertümer von Pergamon, VII*. Berlin: Reimer.

Wiseman, T. P., 1979: *Clio's Cosmetics*. Leicester University Press.

Wycherley, R. E., 1937: '*ΠΗΓΗ* and *ΚΡΗΝΗ*', *CR* 51: 2–3.

Zanker, P., 1988: *The Power of Images in the Age of Augustus* (trans. of *Augustus und die Macht der Bilder*, 1987). Ann Arbor: University of Michigan Press.

Zeitlin, F. I., 1965: 'The motif of the corrupted sacrifice in Aeschylus' *Oresteia*', *TAPA* 96: 463–508.

Züchner, W., 1942: *Griechische Klappspiegel. JDAI Ergänzungsheft* 14.

INDEX

ritual on, 93–5; charcoal-burners and, 83 n. 13

Pelops, 60, 101 n. 106, 130–1 (Pl. 16), 163, 189

Peloros (one of Sown Men), 185

Penelope: in *Od.*, 9, 41, 121, 122, 124, 175, 197; as paradigm, 78, 163, 196; and 'life', 114; betrothal of, 129; in imagery, 123 (Pl. 12)

Pentheus, 88, 92, 153, 173, 201, 202, 211

Pergamon, 63, 64

Persephone, 65, 128, 132

Perseus, 34, 75, 76, 101, 195, 205

Persians, 62, 64, 194

persuasion, 74; Kassandra lacks, 121–2; as rhetorical strategy, 156, 169; of Philoktetes, 170–1; in Pi., 118; in A. *Eum.*, 32, 71–2, 149; *see also* convincingness, *peithō*

Phaethon, 132, 133, 139

Phaiakia(ns), 9, 80, 100, 175

Phaidra, 25, 92, 120

Phanes, 105

Pheidias, 59, 60, 63

Phemios, 27, 175

Pherekydes, 4 n. 13, 49, 185

Philip (of Macedon), and plain/mountain opposition, 94

Philippides, on *oros*, 91

Philoktetes, 103, 106, 112

Philomela, 123–4, 127, 144 n. 60

Philostratos, on old wives' tales, 20, 161

Phineus, 173

Phliasia, autochthony in, 190

phlyakes (type of comedy), 34, 35 (Pl. 2)

Phoenicians, 64, 185, 188

Phoibe, 183

Phoinix, 180

Phrixos, 53

Pieria, 86, 90

Pindar, 29, 163; performance of, 25 n. 39; transcribed, 46; and heroism, 25; and hunting, 92; representation of women by, 117–19, 120, 121, 129; fathers and sons in, 141; brothers in, 144; and gods, 149; and ritual, 155; and bee, 201; rejects stories of

cannibalism, 165; power of song in, 170; and *epitaphios logos*, 171; mythical paradigms in, 197

pine, 202, 203 (Pl. 17)

Pittheus, 137

plain, as distinctive part of landscape, 80, 82, 83, 84, 90, 94, 95, 96

plants, as classifiers, 202, 210

Plataiai: paintings at, 61; and ritual, 93; battle of, 194; siege of, 116 n. 7

Plato, 156, 163; *muthos* and *logos* in, 12–13; on domestic story-telling, 18; myths in, 39; on what is *muthōdēs*, 42; on sense underlying myths, 72–3; on immorality of gods, 140–1; on poetic 'teaching', 171; on poetry, 176–7; on persuasion, 180–1; and Atlantis, 182; *Ap.*, 11; *Crat.*, 88; *Hp. Ma.*, 38–9, 40; *Ion*, 30; *Lg.*, 22, 90, 97, 136, 160; *Lys.*, 20, 171; *Mx.*, 37, 49; *Prt.*, 39, 181; *R.*, 16–17 (Er), 20, 171 (immoral stories), 106 n. 117 (cave), 160 (Underworld), 180–1 (*peithō*); *Smp.*, 10–11

Pliny the Elder, on Kadmos, 186

plurality/pluralism: characteristic of Greek mythology, 11, 17, 36, 69, 177–8, 216–18; of belief, 156–7, 160–3

Plutarch: on *logoi*, 12; on *muthos/logos* distinction, 12; on brothers, 143; on Hom., 174

Pluto, 65

Plynteria (festival), 102

poets: banned from Plato's Republic, 20; prestige of, 21; works taught in school, 22–3; in Hom., 27–8, 30, 40; as myth tellers, 36–7, 39, 165; oral, 46–7; works recited in Hellenistic period, 50; Alexandrian, 50–2; and visual imagery, 62; contrasted with craftsmen, 63; female, 63 n. 36; and spring water, 113; preserve the past, 170–1

pollution, religious, 102–3, 204, 205

Polybios: on gossip, 12; on Arkadia, 23–4; on credulous women, 161

Polybos, 133

Polydamas, 144